FORBEARANCE

FORBEARANCE

A Theological Ethic
for a Disagreeable Church

James Calvin Davis

WILLIAM B. EERDMANS PUBLISHING COMPANY
GRAND RAPIDS, MICHIGAN

Wm. B. Eerdmans Publishing Co.
2140 Oak Industrial Drive N.E., Grand Rapids, Michigan 49505
www.eerdmans.com

26 25 24 23 22 21 20 19 18 17   1 2 3 4 5 6 7 8 9 10

ISBN 978-0-8028-7510-5

Library of Congress Cataloging-in-Publication Data

Names: Davis, James Calvin, author.
Title: Forbearance : a theological ethic for a disagreeable church / James Calvin Davis.
Description: Grand Rapids : Eerdmans Publishing Co., 2017. | Includes bibliographical
    references and index.
Identifiers: LCCN 2017012723 | ISBN 9780802875105 (pbk. : alk. paper)
Subjects: LCSH: Patience—Religious aspects—Christianity. | Church controversies. |
    Conflict management—Religious aspects—Christianity. | Virtues. | Virtue.
Classification: LCC BV4647.P3 D38 2017 | DDC 241/.4—dc23
    LC record available at https://lccn.loc.gov/2017012723

For Elizabeth, Jae, and Kisung

Contents

Preface

What happens when we approach theological disagreement not as a problem to solve or a crisis to endure, but as an opportunity to practice Christian virtue?

In a previous book, I argued that religious communities play an essential role in improving the health of American public life.[1] An unimpeded rise in public vitriol threatens American democracy in our time, but religions could help underwrite an infusion of civility, to make our politics more productive and inspiring. Religions often bring rich histories of moral reflection, including consistent priorities on other-regard and mutual respect, that if shared with the wider public could give us healthier ways of living with difference. As I talk to various church groups around the country, however, the same question comes up over and over again: *how can Christians provide this civic leadership if we cannot get our own houses in order?* How are we supposed to provide a template and resources for respectful dialogue when our own church debates are so often rancorous, divisive, and destructive?

These are exactly the right questions for us to ask, of course, so in this book I try to imagine a better way for us Christians to navigate difference in our own midst, as an opportunity to practice biblical virtue and improve our social witness. In other words, what I offer here is a theological ethic for faithful disagreement in ecclesial community. To describe this new ethic, I adopt and embellish an idea taken straight from the New Testament epistles: forbearance. Written for early congregations riddled with intense theological disagreements, the Letters to the Ephesians and Colossians both challenge their readers to "bear with each other" in spite of their differences.

In this evocative notion of forbearance, I see the promise of a theologically grounded practice where we work hard to maintain the unity of the Body of Christ while we also take seriously the matters on which we disagree. Chapter 1 teases out the meaning of forbearance for our time and place, arguing that the practice of it does not require us to ignore or minimize the real theological and moral conflict that we host in church. The writers of Ephesians and Colossians never suggested that the issues that divided the young congregations in their time were unimportant. But they did insist that there were more and less faithful ways to work through the disagreements, and the practice of forbearance describes the more faithful way.

As we pursue truth and seek justice together, habits of forbearance train us to see theological and moral difference not as impediments to faithfulness but as opportunities to develop Christian character in our relationships with each other. The practice of forbearance relies on the cultivation of familiar virtues in the tradition—humility, patience, wisdom, faithfulness, and love—and is built on fundamental Christian confessions, like the trustworthiness of God and the complicated limitations of human finitude. In chapters 2 through 6, I explore the theological roots for each of these virtues and examine their implications for the commitment to bear with one another through conflict.

Of course, some Christians may be concerned that a call for forbearance sounds like I am asking us to soften or abandon our commitment to what we think is right and true. Can we exercise forbearance when we think parts of the church have abandoned God's truth? Can we honor forbearance without being complicit in the perpetuation of injustice? In chapters 7 and 8, I address these concerns directly, lest my insistence on forbearance resemble a demand that Christians just stop caring so much about doctrine or morals. To the contrary, forbearance invites us to believe, to defend our convictions, and to pursue what we think is right and true in God's eyes. But it invites us to do all of that good work with a certain character and attitude, so that our pursuit of justice and truth itself is reshaped by the practice of forbearance.

Ultimately, forbearance commits us to relationship with other Christians as a testament to God's enduring faithfulness to us, and, through it all, the practice of forbearance provides an opportunity to exhibit to the world a different way of navigating ideological diversity. In the final chapter, I entertain the idea that forbearance just might be the church's primary public witness, offering some antidote to the pervasive divisiveness in contemporary culture.

Throughout this book, I apply the concept of forbearance to contemporary debates that preoccupy the church and our congregations, and I root it in the works of Christian thinkers from the first centuries to the present day. You might think that, in a theological tradition that has seen plenty of rabid disagreement and division, it is farfetched to claim that forbearance represents our better angels. I will admit that many of the most prominent thinkers in the history of Christian thought—and many of the theological heavy-hitters to whom I directly appeal—wrote with an ungracious polemic that runs counter to the virtues I am imagining in this book. At the same time, many of those same theologians provided conceptual ingredients (sometimes despite themselves!) from which we can build a vision of a better way. So this book makes generous use of Christian theological tradition, and claims that the ethic I am describing is consistent with orthodox Christianity, even if we must acknowledge that many thinkers in the tradition have failed to reflect forbearance consistently in their own times and places.

Ultimately, I hope this book offers a constructive way of dealing with disagreement with both integrity and grace, one that may not reflect any one voice from Christian tradition but does faithfully represent the potential of our tradition. Forbearance does not ask us to abandon our convictions. It does ask us to hold them in a profoundly distinct way, the way of Christian virtue, animated by a commitment to preserving the unity of the Body of Christ. In a church that seems to be fighting all the time, would it not be wise to imagine a different way of navigating our differences? Would it not be more faithful to harness the potential for forbearance, stem the tide of division in the church, and channel that energy into our social witness, offering a model for a nation and world desperate for some way out of intractable incivility? Charting a path to this different way is what I have tried to do.

Before we begin, I should acknowledge a few things about the perspective I bring to our task. As philosophers note from time to time, there is no view from nowhere. We all understand the issues before us, and the traditions we call home, by means of a perspective shaped by our particular time and place. This book is no different. I am an American Protestant theologian, and both of those modifiers shape my thinking on church conflict in important ways. My focus here is on the predicament of American *Protestantism*, and the sources to which I appeal draw predominantly from the Protestant wing of Christianity. This is not to say that there is nothing of value here for, say, Catholics, but the theological differences between

Catholicism and Protestantism—principally around issues of tradition, ecclesiology, and authority—are distinct enough that the exploration of forbearance likely would look much different from the perspective of a Catholic theologian than it does in my Protestant hands. Similarly, I am singularly concerned with the *American* Protestant experience. Again, I would not be surprised to discover that the practice of forbearance as I develop it resonates with Christians in other places and cultures, but the American context—with its history of religious voluntarism and disestablishment, and its peculiar political tone—makes our navigation of difference and penchant for division a unique animal. So I am quite aware that I am offering a particularly American Protestant theological ethic in this book, and from the outset I want you to understand that too.

Finally, allow me to share an additional word about my theological and ecclesiastical background. I am a theologian in the Reformed (Calvinist) tradition, so you should not be surprised if rascals from that tradition show up more often than others in this book—though my fondness for Thomas Aquinas will make clear that my theology is sufficiently catholic (with a small "c") to appeal to Christians beyond the Reformed family. I am a minister member of the Presbyterian Church (USA), but as a consequence of geography I currently worship with a congregation in the United Church of Christ. I also write as one raised in evangelicalism but who now identifies as a liberal Protestant. I think the diversity in my religious background informs my vision of forbearance in important ways, not the least being that it equips me to speak the language and see strengths and weaknesses in both Christian traditionalism and progressivism. My intimate familiarity with both evangelicalism and liberalism also helps to explain my optimism that a spirit of forbearance can happen in the church. But I recognize that my mixed theological pedigree increases the chance that members of both groups will find something off-putting in what I describe here. That risk of persuading exactly no one comes with the territory of attempting a rapprochement, but I hope that neither my evangelical family history nor my current liberal disposition will tempt you preemptively to stop reading. Instead, I hope that the theological bilingualism I bring to this task will help me make the case that there is room in the church for both conservatives and liberals, and that these and other divisions in the church cannot be allowed to threaten the unity of the one Body of Christ. At least that is my *hope*. I pray that I am right about all of this, for Christ's sake.

Acknowledgments

My rehearsal of indebtedness must begin with Middlebury College, which provided me a generous sabbatical to begin this project, and in general serves as a supportive environment for teaching and writing—even writing theology! At Eerdmans, James Ernest, David Bratt, and Kelsey Kaemingk have been enthusiastic about this book from the beginning of our relationship, and I am grateful for their vision, improvements, and care. In addition, several organizations and institutions contributed to my thinking on forbearance by providing me opportunities to work through parts of the argument in their midst. Specifically, I thank Dickinson College for the invitation to deliver the 2015 Mary E. Borges Memorial Lecture; the Covenant Network of Presbyterians for welcoming me to their 2011 Annual Conference; Westminster Presbyterian Church in Lincoln, Nebraska (and pastor Bob Snell); St. Stephen's Episcopal Church in Middlebury, Vermont; and Donegal Presbytery (and my old friend Michael Wilson).

Colleagues who have read some of this manuscript include Jason Santalucia, Douglas F. Ottati, Elizabeth Hinson-Hasty, Roger Gench, and Mark Douglas. Conversations with Richard Cizik and David Gushee (exchanges they may barely remember) helped shape my thinking on forbearance's relationship with the pursuit of truth in ways that made chapter 7 easier to write.

This book could not have been written without the generous support of the Louisville Institute, one of the few sources of funding available these days for those of us who study (and write for) American Christianity. I am deeply grateful to Don Richter and the other kind folks at the Institute for the grant that underwrote an essential summer of (relatively) uninter-rupted writing.

The Louisville Institute grant also facilitated a couple of focus groups that gave me a chance to try out some of my ideas with fellow theologians and pastors. One of those groups consisted of fellow Presbyterian ethicists in the Social Ethics Network, convened by Chris Iosso. I thank them for letting me present the outline of my work at our 2015 meeting, and I am especially indebted to a conversation with Letitia Campbell that led to the inclusion of persistence in my discussion of patience and hope. An eclectic group of pastors from Vermont and eastern New York also read a draft of the first chapter and talked with me about the contours of the broader ar-gument. Their feedback was invaluable, so thanks to Tim Franklin, Daniel Wright, Alexandra Lusak, Donna Elia, David Bennett, Mary Kay Schuen-eman, Shannan Vance-Ocampo, David Andrews, Larry Jones, and Susan McGarry for their time and insight. Steve Jewett was supposed to be part of that group until a family emergency pulled him away, but I value the other discussions we have had; Steve's evangelical perspective reassures me that a desire for forbearance is not exclusively a liberal impulse.

My pastor and very good friend Andy Nagy-Benson was also part of this group, and he has been my conversation partner from the genesis of this project. Andy embodies theological forbearance, and he is an abso-lutely perfect model of the kind of pastoral leadership necessary to pull off this ethic in today's congregations. It is not an overstatement to state that this book would not exist without his encouragement, enthusiasm, wisdom, example, and friendship. Thank you, Brother.

Similarly, I must thank the community of faith Andy leads and with whom I worship and serve, the Congregational Church of Middlebury, Vermont. As you will see, I have drawn extensively from my experiences with this group of loving folks, and I have tested many of my ideas in ser-mons and adult education classes in their midst. I am especially grateful for the regulars in the Monday evening study group, a model of forbearance and friendship in their own right. I do not expect that all of my church friends will agree with everything I have written here, but I do hope they recognize their influence on their resident theologian.

Finally, my spouse Elizabeth has read over every word of this volume, as she has done for each book I have written. Her combination of theo-logical literacy and sharp talent for copy-editing undoubtedly made this a better book, but her support for a project that took too long to manifest goes way beyond the editorial. She and our two sons, Jae and Kisung, have been supportive and patient throughout the writing process, especially during the final summer it hijacked. More broadly, their presence constantly reminds me that, as glorious as the calling can be, there is more to life than theology. Elizabeth, Jae, and Kisung practice their own form of forbearance toward a husband and father who almost constantly requires it, but who seldom deserves the kind of virtue they bestow. For their unconditional love, I dedicate this book to them.

CHAPTER 1

Forbearance and Biblical Character

In July 2014, the General Assembly of the Presbyterian Church (USA), that denomination's highest governing body, considered an overture calling for divestment in three companies that provide supplies for Israel's control of the occupied territories. Past overtures labeled Israeli occupation of these lands apartheid, calling for divestment from or boycotts of any corporations that supported "non-peaceful" pursuits in Palestine. Opponents of such overtures argued that the conflict over land between Israel and the Palestinians was more complicated than the denomination's one-sided approach, that the proposed measures would aggravate the situation in the Middle East and alienate Presbyterians' Jewish neighbors here at home, and that such a public expression from the denomination opened the PC(USA) to the charge of being anti-Semitic. The issue was debated heatedly in 2012, with a similar overture for divestment ultimately failing by a stunning two-vote margin, eliciting an audible gasp from the Assembly when the tally was announced. This time around the push for divestment prevailed, and divided Presbyterians struggled to deal with the international implications of this denominational decision while also navigating the complications to interfaith relations in their own neighborhoods.

In 2004, the United Methodist Church opened a new chapter in its decades-long struggle over the issue of homosexuality, when it narrowly voted to add language to its *Book of Discipline* that made it a punishable offense within the denomination for clergy to perform same-sex marriages or themselves identify as "self-avowed practicing homosexuals."[1] Since that vote, a number of clergy have been accused of transgressing these prohibitions. Supporters of traditional views on sexuality have insisted that clergy who run afoul of the *Book of Discipline* should be prosecuted and defrocked. Defenders of ordination and marriage equality for gay and lesbian persons have been just as vocal in their opposition to the disciplinary language; some, in fact, have publicly disobeyed the prohibitions in order to call attention to what they perceive to be an injustice of the church. In the meantime, bishops and other officials have struggled to maintain denominational unity between the groups, with representatives from both sides threatening schism if their views do not prevail. In response, at the 2016 General Conference, the United Methodist Church made a controversial move to delay a final decision regarding LGBTQ equality, voting instead to ask the denomination's Council of Bishops to commission a group to study the issue and report back by 2020. The battles that remain among Methodists are mirrored in similar struggles among American Episcopalians, Presbyterians, Lutherans, and other mainline Protestant denominations.

The evangelical community, too, is increasingly divided over issues of sexuality, but perhaps no topic has caused more consternation among evangelicals in the last two decades than concerns over climate change. For years, environmental stewardship struggled for attention among evangelicals, regularly overshadowed by the higher priority placed on issues such as abortion and gay marriage. But in the first decade of the twenty-first century, a growing number of evangelicals began to see climate change as a pressing theological and moral issue, arguing that the Bible entrusts with human beings the care for creation, and that we are failing that responsibility by contributing to the destruction of the planet. "Creation Care," as many evangelicals call it, got a boost of momentum when Richard Cizik, former chief Washington lobbyist for the National Association of Evangelicals, went public with his insistence that environmentalism should be an evangelical concern. Traditionalist evangelical leaders such as James Dobson and Charles Colson publicly countered that there was no consensus within evangelicalism on either the science or the moral imperatives associated with global warming, and the power struggle within the association eventually cost Cizik his job. But Cizik, ethicist David Gushee, and other evangelical leaders continue to rally more evangelicals to the cause, resulting in a deep rift between Creation Care advocates and their evangelical opponents.[2]

First Presbyterian Church is in many ways a typical college-town congregation.[3] Located near a prestigious school of music, First Presbyterian reflects the community's appreciation for artistic culture. But similar to many college-town churches, First Presbyterian also hosts a deep com-

2

mitment to social justice. Recently the congregation had to deal with an apparent conflict between these priorities. The church's organ was in dire need of work, with replacement estimates exceeding one million dollars, and repair estimates promising only slight savings and ongoing maintenance issues. Supporters of the project to rehabilitate or replace the organ emphasized the importance of music to the church's worship and its contributions to the cultural life of the city. Critics pointed out that the same sum of money might be applied to the congregation's commitment to combatting homelessness and poverty, locally and globally. The congregation remains united in its appreciation of both its worship life and its mission to persons beyond its walls. Increasingly, however, members of the congregation found themselves at odds in a complicated disagreement about which of these priorities—music or mission—would represent a more appropriate commitment of scarce financial resources.

In my own congregation in Middlebury, Vermont, we labor to maintain a sense of community among persons who identify along an extraordinary theological range. While United Church of Christ in denominational affiliation and governance, my church is in reality an interdenominational congregation, peppered with former Catholics, diaspora Presbyterians (including myself), displaced Methodists, implicit Unitarians, and at least one Buddhist, in addition to lifelong Congregationalists. Accompanying those different denominational roots are theological and liturgical preferences that sometimes struggle to mesh. We somewhat regularly find ourselves debating the decision to include a confession of sin in the Sunday liturgy, our relationship with the traditional creeds and doctrines of the church, and the authority of Scripture. None of the debates threatens to rend our congregation, in part because of the theological dexterity of our pastor, but the convictions that animate these disagreements run deep enough that they require deliberate maintenance, and from time to time some in our church family wonder what holds us together—and whether it makes sense for us all to gather as one body on Sundays.

Do you recognize your own congregation or denomination among these portraits? Of course, conflict is not all there is to say about the life of the church in the United States, but truth be told, conflict is increasingly a dominant characteristic of the churches with whom we identify. And the issues that divide us extend well beyond the illustrations I have offered here. Abortion, immigration, evolution, health care, interfaith relations, property rights, the deity of Christ—the list of issues over which congregations and denominations debate and disagree grows longer, while the road between conflict and division grows shorter. We seem to have more over which we disagree and less tolerance for the disagreement. And too often we avail ourselves of the luxury that comes from living in a society of "voluntary associations."[4] We volunteer to disassociate; we gather together our like-minded allies and we split.

Christians have been disagreeing about matters profound and mundane since Peter and Paul. Leaders in the early church famously disagreed about the importance of joining the Jewish community by means of circumcision as a prerequisite for entry into Christian fellowship. Christian leaders in the third and fourth centuries battled over the meaning of the Trinity, and the precise way in which the human and the divine cohabited in the person of Jesus. Throughout the medieval and early modern periods, Christians disagreed over fundamental theological convictions such as the definition of church authority, the best modes of scriptural interpretation, and the nature and extent of salvation. They also debated all kinds of practical implications of Christian faith, like the acceptability of loans with interest or the morality of Christian participation in war. During the Reformation, Protestant Christians divided from the Roman Church, but they also disagreed among themselves over the definition of a "true" church and the proper understanding of the Lord's Supper. Since the Reformation, Protestants have been dividing and dividing and dividing, over theological matters great and small, so that the very character of American religion is division into a seemingly infinite variety of communities and sub-communities.

For as long as there has been a church, then, there has been disagreement and division in it. Seen in this context, the divisiveness we experience in the contemporary American church would seem to be nothing extraordinary. As I write, American Christians remain divided about the wars in Afghanistan and Iraq; were the invasions legitimate by the standards of just war, unjustified by those standards, or unjustified because the standards themselves are a perversion of the priority of peace for which Jesus himself stood? Do those wars make us morally culpable for the atrocities committed by ISIS? American Christians remain deeply divided over the situations in Syria and Palestine, and whether the United States has a right or duty to intervene more directly in either situation. We disagree on what justice requires in the current economy. Does it require government simply to ensure structural reforms in the financial sector in order to provide equal opportunity for all citizens to reap the benefits of capitalism, or does it require government to guarantee a basic minimum income, education, and health care for everybody, underwritten by public aid? Christians disagree over immigration policy, matters of church governance, the role of women in ecclesial leadership, and the authority of Scripture. We disagree about a lot in the contemporary church, but all of the infighting is just the church—as Hank Williams Jr. once crooned—"carrying on a family tradition."

None of these matters of debate is trivial in the eyes of those who fight for or against them. Frequently the combatants understand nothing less than the integrity of the church and its witness to be at stake. To my mind, however, neither the longevity of our tradition of division nor the seriousness of the issues justifies the threat to the unity of the church that we inflict with such abandon. For a tradition that values the virtues of community, that conceives of the church as a "family" of faith and the "Body of Christ," our inability to maintain community would seem to be a significant theological failure, no matter how much historical precedent exists. Especially in an age of shrinking membership and evaporating cultural presence, it also seems practically appropriate to seek another way to approach the matters over which we disagree. Are there ways in which we can negotiate our differences that are truer to the priorities of love, neighborliness, and unity that characterize the message of Jesus? What might it mean to negotiate disagreement in ways that are better governed by the virtues of Christ?

To seek something different from this long legacy of division is natural and just as consistent with the history of the church as our penchant for schism. Once upon a time, we executed for blasphemy and declared war over matters of religion, but since the seventeenth century the church in the west has resorted largely to ecclesial division, not violence, as a response to its disagreements—an improvement in strategy, to be sure. Yes, there were political and practical motivations for the abandonment of "wars of religion" in the modern west. Increasing religious pluralism and the demands of international stability required that we negotiate religious differences without bloodshed. But freedom of conscience, religious pluralism, and the negotiation of difference in nonviolent ways increasingly were seen as important *theological* values as well. Christians began to see that there are better and worse ways to navigate disagreement, and violence was a worse way. So while disagreement and division among Christians are as old as the tradition itself, Christianity has evolved in the manner in which it negotiates all of that difference. Might we continue the evolution, finding ways to approach disagreement in the church that are a more constructive reflection of Christian values, that serve as alternatives to the penchant for division that especially characterizes American Protestantism?

Encountering Difference while "Thinking Theologically"

In recommending a different way of negotiating difference in the church, I do not mean to suggest that we should artificially minimize the differences or eliminate conflict between us. In fact, we should anticipate a plurality of perspectives as people in the church attempt to discern what is right and true in the confluence of Christian belief and our contemporary world. And we should expect some conflict between these different assessments of truth, as Christians together embrace the task of thinking theologically. For "thinking theologically" is what all of us are called to do, not just highly trained academics but pastors and lay members of the Christian community.

What does it mean to "think theologically" as the church? I define the task this way: *Christian theology is the collective project of understanding ourselves, the human community, the world, and the cosmos in relation to God, through the interpretive lens of what Jesus Christ reveals to us about God and in conversation with the best sources of knowledge available in our time and place.* Allow me to highlight a couple of components to this understanding of Christian theology.

First, as I have asserted already, Christian theology is a responsibility of the whole church. Some members of the church will be trained to offer instruction or expertise, and that leadership is important if we are to think theologically with responsible understanding of both the past and the present, but the task of theology ultimately belongs to the entire church.

Second, the objective of theology is to understand ourselves in the most expansive context possible; that is, we seek to understand ourselves in relationship to the human community and the greater cosmos, and to understand the cosmos in relation to God. In fact, when done well, Christian theology pushes us beyond nationalism, anthropocentrism, and other constricted understandings of our own importance to more expansive contexts for truth and responsibility.[5]

Third, we interpret the cosmos, its subsets, and our places in them through the lens of what Jesus Christ discloses to us about the attributes and intentions of God. Jesus Christ becomes the prism through which our speculations about what is "really real" or "really going on" are refracted. Our perceptions of truth strive for consistency with what we believe to be important to the divine character, which we Christians believe we have glimpsed in the incarnation of God in Christ.

Finally, this interpretation of ourselves and our universe in relation to God actively engages the insight of other sources of knowledge available to us—science, history, philosophy, literature, and other disciplines. Christian theology is not done in a vacuum but strives to correlate what we learn from Scripture and Christian tradition with what we know from these other sources of information. For as Douglas F. Ottati writes, "these additional inquiries will be understood, first and foremost, as attempts to develop and refine—in a way that engages culture and takes account of recent knowledge and experiences—the piety and practical vision of human life and the world offered by a particular Christian community."[6] The effort to correlate sometimes shapes our interpretation of the data gleaned from other disciplines, but sometimes it prompts a revision of our understanding of what religious tradition has told us is right and true.[7]

Conceived of this way, the task of thinking theologically includes a number of opportunities for Christians to come to different understandings. In order to view ourselves and the universe through the lens that Jesus Christ provides for understanding God, we must decide what it is exactly that Jesus disclosed about God in his life, ministry, death, and legacy. Of course, Christians have drawn very different conclusions about what we know about God through Jesus. Those possibilities for different interpretations are on display in the Bible itself; the four Gospels tell essentially the same loose biographical account, but in the process they depict Christ in remarkably different ways and commend distinct conceptions of what it means to follow the way of Jesus. Compare, for instance, Luke's depiction of discipleship as solidarity with the marginalized to Mark's frantic apocalypticism, or Matthew's moralism to John's mystical emphasis on love. The diversity of interpretation on display in the Gospels is poignantly magnified in the New Testament epistles, as the realities of living as the community of Jesus created disagreements over the liturgical, theological, moral, and social implications of that identity.

And if the Bible features a plurality of theological interpretations of what Jesus Christ disclosed to us about God, the variety exponentially grows when one turns to post-biblical theological tradition for guidance. A tradition that includes Origen and Augustine, Luther and Aquinas, Calvin and Arminius, Abraham Kuyper and Martin Luther King Jr., and Dorothy

7

Day and Karl Barth hosts a stunning diversity of interpretations of biblical faith. To put it directly, the church has never said only one thing about God (or anything else, for that matter).

Added to the pluralism embedded in the tradition is the diversity we encounter when the tradition engages the world around it. For the task of thinking theologically is necessarily bidirectional; Christians "apply" what their tradition affirms about God to the world in which they live, but they also learn from their world, and the knowledge they glean from the world affects their interpretation of religious tradition.[8] For example, what the natural sciences have taught us about the age of the earth, the interrelatedness of species, and the enormousness of the universe challenges the historical anthropocentrism of Christian theology, pushing many to reconsider how we understand a biblical cosmology that places our world (and human beings) at the center of the moral universe. Social science has revealed to us the depths to which our expectations for what is right or good are constructions of the societies and cultures in which we live, providing us the tools to critique established norms in sexual and social behavior that we have taken as essential truths for generations. Modern medical science complicates how we think about matters as varied as addiction, behavioral diversity, and social deviance, sometimes prompting revision of how Christians think about moral culpability, punishment, and forgiveness. Like the tradition itself, the data we glean from studying the world can be understood and interpreted in different ways, and those differences will affect how Christians understand what is right, good, and true from their theological perspective.

In the bidirectional endeavor to think theologically, then, Christians draw from multiple sources of information, within and beyond their tradition, interpreting and applying that information in diverse ways that reflect, in part, their own loyalties, biases, and limitations of perspective. The result of all of these variables is theological difference. That difference should not surprise us, and we should not regret it. It is part of the theological task.

By extension, it is not necessarily a bad thing that various sub-traditions have arisen as reflections of these different interpretations. Roman Catholicism, Eastern Orthodoxy, Lutheranism, Calvinism, and Pentecostalism represent just a few of the sub-traditions that have developed around particular ways of interpreting the faith. Our effort to think differently about theological disagreement in the church is not necessarily an indictment of the reality of denominations within Christianity. Here I distinguish between denominationalism and schism. Denominationalism is a product of Christians gravitating to a sub-tradition for purposes of self-identification. Schism is the judgmental removal from fellow Christians in order to escape theological difference. Denominationalism can nurture shared affinities, which can be useful for sustaining faith and character and for maintaining theological consistency and a sense of community. Schism, however, takes the virtues of denominationalism and makes them vices, betraying a failure to negotiate conflict and difference productively. Locating the line between productive denominationalism and destructive schism can be difficult, I admit; I suspect the line is not stationary, and that motive is a relevant evaluative factor. But for much of our history—including in contemporary American culture—we have tended to err on the side of schism, often with insufficient consideration of the costs.

The desire for an alternative to destructive conflict and division is not necessarily a rejection of denominationalism, but it may be a warning against excessive denominationalism. It is a desire to find an alternative to the explicit hostility that often accompanies theological conflict and to halt the seemingly unending dissolution of the church into like-minded enclaves. In other words, even within a church that features sub-traditions centered on particular interpretations and priorities of faith, can we imagine a way of approaching theological disagreement that maintains community within and between these denominations, and stems the tide of ecclesial division, at least a little?

Biblical Forbearance

The virtues that lend themselves to more constructive ways of living with disagreement are captured well in the practice of Christian forbearance. *Forbearance is the active commitment to maintain Christian community through disagreement, as an extension of virtue and as a reflection of the unity in Christ that binds the church together.* Admittedly, the term "forbearance" sounds a little antiquated. Most of us do not go around asking for or extending forbearance, unless we are talking about a bank loan. But I confess that the unusualness of the word is part of my attraction to it, because in its very utterance it represents the distinctiveness of Christian practice in the divisiveness of contemporary American culture. And while the word is not part of our normal vocabulary, it does have biblical significance that we might exploit to

9

capture a healthier approach to disagreement. But what does it mean to practice forbearance?

In English, to forbear literally means "to hold back." The several words translated as "forbearance" in English versions of the Bible usually capture the sense of someone abstaining from acting on a judgment. Saul forbears to pursue and kill David even though he has an opportunity. Kings demand that prophets forbear speaking any more of God's judgment. God forbears exacting punishment, despite the people's desert of it.[9] In one common biblical sense of the term, to forbear simply means to delay acting on an opportunity, decision, or conclusion. If that is all we meant by the term "forbearance," though, it would not describe a very satisfying antidote to the disagreements that divide Christians. It might suggest a stalemate or moratorium on our disagreements, but it would not necessarily mean encouraging growth or progress in dealing with the issues that divide us or healing the brokenness that exists. Without a commitment to positive movement through a season of disagreement, forbearance in this minimalist sense connotes the temporary cessation of hostilities, but not in a way that ensures healthier community.

But there is a fuller connotation of the term "forbearance," actually more in line with its literal meaning, and it is this sense of the term that I find appealing. Forbearing also means "bearing for or with," which suggests not just voluntary restraint but actively carrying something or someone for a time. It implies patience, mutual respect, the extension of time, a certain latitude, and perhaps some affection that motivates a person to carry the burden of disagreement. In this sense, forbearance is less a momentary cease-fire than an active extension of concern for one another.

Two specific usages of the word *anecho* ("to bear with" or "to hold up") in the New Testament capture this fuller meaning of forbearance. The Letter to the Ephesians may not have been a letter written to a specific church in Ephesus; it may have been an exhortation meant for circulation among several churches. Whether meant for a single congregation or more, however, the particular issue prompting its writing is clear enough. An offshoot of Judaism in its origins, the early church rapidly became quite diverse in its membership, attracting non-Jewish converts from its earliest moments. Gentile converts entered the church in droves, prompting Christians to ask hard questions about the church's Jewish origins. The apostle Paul had taught that God's grace in Christ freed Christians from the obligation to follow the strictures of Jewish law, thus opening the door for Gentiles to become Christian without first becoming Jews. But some teachers apparently interpreted Paul's teaching on grace over adherence to the law as a license to moral laxity, and in doing so they encouraged new Christians to embrace behaviors from their former lives that Paul would have found problematic. They also exaggerated Paul's rejection of the binding force of the law into an intolerance for the Jewish roots of Christian belief and behavior—as well as for Jewish sisters and brothers within the church.

In response to this growing rift between Jewish and Gentile converts to the faith, the author of Ephesians asserts the unity of the Christian community as it is joined together under its head, Jesus Christ. He describes the church as the family of God's children "adopted" through Christ and bound together with the "seal" of the Holy Spirit. Where once Gentile Christians were outside the family of God, in Christ Jew and Gentile were made "one humanity in place of the two," reconciled "to God in one body" through Christ's death. As a result of God's reconciling grace in Christ, Christians "are no longer strangers . . . but . . . members of the household of God" (Eph. 2:19).

After setting the cosmic context for this claim to Christian unity, with lofty exaltations of Christ and the reconciling grace wrought in him, the letter moves to moral exhortation. Beginning in chapter 4, the letter insists that the practice of unity is an essential expression of the vocation to which every Christian is called:

> I therefore, the prisoner in the Lord, beg you to lead a life worthy of the calling to which you have been called, with all humility and gentleness, with patience, bearing with one another [*anecho*] in love, making every effort to maintain the unity of the Spirit in the bond of peace. (Eph. 4:1–3)

Here the practice of forbearance is specifically identified as a reflection of the church's proper character, its direct response to the grace that brings it into being. Members are encouraged to respond to one another—despite their differences—with humility and patience, committing to the project of living together as a sign of their unity in Christ. To bear with one another in difference, then, is to fulfill their calling, their vocation, as followers of the Christ in whom they exist as one family. The practice of forbearance serves as a display of spiritual maturity. While they retain the responsibility to "speak the truth" to one another, they do so in a spirit of love, refusing to "let the sun go down" on any resentment or anger they hold toward other members of the community (Eph. 4:26).

Clearly Ephesians does not build this call for forbearance on the assumption of uniformity in the church—quite the opposite![10] Commending forbearance does not make any sense absent the existence of disagreement and conflict. Indeed, the occasion for the letter is high-stakes disagreement between members of the church community. But while disagreement is a necessary part of who the church is, so is the way it chooses to negotiate that disagreement, and the writer urges his hearers to practice forbearance, putting away all malice, extending kindness, and forgiving one another as God has forgiven in Christ (4:31–32). Invoking a baptismal creed likely recited in their midst, the writer insists that the practice of forbearance reflects the great act of reconciliation to which they all have been called:

> There is one body and one Spirit, just as you were called to the one hope of your calling, one Lord, one faith, one baptism, one God and Father of all, who is above all and through all and in all. (Eph. 4:4–6)

The Letter to the Ephesians imagines a community that, in living with difference, nonetheless reflects the cosmological unity achieved in Christ and models the character of Christ. In the practice of forbearance, Christians do not create unity; we confess it.

The author of Colossians similarly commends forbearance as a practice worthy of the calling to which Christians are called. Teachers of an alternative theology had infiltrated the church, contesting the Pauline understanding of Christ's divinity and humanity, appealing to Gnostic ideals to urge excessive asceticism and a rejection of the material world.[11] The Letter to the Colossians is not bashful in its opposition to this alternative theology; at the same time, it urges the congregation to practice forbearance with one another as they navigate the crisis:

> As God's chosen ones, holy and beloved, clothe yourselves with compassion, kindness, humility, meekness, and patience. Bear with one another [anecho] and, if anyone has a complaint against another, forgive each other; just as the Lord has forgiven you, so you also must forgive. Above all, clothe yourselves with love, which binds everything together in perfect harmony. (Col. 3:12–14)

12

Pulling no punches in rejecting what he thinks are wrongheaded teachings about Jesus and Christian duty, the author nonetheless recommends that the Colossians put on the character of Christ, and part of that character is the practice of forbearance. As in Ephesians, the commitment to "bearing with one another" is rooted in Christian virtues—compassion, kindness, humility, patience, and love. The author does not ignore the conflict in the community, but he insists that how the church works through that conflict should reflect their character, and that of the one whom they claim to follow.

In the Letter to the Colossians we see not only an acknowledgment that unity and disagreement can exist together but also an illustration of how forbearance can be practiced without the abandonment of principle and conviction. For forbearance is not a recipe for dissolving difference; it is a virtuous means by which to maintain community even in the face of disagreement. To do so is to reflect the character of the God who brings us together, as is made clear in a third use of *anecho* in the New Testament. In the Letter to the Romans, Paul uses references to God's practice of forbearance to indict our own aptness to judge those with whom we disagree:

> You say, "We know that God's judgment on those who do such things is in accordance with truth." Do you imagine, whoever you are, that when you judge those who do such things and yet do them yourself, you will escape the judgment of God? Or do you despise the riches of his kindness and forbearance [*anecho*] and patience? (Rom. 2:2–4a)

For Paul, our presumption to judge others hypocritically for their transgressions ignores the fact that we, too, deserve God's condemnation. But in Christ God forbears us, extending us mercy even as we actively strive to remain estranged from God:

> For there is no distinction, since all have sinned and fall short of the glory of God; they are now justified by his grace as a gift, through the redemption that is in Christ Jesus, whom God put forward as a sacrifice of atonement by his blood, effective through faith. He did this to show his righteousness, because in his divine forbearance he had passed over the sins previously committed. (Rom. 3:22b–25)

The concept of forbearance, then, captures the foundational act of divine grace on which all of Christian belief is built! God acted to extend forbearance to us, to pass over—that is, to refuse to respond negatively to—our sins, instead extending righteousness and patience to us in an act of grace and love embodied in Jesus Christ.

In response, Paul strongly recommends that members of the church extend similar grace to one another, especially in moments of intense disagreement. Toward the end of his Letter to the Romans, Paul wades into a church debate about the importance of certain religious practices. Some in the church believed adamantly that allegiance to Christ should manifest itself clearly in adherence to certain disciplines, including vegetarianism and presumably the celebration of a Sabbath. Others in the church were arguing that faith in Christ frees us from such external scruples. Paul apparently thought the latter group was correct, as indicated by his reference to them as "the strong" and the scruple-focused party as "the weak." Despite his allegiance with those emphasizing Christian liberty, however, he insists that "the strong" welcome the other party in faith, refraining from judgmental contempt for those whom they believed to be wrong in their interpretations of the faith. From Paul's perspective, community can and should be maintained in a church that harbors important theological disagreement, for both "the weak" and "the strong" are united in their intent to live "to the Lord" and in their ultimate accountability to God. As a result, says Paul, we ought to bear with what we perceive to be the failings of the weak, pushing their growth gently, sometimes swallowing our disagreements, seeking not our self-interest but the building up of others (Rom. 15:1–2).[12] For the forbearance we practice in a season of disagreement is a reflection of our gratitude for—and an extension of—the forbearance God in Christ shows us in the face of our alienation. In the end, our maintenance of church unity in the face of difference itself testifies to our faith: "Welcome one another, therefore, just as Christ has welcomed you, for the glory of God" (Rom. 15:7).

Forbearance and Conflict

This biblical idea of forbearance is an underappreciated metaphor for divine grace and an underutilized concept for capturing how Christians ought to replicate that grace in the project of living together in community. To be sure, not much has been made of this idea in classical or contemporary biblical commentary. In his commentaries on both the Ephesians and Colossians passages, for instance, John Calvin leaves the term "forbearance" without comment, skipping past it on his way to elucidating other parts of the passages.[13] Similarly, most modern commentaries do not linger on the idea of forbearance as the lynchpin for the passages we have explored.[14]

Perhaps one of the reasons for its current unpopularity is that the term sounds like a call to yield, which unsurprisingly is not what people want to hear when they are embroiled in protracted disagreements over convictions they consider essential to Christian faithfulness. A couple of years ago, in the run-up to the latest denominational battle over same-sex marriage in the Presbyterian Church (USA), the faculties of two seminaries—Columbia Theological Seminary (GA) and Austin Theological Seminary (TX)—issued statements calling for forbearance in the debate.[15] Insisting that schism in the church is a "profound pastoral and theological problem," the Columbia and Austin faculties implored their fellow Presbyterians to bear with each other in the debate over amendments to the denominational constitution that would allow ordained ministers to officiate at same-sex marriages. In particular, the Columbia Seminary statement notes the way tag-words like "purity" and "inclusivity" have been weaponized in an increasingly hostile ideological environment. Calling on Presbyterians to repent of this hostility and work constructively toward a healthier future for the church, the Columbia faculty modeled this attitude by disavowing their own contributions to the polarization in the PC(USA). Citing biblical authority and denominational precedent, both statements argued that a spirit of forbearance, of "endeavoring to hear and take seriously the convictions of others," was the only way to forestall further division in the church. Indeed, they suggested that a spirit of forbearance in this controversy would testify to the true source of the church's hope, the one who calls the church together.

Predictably, the seminary statements were pummeled in the denominational press, from both sides.[16] Conservatives read the statements as a call to abdicate our responsibility to preserve what they perceive to be biblical teachings on sexuality. Liberals chastised the faculties for abandoning their responsibility to give voice to justice for LGBTQ Presbyterians. For both sides of the debate, the call for forbearance sounded like an appeal to abandon truth and justice in the name of passive nicety or a gradualist pursuit of consensus. Sadly, the statements failed to make a clear impact on the debate that summer.

I think neither the rejection from the theological right nor the dismissal from the theological left represented an accurate reading of the moral vision the faculties of these two seminaries were inviting Presbyterians to adopt. I know that those interpretations of forbearance as an artificial abandonment of debate are not what I have in mind when I commend forbearance. Perhaps part of the explanation for the misreading can be attributed to form. As a genre, the brief public statement could not offer an adequate theological argument; it could not provide the conceptual grounding to understand forbearance as an expression of theological integrity and ecclesiastical faithfulness. (Providing that grounding is what I hope to do in this book.) And to be fair, the Austin Seminary statement does suggest that the church wait for a greater consensus on these matters to emerge, a suggestion that could be interpreted as gradualist obfuscation of the struggle for justice for LGBTQ Christians. But much of the pushback the faculty statements received was rooted in the popular assumption that the pursuit of truth and justice must be engaged as a no-holds-barred contest, that the exercise of forbearance and the pursuit of conviction are mutually exclusive—you cannot have both. In chapters to follow, I consider that assumption carefully, in hopes of discovering ways in which the invested pursuit of what we believe to be true or just can itself be conducted with the virtues of forbearance, without asking us to categorically retreat from our convictions.

To be clear, I am not suggesting that forbearance is necessary because conflict itself is a bad thing. Forbearance is not built on a fear of conflict, but on a desire to work through conflict in a healthy way. Surely it is impossible to completely avoid conflict in any human community, even a church. Conflict is a natural by-product of an association of persons who are not carbon copies of each other. As Stanley Hauerwas notes, "to be a Christian has never meant that we cease to be human beings."[17] Human communities, to the degree that they host any diversity at all, are bound to experience difference and conflict. An ethics of forbearance that depended on the elimination of conflict would be fatally unrealistic.

In fact, not only is conflict inevitable but it can also be a positive force. Conflict can bring differences out in the open, challenge assumptions, and inspire creativity and progress. Conflict can bring attention to strained convictions, expose injustices, and contribute to a healthier and fairer community. As theologian Beverly Harrison once wrote, a society that does not get riled up from time to time is one that does not morally care about anything.[18] In a society whose citizens care deeply about truth and justice, conflict is the inevitable consequence of incompatible but equally passionate perspectives. Similarly, a church that does not care enough about anything to be conflicted is one that does not take seriously its commitment to belief, character, mission, or duty. Nothing I write in these pages should be taken as a desire to avoid or even minimize conflict. Instead, the practice of forbearance represents an attempt to take inevitable conflict and live with it in ways that are constructive rather than destructive. Hauerwas's representation of an Anabaptist understanding of church conflict seems apt for all of us: "That conflict is part and parcel of Christian unity means that the unity of a church is not a unity based on agreements, but rather one that assumes that disagreements should not lead to division but rather should be a testimony to the existence of a reconciling people."[19] The cultivation of forbearance assumes a community of Christians who care deeply about matters of belief and practice, and it does not require ambivalence to principle in order to extend forbearance to others. If anything, to talk of "bearing with" another implies that we often remain unconvinced by their opposition to us. But the physical connotation embedded in "bearing with" another lends us the image of carrying one another through difficult times, and this mutual accord speaks to the distinctive Christian character of the approach to conflict I am commending. Forbearance is more than a *modus vivendi*, an ideological cease-fire. It is instead a positive commitment to living with the productive discomfort of difference as a reflection of the grace of God.[20]

A Ministry of Bearing

Dietrich Bonhoeffer, the German theologian best known for the book *The Cost of Discipleship* and his martyrdom at the hands of the Nazis, understood what he called a "ministry of bearing" to be an integral part of maintaining life together in Christian community. In 1938, Bonhoeffer wrote a little book called *Life Together*, a reflection on Christian community prompted by the Nazis closing his seminary.[21] In *Life Together*, the reader feels Bonhoeffer's longing for the sense of common life he experienced there with other seminarians. In light of that loss, Bonhoeffer reminds us that the enjoyment of "visible fellowship with other Christians" is a privilege, a gift of God's grace to be cherished, cultivated, and protected. Bonhoeffer understood, however, that as a human community the church is not immune from division and self-justification. Christians must acknowledge this inevitability but respond to it with "ministries" or practices of mutual service that maintain the faithfulness of the community. One of these he called the ministry of bearing.[22]

Reflecting the theme in Romans, Bonhoeffer understood bearing with one another to be a response to the divine grace that draws the church together. According to Bonhoeffer, the Christian life in its entirety is an exercise of bearing the cross of Christ. One way we do this is to bear the burdens of others in the community. Often we do this by assuming their concerns as our own, but sometimes they themselves—and the angst they cause us—are the burden that we must carry, joyfully as an act of neighborliness and discipleship. We must bear the burden of others' *freedom*, by which Bonhoeffer meant that we accept the challenge as well as the grace that comes with personalities different from our own.[23] We respect others' individuality and autonomy, and we deal with all of the distinct strengths, weaknesses, convictions, and quirks that come with being in a community with people who are different from us—as Bonhoeffer describes it, "everything that produces frictions, conflicts, and collisions among us" as people.[24] To bear with others is to embrace the sometimes hard or unpleasant confrontations with these differences, and to do so happily. Only by embracing this difference, suggests Bonhoeffer, do we engage others in the church as persons of worth. "To bear the burden of the other person means involvement with the created reality of the other, to accept and affirm it, and, in bearing with it, to break through to the point where we take joy in it."[25] To Bonhoeffer, we not only put up with differences in others but we also engage them, and by doing so we honor them as persons and discharge the hard work of discipleship.

Bonhoeffer acknowledges that conflict in the church results not only from a diversity of perspectives and personalities, but also from the differences of convictions regarding truth that this diversity produces. We believe that what we think is right and true, and what someone else believes, says, practices, or stands for is wrong. Obviously we see this kind of difference at play in the church over matters of sexuality, debates over the authority of Scripture, and a host of other issues. Besides the freedom of other Christians, then, Bonhoeffer argues that we are called to bear with what we might judge to be others' *sins*.[26]

Dealing with what we perceive to be another's sin is a harder project than bearing with generic difference, because what we perceive to be our neighbor's sin may represent (to us) moral or theological irresponsibility, a breach in fellowship with God. Our concerns with those contrary convictions and the threat to Christian community they represent are real and important, but Bonhoeffer argues that to bear with the perceived sinner with patience and love is to mimic the grace of God. As Paul reminded the Romans, God responds to our own alienation with patient grace, without trivializing our sin, and so we bear with others in grace without artificially ignoring the differences between us. In following God's lead, our own forbearance "pays forward" God's forbearance of us. "To cherish no contempt for the sinner but rather to prize the privilege of bearing him means not to have to give him up as lost, to be able to accept him, to preserve the fellowship with him through forgiveness."[27] In the exercise of forbearance, we insist on the maintenance of community even with those we perceive to be in error, acknowledging that the odds are good that we will require forbearance from others in Christian community too.

The "ministry of bearing," then, is the joyful maintenance of community. Forbearance embraces the strengths, weaknesses, and idiosyncrasies of the individual personalities that make up the community. It works faithfully through difference, disagreement, and perceived deviance in the name of grace. Ultimately, for Bonhoeffer the experience of Christian kinship in the church is both a responsibility and a gift: "Christian brotherhood [*sic*] is not an ideal which we must realize; it is rather a reality created by God in Christ in which we may participate."[28] Only a community that practices this kind of mutual regard, says Bonhoeffer, is positioned for the highest service of the church, the proclamation of the word of God to the world.

Forbearance and Christian Virtue

How do we become a community capable of sustaining such a ministry of bearing? We do so by cultivating the necessary character. To talk of character in our Christian life together is to invoke a distinct vocabulary in theological and philosophical ethics. Much of ethics historically has answered the question "how should we live a good life?" by arguing for certain moral rules. Those rules might derive from religious texts or be written in our conscience; they might be absolute or quite pliable, few or many—all depending on the particular philosopher's or theologian's ethical vision. But in this orientation, living the good life means doing the right thing, and the right thing is defined by choices that align with proper moral rules.

The vision of the moral life as rule-abiding is a valuable way to think about ethical decision making, but it is not the only way to think of the moral life. In fact, we could argue that some of the most entrenched conflict in the church has been exacerbated by excessive commitment to the idea that good theology or morality is nothing more than adherence to rules. By contrast, many thinkers down through intellectual history have preferred to understand "the good life" as the project of developing good character, and good character is developed by the cultivation of virtue. The classical Greek philosophers recognized the importance of virtues for moral development; Aristotle taught that virtues are "habits" that are nurtured over time, personal traits that when practiced shape the kind of moral agents we become and regulate how we respond to responsibilities and opportunities for moral action.[29] The language of virtues as a description of "the good life" has biblical roots, too. The apostle Paul argued that faith, hope, and love were the heart of Christian character, and these theological virtues have powerfully shaped Christian theology and ethics for over two millennia (1 Cor. 13). In addition, Paul described the life lived in the Spirit as exhibiting certain fruit: love, joy, peace, patience, kindness, generosity, faithfulness, gentleness, and self-control—expressions of character all (Gal. 5:22–23). Thomas Aquinas, the most important theological voice in medieval western Christianity, appropriated Aristotle's understanding of the virtues as habits and combined it with a biblical theology of spiritual character. He taught that most human beings have a natural ability to develop certain human moral capacities, centered on the four virtues of temperance, fortitude, prudence, and justice. Built upon this natural morality, however, Christian character consists of moral habits cultivated by an infusion of the Holy Spirit, which makes possible the development of those Pauline virtues of faith, hope, and love.[30]

More recently, Stanley Hauerwas has led a rediscovery of the virtues in modern Christian theological ethics, and his work has inspired an industry of contemporary Christian ethicists who prefer the language of virtues to that of rules and principles for defining the Christian moral life.[31] For these thinkers, the cultivation of virtues makes goodness and holiness *a habitual practice*, which then informs and influences the decisions we daily make. For most virtue moralists, these habits of character are best nurtured in community, and in fact they make little sense outside those communities of context.[32] As Hauerwas puts it, "The beliefs and convictions we use to form and explain our behavior are not of our own making. To be a moral self is to be an inheritor of a language of a people."[33] A community, its stories, and its traditions pass on a sense of the ideal character; they help define the good life and shape us into people who rightly pursue it. Friends within the community help to keep us accountable in the development of our character, and in fact for some virtue thinkers friendship itself becomes an exercise in virtue.[34] In other words, community becomes the locus for moral formation. For Christians, the chief community of moral formation is the church.

In the chapters to follow, I describe the practice of forbearance as the expression of Christian character, specifically the virtues of humility, patience, wisdom, faithfulness, and friendship (love). My exploration of the virtues of forbearance will draw (explicitly and otherwise) from the Pauline triad and the fruit of the Spirit. It will depend on this long historic legacy of imagining the moral life this way. And it will take for granted that church community offers a context in which Christians can understand, interrogate, internalize, and practice these virtues. Seen through the lens of the virtues, forbearance can be understood as a commitment to the cultivation of a particular "way of being" in the church, one that lends itself to the navigation of differences in community in healthier ways—for the betterment of the church and the world. Forbearance is not the avoidance of conflict or the abandonment of conviction. Instead, it is a distinctively Christian practice that opens the church to new ways of dealing with difference, rooted in the kind of people God calls us to become.

CHAPTER 2

Humility

The great cartoonist and lay theologian Charles Schulz once drew a *Peanuts* storyline in which Snoopy was writing a book on theology. In one particular strip, Charlie Brown approaches Snoopy and says, "I hear you're writing a book on theology. I hope you have a good title." "I have the perfect title," Snoopy replies to himself: *Has It Ever Occurred to You That You Might Be Wrong?*

As any religious fan of *Peanuts* knows, Snoopy was a pretty orthodox Christian thinker.[1] Yet Christianity is not exactly known for the self-awareness and self-criticism that his title recommends. To the contrary, Christian history is filled with theological title-fights in which all of the participants assumed that they possessed the Truth—with a capital *T*. A lot of ink—and too much blood—has been spilled by Christian caucuses convinced that they represented authentic Christianity and intent on pinning those who disagreed as heretics. Perhaps a preoccupation with defining "right belief" is not so surprising for a religious tradition whose founder claimed to be *the* Truth (John 14:6). Association of Jesus with truth encourages his followers to assert that they *have* his truth. Unwavering confidence, then, quickly becomes an apparent testament to virtuous faith. To be a Christian community that practices forbearance, however, we must cultivate a different virtue, one that also goes the whole way back to Jesus: humility. In our life together, humility is essential to the health of the church, for the virtue of humility conditions us to acknowledge, with Snoopy, that there may be a lot we do not know about an awful lot of things.

The Legacy of Christian Hubris

To emphasize humility as an important Christian virtue is not revolutionary by any stretch. According to the apostle Paul, Christ himself, "though he was in the form of God, did not regard equality with God as something to be exploited, but emptied himself, taking the form of a slave, being born in human likeness" (Phil. 2:6–7). To Paul's mind, Christ exemplified humility, and consequently his followers are called to take on that Christ-like virtue. Jesus practiced humility by ministering not to power but to poverty. In the Gospels, he identified with marginalized persons—the hungry, the poor, the ostracized, and the sick—and instructed his followers that loving those the world rejects is, in fact, equivalent to loving him.[2] Jesus's ministry among people who were culturally discounted exhibited humility, as did his death. The cross, the central symbol of Christianity, is a testament to Christ's voluntary submission to humiliating death on humanity's behalf. One significance of the resurrection is that it vindicated Jesus's commitment to this supremely humble act of love.

After Jesus's death, Paul also exemplified the virtue of humility in his own ministry, if his letters are any indication. He writes of subordinating his own interests for the benefit of the gospel and repeatedly deflects attention from himself and his own successes in the name of Christ.[3] Following his lead, a long list of saints throughout Christian history testified to their allegiance to Christ through the adoption of lives of humility. Often the virtue of humility takes the form of an intentional commitment to live as Jesus did, with marginalized persons. To this day, the idea of the humble saint invokes images of monks, nuns, and missionaries living among the poorest populations of the world. We think of St. Francis of Assisi, Dorothy Day, and Mother Teresa as the embodiment of Christian humility. The overt reflection of humility is certainly one of the reasons Pope Francis is celebrated more popularly than his predecessor. Saints of humility abandon the implicit benefits to which society entitles them as members of the powerful majority, instead living in solidarity with the oppressed, counting themselves among the ones society rejects. In doing so, these saints practice humility as an extension of Jesus's love for the least of humanity, as well as an act of protest against the social injustices that stand between the "haves" and the "have nots."

Humility in service to social justice has been a hallmark of Christian virtue since the beginning of the church. Humility exercised *within* the church, however, has been harder to find. This kind of humility is less about living with the socially marginalized and more about living with fellow Christians with whom we differ. This internal practice of humility within the church has been relatively rare, historically speaking. In fact, from a certain perspective, it might actually seem contrary to the faith, for excessive humility appears to tolerate theological error. In a church charged to witness to the truth, faithfulness requires steadfastness and certainty, not theologically pulling punches. After all, Jesus claimed to be *the* Truth, inviting his disciples to follow him with confidence that they were living as God intended, even when it seemed countercultural to do so. Jesus taught that the world ultimately consists of sheep and goats, and he urged his followers to learn to tell the difference. In that spirit, Christian theology traditionally has asserted that there is a substantial distinction between the saved and the reprobate, between saints and sinners, and the point of Christian subscription is to be counted among the former in these pairs. In general, Christianity seems to be a worldview built on the certainty of conviction in an uncertain world, emphasizing faithful stead-fastness against the tides of doubt and tribulation. Where is the virtue in waffling, in retreating from an adamant commitment to the truth?

In a later chapter I will explore the ways in which a strong commit-ment to conviction can be appropriately held in tandem with the practice of forbearance. Not all strong conviction is virtuous, however. Too easily the celebration of faith's certainty slips subtly (or sometimes not so subtly) into theological arrogance, so that our level of confidence in our discern-ment of God's wishes exceeds what can be reasonably justified, and the faith that was a message of comfort for life in a stormy world becomes a weapon with which to make more storms. The authority of Scripture, the meaning of the Lord's Supper, the significance of good works, the bound-aries of good sex, and the need to be "born again" are all matters of faith over which Christians have divided, because believers on different sides of these issues claimed to know for certain the will of God. Theological confidence morphs into arrogance, arrogance fuels the demonization of the other, and all kinds of evil are wrought from the disqualification of others from the Christian (or human) family. For as long as there have been Christians, there have been believers who so zealously assumed they understood better than others what the truth of God in Jesus Christ really is that they did not hesitate to ostracize and villainize those who disagreed.

Even some of the great statements of common confession celebrated in many of our churches betray this kind of theological hubris. The Nicene Creed is a fourth-century presumption of shared Christian orthodoxy, an attempt by leaders in the early church to "settle" enduring theological questions, especially around the relationship between Jesus and God. The metaphysical descriptions of the Trinity that we take for granted as classical Christian confession (whether we like those classical formulations or not) actually were attempts to resolve open theological questions in the early church. How could Jesus be God incarnate, perfectly divine *and* created humanity? How could Christians believe in one God if they counted the Father, Son, and Holy Spirit all divine?

In formulating different answers to these questions, Christians attempted to hold together claims that on the surface might appear to contradict one another. The nature of Christ and the Trinity were theological puzzles that preoccupied early generations of Christian thinkers. Some Christian leaders argued that Jesus was not really human at all, just the façade of humanity that allowed God to walk among us while protecting the integrity of his divinity. Others argued that Jesus was a real person whose faithfulness caused God to adopt him as a kind of demigod, a theory meant to maintain the integrity of his humanity, even at the apparent expense of his full divinity. The Nicene Creed was an attempt to settle some of these apparent contradictions once and for all. The creed asserted faith in one God, but a God known as Father, Son, and Holy Spirit. The Son was described as "becoming human," but also "begotten of the Father . . . God from God, Light from Light, true God from true God, begotten, not created"—a formula clearly meant to reject the idea of Jesus as an adopted creature.[4] Ultimately the creed described the Father and Son as being of "the same essence," an unbiblical and largely unexplained term employed to bridge the gap between assertions of Jesus's humanity and his divinity.[5] Since its adoption, the Nicene Creed has become a widely shared summary of classical theology for much (not all) of global Christianity—although the version most of our congregations use is actually an elaboration of the Nicene Creed that came out of the Council at Constantinople about fifty years later. Nonetheless, its recitation in churches across a wide variety of denominations serves as a unifying symbol, connecting local congregations with "the church in every time and place."

Yet there is a part of the Nicene Creed that congregations do not normally recite in worship, and that unspoken part betrays a backstory that runs against this unifying grain. What we do not say together are the "anathemas" that accompanied the original version of the creed. To say that something is anathema is to label it as so far off the mark of proper belief that it does not qualify as Christian; it is to reject and condemn those convictions and the people who hold them. That is exactly what the winners of the Nicene "compromise" did to their opponents. Again, one of the important theological questions at stake in the church at the time was the understanding of Jesus Christ. What did it mean to refer to him as the Son of God? For the Christians who were at pains to protect Christ's divinity, it was imperative that they described the Son of God as "co-eternal," without beginning or end, just like God the Father. Other Christians were concerned that this jeopardized pure monotheism, the confession of God as one. These Christians preferred to talk of Jesus Christ as created by God the Father, a little less than the Father but a lot higher than human beings and the angels, a being adopted by God but with "a beginning" in the will of God. The group that insisted on the Son's full divinity won the day (for the most part), which is why the creed asserts that the Son is "God from God" and "begotten, not made." After the summation of what was to be considered orthodox faith, the gathered bishops sharply ruled out the alternative (and those who held it) with unambiguous dismissal:

> And whosoever shall say that there was a time when the Son of God was not, or that before he was begotten he was not, or that he was made of things that were not, or that he is of a different substance or essence [from the Father] or that he is a creature, or subject to change or conversion—all that so say, the Catholic and Apostolic church anathematizes them.[6]

Attempting to capture the nature of God and the miracle of grace in human language is a job for poetry, but the claims of the Nicene Creed quickly morphed into propositional assertions of theological fact. The promulgators of the creed were so certain that they had defined the truth and believed so strongly that the viability of the church depended on doctrinal uniformity that they disqualified those who disagreed with them. This anathema is only one of a series at the end of the creed, defining who is "out" as a corollary to what convictions are "in." While most Christians are unaware of the creed's anathemas, there they are, ironically attached as an intolerant appendix to a historic confession of theological unity.

The theological intolerance on display in the Nicene backstory became a popular tradition in the history of Christian thought, never more clearly on display than in the Reformation. In the sixteenth century, Protestants broke with the Roman Church over perceived theological and moral errors (not to mention the influence of national allegiances). Not oblivious to the church's problems, Rome eventually called the Council of Trent to respond to the Protestant irritation and address the need for reform themselves. Besides reasserting and reforming points of belief and practice important to Catholic Christianity, the Council of Trent also anathematized a long list of doctrinal deviations that Protestants were making popular, on matters such as justification by faith, the importance of good works to salvation, the interpretation of the sacraments, and the proper understanding of church authority. In the creed developed by the Council of Trent, good Catholics everywhere were encouraged to pledge:

> I acknowledge the holy, Catholic, and apostolic Roman Church as the mother and teacher of all churches; and I promise and swear true obedience to the Roman pontiff, vicar of Christ and successor of Blessed Peter, Prince of the Apostles.

Harmless enough, but then the creed goes on to encourage Christians to attest:

> I unhesitantly accept and profess all the doctrines (especially those concerning the primacy of the Roman Pontiff and his infallible teaching authority) handed down, defined, and explained by the sacred canons and ecumenical councils and especially those of the most holy Council of Trent. . . . At the same time I condemn, reject, and anathematize everything that is contrary to those propositions, and all heresies without exception that have been condemned, rejected, and anathematized by the Church.[7]

This encouragement to reject all belief that did not align with the Roman Church was an obvious swing at the Protestant movements. The treatment of Protestantism at Trent, however, was in part a response to the prior rejection of Catholic principles by Protestant thinkers, often done with unflattering rhetoric to say the least. For instance, in a diatribe of theological objections that gave rise to the Reformation, Martin Luther referred to his Catholic antagonists as "toadies" and their arguments as "drivel," the "sludge of [a] foul drain"—which I am pretty sure is a reference to septic runoff. Ultimately Luther described spokespersons of the Roman Church as "instigated by an angel of Satan."[8] Luther is infamous for his colorful habit of theologically disqualifying and even dehumanizing his opponents; the language I have quoted is pretty typical of his writings, whether his targets were officers of the Roman Church, Jews, or peasant revolutionaries who he thought were dangerously radicalizing the Protestant movement. Some of the other Protestant reformers were more refined in their rhetoric, but they shared Luther's dismissiveness toward Catholic antagonists, an attitude that was itself instigated by Roman rejections of (and threats against) Protestants—a vicious cycle, to be sure.

As the Reformation progressed, Protestants began to turn on each other, taking other Protestants to task for perceived errors and exaggerations of the cause, and bequeathing to us the tradition of seemingly infinite subdivisions within Protestantism. This spirit of unmovable certainty—"you are either for us or against us," we can hear those sixteenth-century Christians shouting at one another—continued beyond the Reformation. In the early part of the twentieth century, Christian progressives and fundamentalists attacked one another over which beliefs were essential to Christianity and what effect modern science ought to have (if any) on Christians' understanding of the historic faith. Liberals subjected even the most central Christian doctrines to rational scrutiny, dismissing their fundamentalist antagonists as simpleminded and backward. For their part, fundamentalists boiled down twenty centuries of theological reflection into five propositions, anathematizing any who refused to acknowledge those propositions to be timeless and essential Christian subscriptions.[9] Their descendants continue to fight along these lines, within and between denominations. Conservative Christians accuse liberals of abandoning the central tenets of the faith, subjecting God's eternal truth to the litmus test of secular rationalism. Progressives charge conservatives with incapacitating Christianity in the modern era by refusing to revise traditional beliefs in light of what we know through scientific inquiry. These battles wage between evangelical associations and the so-called mainline churches, but many mainline churches host micro-versions of these theology wars within themselves, with conservatives and liberals battling for the soul of their denominations.

The history of ecclesial division has been propelled by Christians assuming that they grasp God's truth categorically better than others and that their antagonists are so far from a proper understanding of truth that they do not qualify as Christian. Taken to such an extreme, confident faith becomes hubris, an arrogance that prevents us from regarding others as Christian sisters and brothers. Now certainly the pursuit of truth itself is a legitimate Christian preoccupation. My Reformed (that is, Calvinist) tradition celebrates the "preservation of the truth" among what it calls the

Great Ends of the Church.[10] As we will explore more deeply in later chapters, there is nothing wrong with Christians committing to the discovery and knowledge of God's truth. In fact, to do so is one of the highest priorities of the Christian life. But our pursuit of truth dissolves into arrogance if we do not engage that task with virtue, specifically with a healthy spirit of humility. Humility prompts us to accept and honor that there will be differences among Christians as they pursue God's truth and that some of those differences may be the result of our own misunderstandings. Humility therefore commends to us a certain amount of reserve as we make truth claims. Humility reminds us that none of us has a monopoly on truth, so we might stand to learn something from those in the church who discern God's intentions differently. Ultimately, the cultivation of Christian humility shapes our character, so that we approach theological debate with the awareness that, as Doctor Snoopy suggests, we could be wrong about a great many things.

But why should we be humble about our faith? Why is it necessarily virtuous to be tentative in truth claims? To practice humility in the form of solidarity with the world's marginalized is obviously virtuous, for to do so is a clear reflection of the life Jesus lived. But why should we be *theologically* humble? I want to argue that theological humility is a virtue because it is a form of Christian confession. Theological humility is rooted in fundamental Christian affirmations about who God is—and, by extension, who we are. To practice the virtue of humility, then, is to say something profound about Christian understandings of the nature of God and human beings—convictions that draw us together and underwrite the patient navigation of difference in the church.

God Is God

Back when he was on *Saturday Night Live*, Chevy Chase used to begin his broadcast of the "Weekend Update" by saying, "I'm Chevy Chase . . . and you're not." Imagine God opening that skit instead and you have an elementary confession of Christian belief that has powerful implications for how we conduct ourselves in the church and the world. Foundational to Christian wisdom surely is the reminder that God is God—and we are not. In this distinction is rooted the virtue of humility.

Christian confession of the greatness of God derives, of course, from the consistent biblical portrait of God as the Creator, Redeemer, and Sustainer, the source of not just physical reality but also truth, beauty, and wisdom. All good things come from God, proclaims the Bible, and God's truth and wisdom extend well beyond the limited capacities of humans to understand and appreciate. Psalm 8 regales God with praise: "O Lord, our Sovereign, how majestic is your name in all the earth!" (v. 1). It celebrates God as the author of the created universe, the complexity of which prompts the psalmist to ask: "What are human beings that you are mindful of them, mortals that you care for them?" (v. 4). In the Psalms, God is frequently sought and praised as a source of wisdom and knowledge, whose ways are ultimately unknowable and whose majesty inspires awe. This poetic celebration of God's greatness is repeated time and again in other books of the Bible.

The Old Testament figure Job came face to face with the inscrutable ways of God. The story of "suffering Job" is well known, if a bit misunderstood. Job has calamity after calamity piled onto him in a mythical contest between God and Satan, who appear to be taking bets on whether or not Job will crack. Job does not curse God, but his response to his plight is not as enduringly patient as his reputation suggests. Job actually gets intensely frustrated, and he engages in an extended accusatory lament of the suffering he has endured, questioning why God would pile misery on him this way:

> I cry to you and you do not answer me;
>> I stand, and you merely look at me.
> You have turned cruel to me;
>> with the might of your hand you persecute me.
> You lift me up on the wind, you make me ride on it,
>> and you toss me about in the roar of the storm.
> I know that you will bring me to death,
>> and to the house appointed for all living. (Job 30:20–23)

Job accuses God of abandoning him for reasons that are unclear, and, in response, God reminds Job that God's ways are majestic and incomprehensible. God thunders from a whirlwind: "Who is this that darkens counsel by words without knowledge?. . . Where were you when I laid the foundation of the earth? Tell me, if you have understanding" (Job 38:2–4). What follows is an impressive list of God's cosmic accomplishments and a pointed reminder to Job that human beings have no real perspective on the causes, consequences, and significance of the events around them. I am God and you are not, says God!

Appropriately chastised, Job acknowledges that God's wisdom extends well beyond what he (or any other human being) can understand:

Then Job answered the LORD:
"I know that you can do all things,
    and that no purpose of yours can be thwarted.
  'Who is this that hides counsel without knowledge?'
Therefore I have uttered what I did not understand,
    things too wonderful for me, which I did not know."

(Job 42:1–3)

Job's confession that he ventured into the realm of "things too wonderful for me" is one of my favorite lines in all of Scripture, for it speaks to a respect for the reality of mystery, a respect commended throughout the Bible. The writer of Ecclesiastes admits with resignation:

When I applied my mind to know wisdom, and to see the business that is done on earth, how one's eyes see sleep neither day nor night, then I saw all the work of God, that no one can find out what is happening under the sun. However much they may toil in seeking, they will not find it out; even though those who are wise claim to know, they cannot find it out. (Eccles. 8:16–17)

More hopefully perhaps, Paul reassures that "now we see . . . dimly," but there will come a time when we will gaze on God's truth "face to face" (1 Cor. 13:12).

Christian theology has honored the "unknowable" aspects of God's truth in different ways. Many of the early Christian fathers utilized the idea of apophatic or "negative" theology, by which they respected the insufficiency of human concepts and language to capture the essence of God. For apophatic theologians, the best we can do is describe what God is *not*, because what God actually is surpasses human understanding and articulation. God is not created or limited, for instance, but what God is (positively) is impossible for human beings to adequately represent in words. Medieval mystics celebrated God's ultimate unknowable nature poetically, and Martin Luther talked about the active hiddenness of God, by which he meant God's deliberate refusal to disclose the complete divine self to human beings—perhaps to encourage us to live to Christ, perhaps in a Jack Nicholson–like assumption that we "can't handle the truth" of God in its entirety.

John Calvin counseled his readers to accept that there are things we cannot understand about God's ways, including some things God commanded us to do. Calvin's exploration of the Lord's Supper, for instance, included hesitance to over-explain the spiritual union with God that the Christian experiences in it. Do the elements turn into the body and blood of Christ? Or is the Supper simply a remembrance of Jesus? Calvin rejected both of these options, but when it came time to explain exactly how the Christian experiences the divine union that he insisted was at the heart of the Supper, Calvin appealed instead to a reverence for mystery:

> Now, if anyone should ask me how this takes place, I shall not be ashamed to confess that it is a secret too lofty for either my mind to comprehend or my words to declare. And, to speak more plainly, I rather experience than understand it. Therefore, I here embrace without controversy the truth of God in which I may safely rest. . . . In his Sacred Supper he bids me take, eat, and drink his body and blood under the symbols of bread and wine. I do not doubt that he himself truly presents them, and that I receive them.[11]

Respect for the mysteries of God is a recurring theme in Christian tradition.

This respect is evident even for those of us who do not spend our time reading theologians or mystics. Many of the hymns that our congregations cherish linger over this theme of God's gracious incomprehensibility. The first and third stanzas of "Immortal, Invisible, God Only Wise" especially capture the distinction between God's greatness and mystery and our own limitation:

> Immortal, invisible, God only wise,
> in light inaccessible hid from our eyes,
> most blessed, most glorious, the Ancient of Days,
> almighty, victorious, thy great name we praise.
>
> To all, life thou givest, to both great and small;
> in all life thou livest, the true life of all;
> we blossom and flourish as leaves on the tree,
> and wither and perish, but naught changeth thee.[12]

Whether in the words of our classic hymns or of our great thinkers, Christian doxology regularly acknowledges that our God-talk ultimately depicts a Power whose ways, intentions, and being are beyond the capacities of any of us to discern perfectly. God is more than what we can discern, and that greatness—call it mystery, otherness, inscrutability, or Something More—ought to temper the confidence with which we speak for or about God. "Good and upright is the LORD," says the psalmist. "He leads the humble in what is right, and teaches the humble his way" (Ps. 25:8–9). Humility is a Christian virtue precisely because we confess that God is great.

We Are Not God

The second half of God's impersonation of Chevy Chase is also important for inspiring humility. God is God—and we are not. As much as we celebrate God's majesty and mystery, the virtue of humility prompts us to confess our own limits. This is a theme that runs through the Christian theological narrative: human beings are creatures, but special among the rest of creation. And one of the things that sets us apart is our existential awareness of our limitations. We exist in the tension between our finitude and our freedom. We are limited, mortal creatures, but we also possess the capacity to recognize our limits and to yearn to transcend them. So we routinely challenge the boundaries of our knowledge and capabilities in an attempt to be something more than the limits that define us.

We push those limits when we presume knowledge or power that we cannot or should not possess. "Playing God," we sometimes call it. By virtue of the limitations of being finite, we do not know everything, but we like to act as if we do. We cannot do everything, but we like to pretend that there is nothing beyond our reach. We do not control everything, but we try awfully hard to behave as if everything on, above, and below the earth should bow to our power. God is God and we are not—but sometimes we lose sight of the distinction.

The perils of "playing God" are commonly raised in discussions of scientific or medical advancements, where many critics argue that fiddling around with cloning or genetic manipulation is a dangerous reach beyond what human beings ought to control. Some Christians regard abortion and assisted suicide as immoral attempts to "play God" by determining for ourselves the acceptable circumstances for birth or death. Now I think there is room to debate whether or not scientific or medical intervention in any of these arenas amounts to "playing God"—and whether that would be a bad thing. After all, the Bible suggests that God commissions human beings to be stewards of creation in God's stead. Our sister tradition, Judaism, refers to human beings as "co-creators" with God, as a way of capturing the mandate God gives human beings to apply their creativity and intelligence to governance of the world. Maybe "playing God" is not always a bad thing, if by doing so we are using what God has given us to make the world better—more human, more just, more enjoyable—in God's name.[13]

More often, however, the phrase "playing God" connotes a reach beyond what is proper for human beings to do. It emphasizes a distinction that it is hard for our species to accept, a distinction that lies at the heart of humility. We are not God. None of us knows the ways of God perfectly. There are matters of truth to which we do not have access. There are seemingly infinite opportunities for us to learn and grow in knowledge.

In his classic book *The Nature and Destiny of Man*, the twentieth-century Christian thinker Reinhold Niebuhr agreed that what distinguishes human beings from the rest of the created world is our rational imagination, our awareness of our limits combined with our ability to imagine (if not completely achieve) transcendence of those limits. We possess the capacity to understand our finitude as well as the freedom to contest it. Ultimately, however, we cannot escape our limits entirely, and, as a result, we live in a state of existential anxiety, pushing against the limits of a mortality we cannot change:

> Man is both strong and weak, both free and bound, both blind and far-seeing. He stands at the juncture of nature and spirit; and is involved in both freedom and necessity. His sin is never the mere ignorance of his ignorance. It is always partly an effort to obscure his blindness by overestimating the degree of his sight and to obscure his insecurity by stretching his power beyond its limits.[14]

A common form that intentional and insecure obscuration takes is our assertion of power over our circumstances, environments, and neighbors. We exert our interests at the expense of others; we dominate in a futile attempt to "play God." According to Niebuhr, an astute observer of domestic and international affairs, human social and political conflict can be understood largely as the "will-to-power" of human collectives motivated by the uncertainties and insecurities that result from our keen awareness of our own natural, social, and historical limits.[15] Similarly, the assertion of intellectual and moral superiority over others represents a claim to transcendent knowledge of truth, a claim that conveniently masks the limitations of perspective of anyone claiming to have universal knowledge of what is right and wrong.[16]

Despite our best efforts, we will never be able to control, predict, or know everything. From a theological perspective, God is God and we are not. The limits to human knowledge and capabilities should temper our confidence in our own moral or theological pronouncements. We will never enjoy the perspective on what is right, true, and good that we Christians attribute to God. As human beings, we will always have a less inclusive view of the world than God. Our field of theological or moral vision always will be restricted to some degree by our experiences, and usually it will center (implicitly or explicitly) on our own interests. We necessarily suffer from *myopic worldviews*.

"Myopia" is the technical word for nearsightedness, and metaphorically speaking it is an apt description of how we navigate life. Our view of the world and our place in it begins with what is nearest us—our experiences, perspectives, values, and interests. For some of us, our worldview does not extend very far beyond what we know; we are socially, culturally, and perhaps theologically quite nearsighted, and we tend to interpret and judge the world through the lens of the small corner we occupy. For others of us, our worldview is more expansive, with a broader encounter with the world providing opportunities to critique and revise our personal experiences, perspectives, values, and interests. But none of us escapes myopia entirely; we all necessarily operate with worldviews that are at least somewhat bound by the limits of our life perspective. This natural limitation to our knowledge, capacities, and experiences, as well as our penchant to pursue our own interests as the lens through which we view the world, has a number of consequences for understanding God, the world, and what is right and wrong.

First, our natural limitations and tendency toward myopia result in what we might call *informational limits*. Because of physiological restrictions on human memory and the boundaries that experience and exposure create, there is a limit to what any one person can know. None of us can be an expert on all of the information that is relevant to the issues on which we disagree. Moral debates require facility with moral reasoning plus sufficient technical knowledge of the issues that divide us—human sexuality, economics, biotechnology, or environmental science, for instance. Debating theological controversies requires additional mastery of biblical and historical materials, but few of us possess that background adequately to say for sure what is consistent with the tradition. The restriction on the stuff we can know is true of individuals, but it also can be true of communities, especially fairly monolithic ones.

Second, our perspectives are limited not just by our capacities to gather current information but also by our location in a particular moment in history. We might call this inability to completely escape the restriction on our historical vantage point the *temporal limit* under which we all operate. By virtue of being products of the twentieth and twenty-first centuries, we cannot perfectly know what it was like to live in another time and place. Yet we often fail to appreciate the effect that historical location (including our own) has on a person's understanding of the world. I see this all the time in students (and far too many faculty colleagues) who are eager to dismiss differences in perspectives from ages past as ignorance or willful malice (especially if they were influenced by religion), without trying to imagine what it might have been like to live through certain moral moments without the benefit of modern knowledge. Progressive Christians who are dismissive of what they judge to be premodern understandings of God, or who are bewildered by support of slavery among nineteenth-century Christians in the American South, or who are embarrassed by the slow pace at which American Protestants embraced the ordination of women often write off perspectives of the past as simple and closed-minded moral failures without sufficient appreciation for how these views were in part products of what people thought they knew in a certain time and place. For their part, some conservatives *adopt* positions from the past without sufficiently considering how those convictions are historically conditioned, without asking how the progression of time ought to influence our understanding of those same issues in a very different time and place. In either case, by judgmentally dismissing perspectives in the past or uncritically adopting them, we betray an inability to appreciate the temporal limits on those perspectives, or on our own.

Similarly, we cannot predict the future, and that limits the information we have at our disposal. To be sure, in this data-loving era in which we now live, lots of people make a living claiming scientific clairvoyance. Economists create models, sociologists posit theories, political scientists do polling, and natural scientists run experiments—all meant to minimize the mystery in how human beings or the natural world will respond to circumstances in the near and distant future. Yet we cannot take the surprise out of living. For good and for bad, people sometimes fail to behave the way social scientists expect we will. Diseases respond more quickly or slowly to human intervention than medical researchers predict. The economy plods on sluggishly or enjoys a notable uptick that challenges Wall Street models. As breathtaking as human scientific and technological advances have become, we have not managed to free ourselves completely from the surprising, the mysterious, or the apparently miraculous. We do not always know what will happen in the future, just as we do not always sufficiently understand the past.

Third, the myopic restrictions on what we may confidently claim to know go well beyond the limits of *what* we can know of current information or past and future perspectives. Our perspectives on God and the world are also consistently nearsighted because of the influences on *how* we understand the information at our disposal. Call this our *interpretational limits*. Not only what we know but how we understand it and its significance can be affected by the boundaries of perspective. What we have experienced (and what we have not) shapes what we believe is right or true. Whether I grew up male or female, black or white, wealthy or poor, religious or not, in an urban environment or as a farm kid—all of these particular experiences (and many others) affect how I interpret the world and the information I glean from it. My evaluation of the effectiveness of welfare policy may be affected in part by my economic circumstances; while an upper-middle-class American with no exposure to poverty may be tempted to interpret state welfare as enabling laziness, the firsthand experience of poverty might incline another to recognize poverty as partially the result of systemic factors that make it difficult for citizens to achieve self-sustenance. My assumptions about the success of racial justice in the United States likely are shaped by whether I am Caucasian, African American, Asian, or Latino. My perspectives on homosexuality can be profoundly changed by whether or not I personally know anyone who is gay. My assumptions about how Christians "normally" talk, think, pray, and worship will be different depending on whether I regularly worship in an evangelical megachurch, a Roman Catholic parish, or a liberal-leaning urban mission church. The experiences we have had (or not had) affect how we interpret what is truth, what is reality, what is really going on and really ought to be.

Our choices for where we get our information also affect our interpretation of truth and reality, for as one philosopher rightly put it, there is no "view from nowhere."[17] All knowledge carries interpretive bias. As Niebuhr put it, "All human knowledge is tainted with an 'ideological' taint.

It pretends to be more true than it is. It is finite knowledge, gained from a particular experience; but it pretends to be final and ultimate knowledge."[18] If I watch nothing but Fox News for my information about the world, then the information I possess and how I understand the world will be shaped by the values to which my exclusive source subscribes. The same is true if I watch nothing but MSNBC. If I watch nothing but MSNBC or Fox, I may erroneously conclude that what I am seeing on those news programs is "objective truth," because I will lack any comparative vantage point. I will lack sufficient perspective from which to be self-critical about my own biases and those of my favorite news source. I also will lack any basis by which to understand devotees of other news sources, because I will have no exposure to those alternative interpretations of the world. That, in turn, may lead me to make uninformed assumptions about what "they" believe, assumptions that themselves reflect the interpretive biases of my sources as much as they do the reality of my antagonists' beliefs.

Fourth, related to the factors that necessarily make our interpretation of "facts" myopic is our inability to adequately comprehend other people's perspectives, what we might call *interpersonal limits*. As often as we say to others, "I know what you mean," or "I can imagine what you're going through," the truth is that we cannot know exactly how someone else is thinking about an issue or situation, especially when their perspectives are shaped by capacities, experiences, and circumstances that are substantially different from ours. For instance, the fairly localized coal-mining town in western Pennsylvania in which I grew up in the 1970s and 1980s did not in itself provide much of a platform for me to understand the world beyond it. The entire time I was in public schools, I shared the classroom with one African-American kid and (to my recollection) one Jew. I did not know anyone with substantial wealth (although my best friend's family seemed pretty rich, compared to mine). I did not know anyone who openly claimed to be gay, and in fact I knew the term "gay" only as derogatory. The only two ways I could imagine interpreting my Christian faith were the evangelical-leaning traditionalism of my Protestant congregation (which of course seemed an authentic and accurate interpretation of biblical faith) or the Roman Catholic tradition at which we Presbyterians often looked askance. Progressive Christianity seemed an oxymoron in that context, Judaism was largely a foreign concept (including in public schools that still largely subscribed to the Christian calendar), and I had no memorable encounter with any other world religion. I could not possibly imagine what it was like to be rich, black, Jewish, urban, Hindu, or gay. It took going off to college for me to encounter these "others" and revise my understanding of the world accordingly.

Then again, the New England college town in which I now live and work—which prides itself on a high degree of inclusivity—at times betrays its own brand of insularity. It hosts very little understanding of the experiences familiar to a coal-mining community, a fact made quite clear by the widespread bewilderment in my current community over the Rust Belt's role in the 2016 presidential election. My neighbors struggle to imagine the economic and psychological trauma of feeling "left behind" by the progression of American history and culture. They do not possess nearly the appreciation for the importance of labor unions to economic fairness in the United States that my parents and grandparents did, and that limits their understanding of the effect that the demise of unionization has had on the current economic circumstances gripping many parts of the United States. Here in northern New England, religious literacy also is astonishingly low, but in different ways than in my hometown. Buddhism enjoys a certain level of boutique interest, but many folks here do not know much at all about Christian history or its classical teachings, and they are not personally acquainted with a lot of religious conservatives. Neither their unfamiliarity with traditional Christianity nor their lack of real contact with conservative Christians (like the people who raised me) keeps them from dismissing such people as unlearned, backward, and bigoted. In fact, the New England liberalism rampant in my current community often leads to a certain intolerance toward religious conservatives—an ironic demonstration of the myopic perspective that results from our interpersonal limits.

Of course, the larger and more diverse a community becomes, the more likely it is that different members of that community will bring different perspectives to the collective reservoir of knowledge. This often results in an expansion of the collective perspective of the community, and individuals who live in this kind of community are potentially less myopic in their views because they enjoy daily encounters with different people— if, that is, they take the time to get to know and listen to other members of their community. (I will have more to say about the importance of listening in the next chapter.) Diversity, then, serves as a fruitful (if imperfect) antidote to the nearsightedness that our finite perspectives place on us.

The point of all of this is to reveal several fronts on which our natural limits as human beings restrict our perspectives on what is right and true. We lack complete information. Our interpretation of events around us is naturally skewed by our vantage point. We live in a particular time and place that impedes our perfect understanding of histories, communities, and events that have come before us. We cannot predict the future. We cannot perfectly walk in another person's shoes, especially if we have limited exposure to people who are not like us. For all of these reasons, we should expect that our perspective is not the only one to be had on any issue. For all of these reasons, Christians have frequently referred to the lifelong discovery of faithfulness and truth as a *pilgrimage*, a journey to closer intimacy with God that remains by necessity a work in progress through this life. For all of these reasons, we should take Snoopy's advice and consider for a moment that we could be wrong about lots of stuff, including what God loves and desires. In light of the likelihood that we are wrong about *something*, should we not engage one another with considerable humility?

Biblical Humility

Now perhaps you agree with me that there are clear limits to human intellect and experience, limits that therefore restrict what we can confidently claim to know about the truth. Nonetheless, perhaps as a Christian you are inclined to remind me that this is why we have the Bible. "All scripture is inspired by God and is useful for teaching, for reproof, for correction, and for training in righteousness" (2 Tim. 3:16). Scripture is the corrective to what human beings cannot naturally know about truth by themselves. John Calvin certainly thought so. Calvin believed that sin had tragically compromised our ability to know God's truth, but for that reason God provided Scripture, to serve as the "spectacles" that correct our myopia and point us toward the ways of God:

> Just as old or bleary-eyed men and those with weak vision, if you thrust before them a most beautiful volume, even if they recognize it to be some sort of writing, yet can scarcely construe two words, but with the aid of spectacles will begin to read distinctly; so Scripture, gathering up the otherwise confused knowledge of God in our minds, having dispersed our dullness, clearly shows us the true God.[19]

For Calvin, Scripture offered a perfectly reliable source of God's truth, the study of which makes that truth "unmistakable" to the faithful reader.[20]

Human beings' natural knowledge of God may be limited and corrupted in all sorts of ways, but Scripture provides us with a necessary corrective.

Now the nature of scriptural authority is a complicated and highly contested issue among Christians, and this is not the place for a full treatment of the subject. It will have to suffice to say at this point that I do not quite share Master Calvin's optimism about the certainty we may enjoy regarding the truth of the Bible, for two reasons. First, in suggesting that the Bible completely cures us of our myopia, Calvin seems to be underestimating the need for Scripture to be interpreted, which introduces all kinds of opportunity for human shortsightedness to influence our readings. Each of the limits to human understanding we reviewed above affects how we read Scripture. Our temporal and informational limits regarding ancient Near Eastern culture or the first-century Roman world affect our interpretation of the context to which the biblical writers were responding (though archaeological and historical scholarship continues to push those limits farther and farther). Our interpersonal limitations prevent us from perfectly inhabiting the biblical authors' worlds and understanding their words from the perspectives that gave birth to them. Our interpretational limitations result in alarmingly different readings and responses to the words on the page, influenced by the contemporary perspectives we bring to the Bible as well as the different ways in which the diverse history of Christian interpretation may influence our reading of the texts.

For example, Paul's apparent condemnation of homosexual behavior in the first chapter of Romans is read very differently by different groups in today's church:

> For this reason God gave them up to degrading passions. Their women exchanged natural intercourse for unnatural, and in the same way also the men, giving up natural intercourse with women, were consumed with passion for one another. Men committed shameless acts with men and received in their own persons the due penalty for their error. (Rom. 1:26–27)

Many self-identifying conservatives read this passage at face value, as a condemnation of homosexuality as a reflection of the degradation of human nature by sin. By contrast, many Christian progressives insist that Paul is not condemning what we now debate in the modern church—the appropriateness of stable same-sex relationships—because that dynamic was relatively unheard of in the first-century Roman world. Instead, they read these verses as a condemnation of sexual practices that are demeaning and objectifying, and almost incidentally happen to be homosexual in nature. This debate is much deeper and more complicated than I have just summarized here, but at play in the different readings of this same scriptural text are different understandings of this historical context and intention (temporal and informational limits) as well as the distinct perspectives, assumptions, and needs each group of readers brings to the text (interpretational and interpersonal limits). In other words, this is not a debate between those who take this scriptural passage seriously and those who do not, but instead a contest between readings of a shared text, readings that are affected, shaped, and skewed by human myopia brought to the exercise of reading.

And that brings us to the second reason I do not quite share Calvin's optimism about the certainty we may enjoy regarding the truth of the Bible. Given the importance of interpretation to the reading of Scripture, and the consequences that our myopic understandings can have on that interpretive exercise, it should not surprise us that different Christians have different readings of the Bible, with the result being that the "true" message of Scripture is seldom as clear as Calvin implied it should be. But human limitations affect our appeal to the Bible's authority in another way, too. Scripture itself is in part a human product. Christian theology has never understood the Bible simply as divine dictation. Given the way appeals to Scripture come off in some Christian circles, perhaps it would be wise to repeat that last observation: Christian theology has never understood the Bible simply as divine dictation. As Brian McLaren points out, Christians who subscribe to such a theology of Scripture have more in common with classical Islam than with classical Christianity.[21] Christians have always understood the Bible as God's word mediated through the words of human beings. Certainly since the advent of modern historical-critical approaches to biblical interpretation, we have an even better appreciation for the authorial complexities embedded in the books of the Bible. We understand that the Torah was not written by Moses, despite what the KJV told us, and in fact likely reflects multiple voices from different moments in Israel's early history. We understand that most if not all of the Gospels were written by people other than those with the names they bear, and that some of the New Testament epistles were written in the tradition of Paul rather than by Paul himself. None of these historical clarifications undermines the authority of Scripture, in my view, but they ought to make us more circumspect in how we interpret and apply that authority, recognizing that Scripture's truth comes to us through the perspectives of humans articulating their experience of God.

Not only the authorship but also the arrangement of the Bible betrays the fingerprint of human beings. The decisions in the early church regarding which books to include in Christian Scripture, and which to exclude, reflected in part the myopic perspectives of leaders in the church at that time. The "canon" of Scripture—the sixty-six books we now call the Bible—was determined over the course of centuries and reflected regional preferences and political considerations as much as theological discernment. And it is still a matter of dispute today, as several denominations include books in their Bibles that other churches consider "apocryphal" and not (or less) authoritative. There are also limits in the range of issues the Bible addresses. The Bible does not have much to contribute to a scientific explanation of the earth or cosmos, since its books were written in an age in which we thought the world was flat and at the center of the universe. The Bible has a lot to say about poverty but no clear commentary on capitalism, an economic system that obviously would come much later. Despite the way it is wielded in the culture wars, the Bible has very little to say directly on the matters of abortion and homosexuality.[22] It has no direct commentary on gun control or genetic therapy. As God's word mediated by human hands and in historical time, the Bible reflects some of the same limits of perspective that we know in our own lived experience of God.

So despite the popularity of the Reformation bumper sticker, *sola scriptura*, appeals to biblical authority offer no *easy* access to God's truth. Biblical authority is complicated by the limitations and pluralities of human interpretation, both in contemporary times and in the diverse tradition of Christian biblical interpretation. Given the differences in perspectives that can result from both the human origins of Scripture and the human reading of it, it makes sense for us to temper any confidence we may harbor that we understand the truth it portrays exactly.

Fortunately for us, Scripture itself actually celebrates the humility I am commending here: "And all of you must clothe yourselves with humility in your dealings with one another, for 'God opposes the proud, but gives grace to the humble.' Humble yourselves therefore under the mighty hand of God, so that he may exalt you in due time" (1 Pet. 5:5b–6). Humility is a biblical virtue, and it is an essential component to the practice of forbearance. Humble acknowledgment of the shortcomings in our perspectives ought to give us pause before we conclude that those with whom we disagree are not only wrong but irredeemable. It should incline us to habitual self-criticism, as well as make us eager to test, refine, and enlarge our perspectives by hearing other voices, both around us and from different times and places. Humility ought to engender openness, listening, study, conversation, and reflection. But these exercises require time, a commitment to taking the long view on the pilgrimage of faith. That, in turn, requires a certain amount of Christian patience, born of the hope that God will "exalt us" in God's time. To the exercise of hope and patience we turn next.

CHAPTER 3

Patience and Hope

Patience is a lost virtue in contemporary American culture. Once upon a time, professional sports teams built championship squads through the draft, with a multi-year plan and coaches who remained in place for a decade or more. Now franchises bid for mercenary free agents, and they hire and fire coaches with the expectation that "winning it all" should happen in a year or two. As annual divorce statistics testify, fewer American couples embrace the longevity of marriage. The reasons for the increase in divorce are complicated, and a significant factor surely is women's greater power to leave abusive or oppressive relationships. That development is a very good thing, but some of the increase in the divorce rate reflects a more transient understanding of the commitment to marriage through the ebbs and flows of careers, children, and changing aspirations. Politicians used to be able to count on a honeymoon after an election, a season of good will during which they were given the benefit of the doubt as they acclimated to new responsibilities and began their efforts at governance. Now we expect our leaders to show immediate results, even in the address of longstanding and intractable social problems, lest they pay the consequence for their apparent lack of progress in the very next election cycle. And in our contemporary celebration of charismatic leadership, decisive action is assumed to be an essential sign of conviction, even if it betrays a stunning failure of thoughtfulness and care.[1]

In lifestyle, economics, politics, and entertainment, contemporary American culture celebrates immediate gratification and quick responses. We Americans do not sit with things very well; we are not particularly good at waiting. As a culture, we are not comfortable wading through

45

nuance and ambiguity, which explains why we have little appetite for the slow, hard work of reconciling a society divided over so many moral and social issues, from foreign affairs to sexual ethics to racism to gun violence. We display little interest in learning why so many of our fellow citizens think differently about these issues, and we do not often gravitate toward leaders who exhibit that kind of patient engagement either. Patience and deliberation are seldom celebrated as virtues of leadership these days; in fact, these attributes are often viewed as liabilities of character, the equivalent of indecisiveness or a lack of courage—as "waffling." We do not insist that our political leadership engage in serious deliberation or compromise, preferring instead that they employ whatever obstructionist or deceptive strategies necessary to win the culture war. So we end up with a political culture built on bullying and trench-digging rather than the long-term work of getting to know ideological opponents, their arguments, and their reasons for holding them. Negotiation, conversation, and compromise take time that we are unwilling to invest.

Of course, not all of us conform to this description of contemporary American culture. Even among those of us disgusted by the impulsivity and divisiveness that surround us, however, we often react with another by-product of impatience. When we have had enough of the incivility in American politics and culture, we often respond with apathy and withdrawal. Political observers tell us that only 55 percent of Americans voted in the 2016 presidential election.[2] Think about that number! Nearly half the citizens entitled to select the world's most powerful leader failed to participate.[3] Many chose not to come to the polls because they were disenchanted with the tone of American politics, the limited choices our two-party system presents, and the inability of today's politicians to move past fighting to get anything done. But one could argue that this disgust or apathy is just another sign of our impatience. When we walk away from our responsibilities as citizens, we yield our chance to improve politics by participating in it. Rather than asking, with John F. Kennedy, what we can do for our country to restore some civility and productivity to the political process, we tune out and stay home.

The same by-products of impatience that dominate American society are on display in our churches. As in the broader culture wars, we Christians often find quick judgments and decisive action more satisfying to our convictions than long-term dialogue and the prospect of compromise. We would rather make up our minds that our opponents are insufferable, so we can write them off quickly and move on to the consequences of our divisions—which is often to cut and run. This drama is playing out in several mainline denominations these days. The Presbyterian Church (USA), for instance, has been debating issues surrounding same-sex marriage and ordination standards for years. Over the past decade, many congregations decided that they knew right from wrong on these matters and they were not going to find what was right within the PC(USA). So they left in droves, leaving the denomination for more like-minded caucuses elsewhere.[4] Those that remain in the denomination sometimes push for non-geographical judicatories (geography is the traditional way Presbyterians draw governance boundaries) in an attempt to group ideologically aligned congregations together, presumably as a way of staying in the denomination without the need to deal intimately with difference.[5] The General Conference of the United Methodist Church recently decided to refer the same issue to study, rather than make a definitive decision about the future of their denomination, and the move was met with groans from people on both sides of the debate who preferred action to deliberation. Other mainline Protestants are experiencing similar divisions, with Christians preferring ideological ghettos and lawsuits over property rights to any deep investment in theological reconciliation.

While the combatants brawl, more and more people are so turned off by the battle lines that they stay home, giving up on church altogether. Over the last ten years, the mainline Protestant churches in the United States have lost approximately five million members, despite significant growth in the US population over that same span.[6] Of course there are many explanations for the membership challenges mainline Protestantism has been facing, but one contributing factor may be the role our ideological infighting plays in a growing indifference or hostility to religion among Americans. Whether in our antagonism or in our abdication, we betray our impatience—an unwillingness to be church with one another for the long haul—through all of the hard disagreements that divide us. Christians often are no more patient with each other than the gladiators in the culture wars around us, and people outside the church have noticed.

Patience *Is* a Virtue

Yet Scripture heralds patience as a fruit of the Spirit, central to the life of Christian faith and virtue. In his Letter to the Galatians, the apostle Paul lifts up patience as a sign of the Spirit's presence with a Christian (Gal.

5:22). He does so by contrasting it and other fruit of the Spirit with the works of "the flesh," destructive attributes that derive from our baser instincts. Among the works of the flesh Paul identifies, preachers gravitate toward the warnings against "fornication, impurity, licentiousness, and drunkenness." Juicy as these moralistic concerns are, however, they are dwarfed in the list by habits like making "enmities, strife, jealousy, anger, quarrels, dissensions, factions, [and] envy." In other words, the bulk of Paul's list of vices consists of inclinations to sabotage community through divisiveness and destructiveness. By their prominence in his list, these sins of divisiveness apparently were the most insidious signs of "being of the flesh" in Paul's eyes. In this context, the fruit of the Spirit clearly are virtues that have the opposite effect: they build up community. Paul cites love, joy, peace, kindness, generosity, gentleness, self-control, and faithfulness as fruit of the Spirit—all are other-regarding inclinations, all are dispositions that direct our priorities toward the needs of others. Nestled in the middle of this list of community-building spiritual virtues is patience.

But what is patience? At a most basic level, we may define patience as "waiting without complaining," though St. Augustine quickly would remind us that for patience to be Christian, we must be waiting for something good, something we perceive to be compatible with God's intentions.[7] So perhaps a slightly fuller definition of Christian patience might be "waiting to achieve or experience something godly, without complaint." Charles Pinches elaborates on this definition even further, explaining that Christian patience "keeps us moving toward where we are rightly headed, especially when we face evils that threaten to divert us from this way." For Pinches, Christian patience has direction; it represents reasonable endurance of obstacles on the path toward "becoming fully the person God meant us to be."[8] For the idea of patience to be theologically complete, however, we need to include the church, and not just the individual faith pilgrimage, in its vector. We also need to recognize that the marks of *impatience* go beyond complaining. If my children are any indication, impatience sometimes manifests itself in acts of lashing out over delayed gratification. So perhaps a sufficient definition of patience might be "waiting for the fulfillment of God's purposes for ourselves, the church, and the world, without complaint or destructive reaction in the meantime."

Broadly speaking, to have patience is to possess a capacity to bear difficult circumstances with perseverance, a positive attitude, and an investment in the time to find resolution or relief. Each of these elements is important. To *persevere* in the face of difficulty is to muster the courage and inner strength to stick with things, rather than taking the easy out. As difficult as our disagreements in church are, and as sure as we are that the integrity of Christian faithfulness is at stake in some of them, the biblical virtue of patience reminds us that it is seldom a virtuous response to cut and run when the unity of Christ's body lies in the balance. If we choose to muscle through disagreement, a *positive attitude* distinguishes patience from other ways of enduring. Christian patience keeps us from wallowing in sadness or simmering with anger. The medieval theologian Thomas Aquinas described patience as "a virtue to safeguard the good of reason against sorrow," particularly the sorrow other people cause us. This is not to say that patient people never get frustrated by the ordeals they endure, but they refuse to let their frustrations and disappointment turn into despair or resentment. Their ability to stay relatively positive reflects the *investment in time* that characterizes Christian patience. The patient Christian does not think only in the short-term, but takes a long view of piety. She keeps her aspirations for the church constantly in sight, and this vision of the future motivates her to endure present circumstances. Quoting St. Augustine, Thomas wrote that "a man's patience it is whereby he bears evil with an equal mind . . . lest he abandon with an unequal mind the goods whereby he may advance to better things."[9] Armed with the promise of the goodness of God, the patient person refuses to let present suffering distract him in the exercise of hope and faith. Together the perseverance, positive attitude, and far-thinking capacity that make patience a virtue allow us to live and labor through hardship, annoyance, misfortune, pain, or provocation without becoming irritable, contrary, violent, desperate, or divisive.

The exercise of patience is key to the broader practice of forbearance, for it equips us to maintain community in the face of conflict. Through disagreement that many of us experience as real hardship, the charge to bear with one another and maintain community requires that we each foster the capacity to absorb some of the discomfort and pain that comes with enduring protracted disagreement without extreme or divisive response. The New Testament commends patience as essential to the practice of forbearance in community. In the Letters to the Colossians and Ephesians that we considered in the first chapter, the writers invoke patience immediately before they plead for forbearance, indicating that patience is a core ingredient to the broader disposition that allows us to bear with one another in difference.[10] The Book of Colossians goes so far as to describe patience as an article of virtuous clothing that should adorn every member of the church, especially in moments of uncertainty, in order to maintain the spirit of unity in Christ. The Second Letter to Timothy encourages patience as a necessary trait for Christian preachers and teachers, warning those leaders that their instruction will compete with more alluring (but less sound) doctrines for hearers' ears, but assuring them that truth and love will prevail if they are patient with the pace of the Spirit's work (2 Tim. 4:1–5). By commending patience to the church, the New Testament reshapes the normal human tempo and tenor of disagreement.

For we must admit that there is something natural about the alternative reactions to conflict: fight or flight. Scientists tell us that a "fight or flight" impulse is rooted in our evolutionary development, so that (to a certain degree) we are hardwired to respond to confrontation with aggression or fear. To the degree that it charts a different response, patience is a "super-natural" virtue in its call to something higher than the inclination toward self-preservation. Or at the very least it tempers these natural reactions with another dimension of human being, namely, our inherent need for social and moral association. Patience appeals to our need for community by shaping our response to collective challenges with a community-building impulse. It equips us to deal with uncomfortable relationships or circumstances with an eye toward the good of the whole.

Rather than running from conflict, the patient person "hunkers down," as they say back home. In this way, Thomas Aquinas imagined patience as a corollary to a virtue central to common morality, fortitude. For Thomas, fortitude represents "firmness . . . in bearing and withstanding those things wherein it is most difficult to be firm."[11] In other words, fortitude is the practice of endurance in the context of things that disturb us, the resistance to "fear, which of itself evokes flight which fortitude avoids." In a church and culture in which we much more commonly respond to conflict with demonization and separation, both motivated largely by fear of what is different, the exercise of fortitude is essential to the maintenance of relationships and community. If we leave as a response to hardship, we foreclose on the possibility of building understanding and affection between us and those with whom we differ. Working through uncomfortable situations to build relationships takes time, however. Patience gives us the gift of time by providing the energy to persist, the positive attitude to hope for good, and the long view necessary to sustain that hope. In all of these ways, patience roots us in the character necessary to deal with difficult circumstances constructively and positively.

If patience helps us to resist the temptation to leave when we are faced with difficult circumstances, it also curbs the impulse to fight, or to respond to tough moments with anger and aggression. Thomas described patience as a willingness to suffer rather than cause harm through a destructive response to that which frustrates or disappoints us. According to Thomas, "properly speaking those are patient who would rather bear evils without inflicting them."[12] Patient character refuses to go on the attack, instead pushing us to live and work with—and sometimes simply endure—those who wrong us, in order to effect a greater good.

As I have been suggesting since the beginning of this book, with the practice of forbearance, the character with which we engage differences serves as a reflection of the gospel that draws us together in the first place.[13] This is certainly true of patience, where in exercising this virtue we choose to adopt a bit of the character of God, at least as God is known to us in Jesus Christ. Divine patience is, in fact, the central thesis of the biblical narrative of salvation. Like a jilted lover, God heroically pushes through our betrayal and patiently waits for us to find our way home (Hos. 1–3). Like a disrespected father, God waits at the gate, patiently hoping his prodigal children will return (Luke 15:11–32). God is not *passively* patient; the story of divine grace is one of active longing, persistent entreaties, and increasingly creative strategies for helping us find our way back to God. God also reflects a willingness to take the long view, to invest in the time that reconciliation apparently will require. In fact, as Karl Barth once wrote, "the fact that [God] has time for us is what characterizes his whole activity toward us as an exercise in patience."[14] The Great Thanksgiving prayers that many Christian traditions use when they gather at the Lord's Table lyrically celebrate the historical narrative of God's persistently patient grace:

> When we rebelled against you, refusing to trust and obey you,
> you did not reject us, but still claimed us as your own.
> You sent prophets to call us back to your way.
> Then in the fullness of time, out of your great love for the world,
> you sent your only Son to be one of us, to redeem us and heal our
>   brokenness.[15]

We extend patience to others because God has been patient with us, through the "fullness of time." In our exercise of patience among ourselves, the church testifies to God's patient grace with the world.

The translation of divine grace to human form is modeled for us in the life and ministry of Jesus, so that our exercise of patience also represents an effort at *imitatio Christi*, the imitation of Christ. Patience was an important part of Jesus's ministry on earth. To great entertaining effect, the Gospels describe many of those around Jesus bumbling around in partial understanding, especially the disciples, with whom Jesus exercised seemingly unending patience in the wake of their mistakes and dimwittedness. Jesus catches the disciples bickering among themselves about what it means to be the greatest of his followers, and he has to instruct them on the way he is turning worldly definitions of greatness on their heads (Mark 9:33–37). The disciples rebuke a woman for wasting expensive oil on a ceremonial honor for Jesus, when that ointment could have been sold for relief of the poor, but Jesus responds with a vindication of the woman's gesture that continues to perplex readers today (Matt. 26:6–13). And when the most prominent of his disciples resists all of Jesus's doom-and-gloom talk of crucifixion, he chastises Peter and points out for the umpteenth time that the cross is the orienting axis on which the entirety of his ministry is to be understood (Mark 8:31–9:1). Throughout the Gospels, characters consistently miss the point of Jesus's life and message. Scripture depicts the disciples in particular as spiritual amateurs of varying degrees of reliability in their understanding of and commitment to Jesus's way, while Jesus embraces them with enduring patience.

The virtue of patience, then, offers Christians an opportunity to model the character of God. Even if we are convinced that our understanding of Christian faith and morals is truer than others' in the church, to extend them patient commitment is an opportunity for discipleship, a reflection of our gratitude for the grace God extends to us in Christ. The practice of patience is undoubtedly difficult; from our perspective some of our sisters and brothers in the church may resemble those first bumbling disciples, tragically misunderstanding the desires of God. Their misunderstandings may frustrate us, disappoint us, and even give us grave concern for the faithfulness of Christ's church. But when we exhibit patience to fellow Christians, even when we think they are wrong, we witness to the beautiful persistence of God, and we contribute to the cultivation of a church that reflects that godly character. In our unwillingness to give up on them, we proclaim God's unwillingness to give up on us.

Hope

Ultimately our exercise of patience in the face of difference—even difference that brings us great sorrow for the church—testifies to our hope in a future that remains in God's hands. Just as we saw with humility in the last chapter, so the virtue of patience reflects a fundamental confession of Christian faith. Christians are patient with the challenges of time because we insist that time ultimately belongs to God. Our trust in God as the guarantor of the future, then, gives us hope, and hope in the reliability of God underwrites our practice of patience. As the old gospel hymn reminds us, "our hope is built on nothing less than Jesus' blood and righteousness." In the life, death, and resurrection of Jesus Christ, God declared the triumph of love. As one of the statements of faith in my denomination puts it, through Christ we are assured that "in life and in death, we belong to God."[16] Through Christ God is working in the world to reconcile the world to God—that assurance *is* the gospel, and in the midst of all of the uncertainties that life throws at us, that assurance remains our ultimate hope.

As Paul wrote to the Romans, what gives us the power to endure unfortunate circumstances is our firm belief that "the sufferings of the present time are not worth comparing with the glory about to be revealed to us" (8:18). Like the rest of the cosmos, we sometimes groan under the weight of conflict, destructiveness, and animosity around us. Yet in Christ, says Paul, we are assured that nothing can separate us from the love of God (8:38–39). In the meantime, we maintain our hope in God's future, for "we know that all things work together for good for those who love God, who are called according to his purpose" (8:28). What greater source of patience and fortitude could the church ask for than this confession? We hope, not out of confidence in ourselves, but in the God who is much more than even the sum of our parts. We hope, not just in the potential of the present, but in a future yet to be shown to us. "Now hope that is seen is not hope," reminds Paul. "For who hopes for what is seen? But if we hope for what we do not see, we wait for it with patience" (Rom. 8:24–25). With our patience, we testify to our reliance upon God.

Hope that God will secure our future has been a central confession of Christians ever since there has been church. Historically Christians have imagined this hope in the expectation of the coming kingdom of God. The Gospels regularly depict Jesus as preaching the coming of God's kingdom. What precisely he meant by the coming of the kingdom has been the subject of generations of biblical scholarship. At times Jesus seems to be describing an entirely future event, as if the kingdom of God would usher in the end of temporal history and the dawn of a new age. At other times Jesus seems to be describing an era or an ethos that is breaking into human history right now, what theologians have called the "now, but not yet" character of God's reign—part present experience, part future fulfillment. From this perspective, Christians live in the overlap between human history and the triumph of God's ordering. While Christians have never quite agreed on one reading of the kingdom in the Gospels, the vast majority of us pray for it each Sunday when we say together, "Thy Kingdom come, thy will be done, on earth as it is in heaven." In praying this way, we confess our hope for a future that belongs to God.

If the future is truly God's to accomplish, that assurance takes some of the pressure off of us to make the right future happen. When we practice active trust in the big picture of God's reign, we acknowledge that the big picture is not ours to secure. Here we see the direct connection between patience and the humility we considered in the last chapter. When we exercise patience, we remind ourselves that God is God and we are not, that we are finite creatures limited in what we can control. The future is not ours to ensure; the circumstances in church and world that we deem less than ideal are not entirely ours to fix. Sometimes the frustrations we experience are dissatisfactions to endure or occasions from which to learn. Sometimes they are moments for us to grow in character. But they may not always be ours to correct. We do not know perfectly what is right. We cannot know for sure what God intends. So when we exercise patience, we testify to our faith in God's future in a way that also exhibits a humble confession of the greatness of God.

All of this talk of patient endurance and reliance on God to secure the future can be taken to an extreme, of course. When exaggerated, hope can begin to resemble fatalism, throwing up our hands in inert response to the difficulties that surround us, abdicating our responsibilities to the challenges we face in church and the world. Properly understood, Christian hope cannot be license for laxity or resignation. While Christians trust in God to secure the future, we also know that God works out that future through the events and actors of this world, including ourselves. So while our ultimate hope for the future rests with God, we constantly look for ways in which God is calling us to participate in the emergence of that future. In this way, patient hope is also persistent hope, doggedly continuing to do God's work as we understand it.

Hope as patience and hope as persistence would seem to be at odds, however. How do we know when to endure and when to struggle for change in the name of God's kingdom? How do we tell the difference between faithful labor and the arrogant usurpation of the prerogative of God? How do we tell the difference between patient endurance and lazy fatalism? If there were an easy recipe for making these distinctions, then Christian navigation of the perils and perplexities of church and world would be a whole lot more straightforward an exercise than it actually is! In reality, telling the difference between moments that call for endurance and times that call for persistent action requires discernment, a virtue we will explore in a chapter to come. What we can say for sure is that patient hope in God's future is an attitudinal approach to difficult circumstances that reshapes the character we apply to those moments, whether we push for what we believe to be right or hold back and endure what we think is wrong. In fact, as we will explore later, persistent pursuit of conviction can be an act of patience. The cultivation of hopeful patience ensures that whatever we discern to be the right act in a particularly difficult moment, it will be accompanied by a spirit of cosmic optimism in God's goodness. It requires willingness to invest in the time it takes for goodness to manifest, respect for other pilgrims also engaged in the discernment of God's wishes, and commitment to maintaining the unity of Christ's church through the uncertainties we encounter together.

So much of the frustration we have with theological or moral disagreement in the church stems from our commitment to God's truth and purposes, and our concern that some of the convictions our sisters and brothers assert undermine the church's fidelity to God's wishes. Impatience with others' inability to see the right as we do often derives from our love of the church and our concern for its future. Why can liberals not see, for instance, the cultural erosion of the vital institution of marriage and the church's responsibility to protect it? Why can conservatives not see that the world has changed and that the extension of marriage and service to all persons is an opportunity to be on the right side of justice? Why can others not see the truth? For many who care deeply about issues such as these, righteous impatience grows with every additional iteration of these debates, until fatigue prompts us to go our own way, to be church somewhere else.

Or perhaps we are frustrated with the dominance of discord itself. Perhaps we feel that divisiveness itself is what robs the church of its integrity and efficacy. We tire of visiting denominational news sites and reading nothing but the latest chapter of eternal debates over marriage, abortion, or divestment. We long for a time when uncertainty, confusion, and infighting cease to dominate the inner life and public caricature of the church. We yearn for clarity, for singularity of purpose, and for a clear calling in this world. We hunger for a sense of what we ought to believe, and the chaos that reigns in the church tries our patience so much that some of us are tempted to disassociate, either by splitting or rethinking our commitment to church altogether.

Rooted as they often are in genuine piety, these frustrations are understandable, but to exercise patience in the face of such disappointment is to witness to our hope in God as the ultimate guarantor of the church's future. The exercise of patience acknowledges our responsibility to serve God's reign while also admitting that God's reign is not in our power to define or assure. In that confession, patience proclaims that what is seemingly impossible for us to resolve is possible for God. To exercise patience is not to capitulate or lose our nerve in matters of deep importance, but instead it testifies to God's grace, signaling our confidence that God will give us the time and wisdom to get some things right.

In this light, patience is an act of grateful worship. Our respect for the slow pace at which others apparently discover truth and justice is itself an expression of thanksgiving to God for the gift of time. Theologically, patience is an entirely appropriate response to the grace that brings us together and makes us the Body of Christ in the first place. Justified by faith in Christ, sanctified and empowered to live a life for God, Christians live as expressions of gratitude, by loving others as God first loved us. Laboring for God's kingdom, we do so with patient love for others, entrusting the church's future ultimately to God. The practice of patience with one another testifies with grateful praise to the graceful patience with which God first called us to be church.

Practicing Patience: Listening

If patience is a theological virtue rooted in the Christian confession of hope in God's future, then we ought to cultivate it in the church and model it for the world. But what does patience look like in practice? When we commit to the long view, what do we do in the meantime beyond grin and bear the things that disappoint us? How does patience shape the practice of forbearance?

One important way we exhibit patience in the life of the church (and beyond) is through taking the time to *listen* to one another. Listening is an uncommon practice in our active, extroverted culture. To be honest, we Americans generally do not know when to shut up. We have our opinions and we share them loudly, and like most other things in American culture, the biggest and baddest is what we give the most attention. Our penchant for talking and arguing without the benefit of listening to the other side is reflected in our political climate, where actual debate is a lost art form. Rather than an exchange of ideas, what passes for debate in American politics is manipulation and positioning, often based in the intentional misrepresentation (or at least negligent misunderstanding) of an opponent. Candidates for office do not respond to an opponent's actual position on foreign policy, the budget, immigration, or education, but instead exaggerate and distort the positions of the other side to set up a convenient springboard for their own partisan views. The refusal to listen also is on display in the American news media, where "debate shows" draw big ratings as conservative and liberal pundits shout past each other in a contest of rhetorical bullying.

In American politics, it seems true bidirectional discourse is neither sought nor desired. In the context of moral and political debates that preoccupy us as a national community, however, taking the time to listen to one another would give us the chance to understand one another's positions. Listening gives us a better appreciation for how our ideological opponents arrived at such different convictions than ours, why those convictions are important to them, and how they feel they are harmed by our stances. Heaven forbid, listening also opens us to the possibility that we could learn from our opponents, conceivably so much that we change our minds on some things—perhaps a little, perhaps a lot. Patient listening to one another at least promises to help the task of infusing our public debates with more civility. We can only hope that it helps us find a bit of compromise or consensus on the issues that divide us.

With deliberate contrast to contemporary political culture, a forbearing church should advocate for respectful listening, animated by a patience which itself reflects Christian hope that the future belongs to God. In fact, Luke Bretherton has suggested that "double listening" for the word of God in the engagement of others is the essential thesis of faithful Christian participation in political life.[17] For Christians, listening to one another promises practical benefit in the debates that divide the church as well as the nation. As in the greater culture, listening to our opponents in the church gives us an opportunity to learn about them and from them, for the good of our coexistence. It serves as an antidote to some of the myopia that we explored in the last chapter, because engagement with other perspectives enlarges our own. Through a theological lens, when we shut up and stop moving and take the time to listen to others, we open ourselves to the voice of God, whether that voice speaks to us through the voices of those to whom we listen or in the silence that comes from everyone ceasing their chatter for a moment.

True listening as an extension of patience also conveys respect to our sisters and brothers in the church, for it affords us the chance to know better the character, story, and needs of others. When I was in seminary, my pastoral care professor hammered into us the need to listen to the parishioners we visited. During pastoral calls, he encouraged us not to respond with pithy suggestions for how our parishioners might approach their illness more positively, or what steps they should take to get over their anxiety or depression, or how they might think more accurately about the church business that was frustrating them. Instead of advice, he suggested that we respond in those conversations with remarks that began with this form: "What I hear you saying is. . . ." In other words, our primary contribution in those pastoral care conversations was to reflect back to our parishioners what they were saying was most important to them. To be honest, the formula our teacher recommended seemed a bit of a gimmick to several of us in the class. What we did not understand, however, was that our teacher was passing on to us a deliberate practice that would help habituate the art of listening. With time, we would lose the formula, but the habit would remain. Responsible to the task of pastoral listening, we would develop more natural and nuanced ways to indicate to our parishioners that we were truly hearing what they had to say.

Patient listening requires real attentiveness. More fundamentally, it conveys respect and a sense of value to our fellow Christians, assuring them that we are paying attention to who they are, what they believe, and what they need. As an act of mutual respect and concern, listening is a building block for true fellowship and understanding. At a basic level, having the patience to listen to one another demonstrates a profound faith in God, for taking the time to listen means that we are releasing time to God, trusting that the God who rules as sovereign over time will bless our investment in the good work of building friendships, searching for wisdom, and preserving the unity of the Body of Christ.

A number of years ago the Presbyterian Church (USA) hosted a wonderful example of how listening can testify to this kind of faith, and in the process empower efforts to replace division and antagonism with unity and discernment. The denomination responded to persistent debates over constitutional restrictions on ordination and marriage of gay and lesbian persons by commissioning what it called a Task Force on Peace, Unity, and Purity. Consisting of pastors, theologians, and lay persons from across a theological spectrum, the group was tasked with discerning a way through the impasse, one that would respect the calls for purity in the church while also protecting the peace and unity of the denomination. The group embraced its charge by committing to meeting with and getting to know one another deeply, as a foundation for their conversations. They shared fellowship with one another and engaged in study together. Most importantly they listened faithfully to each other as an act of love and mutual respect. The result was, from all accounts, a life-changing experience for members of the group. Many of the participants emerged from their time together with essentially the same position on ordination and marriage, although at least one participant changed his mind dramatically as a result of these encounters.[18] All of them grew to know each other better and to understand positions diametrically opposed to theirs much more accurately and sympathetically. The outcome of their work was a call to patient discernment over time that reshaped the denomination's subsequent wrestling with matters pertaining to homosexuality, perhaps more than many in the denomination appreciate. The Presbyterian Task Force on Peace, Unity, and Purity was a wonderful example of building community with patience, as Christian sisters and brothers trusted God and truly listened to one another through their differences.

Allow me one more example. Andy and Anna were both students in my introductory class on religious ethics. Anna was raised by progressive Christian ministers and considers herself a liberal feminist Protestant. Andy was raised in a traditional Roman Catholic family. Andy and Anna are both Christians, but there the similarities end, for they saw eye to eye on very few issues. While they shared my class, the issue that taxed them most was abortion. As a traditional Catholic, Andy believed that a fetus is a person with moral value akin to yours and mine, and that therefore abortion is the unjustified killing of an innocent person. Anna believed that a fetus has moral value but is not a person in the same way infants, children, and adults are, so that the value of a fetus is more easily outweighed by the medical, mental, or emotional needs of the woman carrying it. For Anna, the central moral issue in abortion is almost always a question of justice—a woman's right to control decision-making over her body, and her right to access health care resources to do so. For Andy, the abortion debate is fundamentally about the inviolability of innocent life.

Andy and Anna were at opposite ends of the ideological spectrum when it came to abortion, and the semester could have dissolved into a weekly shouting match between the two. But partly because of the rules I set for my classroom, and partly because of the virtuous disposition of my two students, that did not happen. Instead of seeing class as a contest to win, Anna and Andy approached it as an opportunity to understand a position within their own faith tradition that heretofore had perplexed them. So they listened, they prodded each other, and they carefully considered what the other had to say. As a result, they left the semester with what they were seeking. They did not change their respective minds on the morality of abortion, but they understood better how someone could come to such a remarkably different conclusion than theirs, from within the same general set of Christian convictions. They also developed profound respect for each other, as moral thinkers and persons of deep faith.[19]

When we shut up and truly listen from time to time, we make room for others to share and inquire. We also create space for people to say nothing at all, and the enjoyment of occasional silence can be instructive as well. I firmly believe that silence is underappreciated, perhaps because I am an extreme introvert living in a world run by extroverts. Introverts like me are naturally wired to value silence and a slower social pace, because we actually depend on a significant amount of "alone time" in order to get back the considerable energy we expend in situations with other people. By contrast, extroverts, who actually get energy from social situations, often seek to maximize occasions to work, play, and talk with other people, with the result that they are often too preoccupied with moving, doing, and talking to have much time for quiet. As Susan Cain has demonstrated in her remarkable book *Quiet: The Power of Introverts in a World That Can't Stop Talking*,[20] American culture is dominated by extroverts and the character traits that predominate among them. The cultural gravitation toward charismatic leadership (believe it or not, there are other types of leadership styles), the popular preference for action over contemplation, and the prevalence of "group think" models in contemporary business strategies all speak to the way American culture honors, values, and takes its cue from an extroverted view of the world. In this kind of ethos, there is little room for cultivating stillness and silence. Cain argues, however, that the political and business arenas would do well to adopt more introverted ways of thinking—or at least to make more room for introverted individuals to contribute the strengths of their personalities to the common good, instead of feeling like they need to masquerade as extroverts to be accepted. Using the 2008 Wall Street crash as the quintessential example of an extroverted world run amok, she argues that we could use a little more introverted character. Introverts display, among other things, an ability to think and work independently, a penchant for thoughtful analysis, the discipline to develop a plan and stick with it (the opposite of impulsiveness), a heightened radar for risk, and a greater capacity than extroverts for reward deferral. All of these traits would have helped stave off the financial crisis, she argues, had they been in greater supply in contemporary business culture.

Cain helpfully illustrates the practical advantages that come from placing more priority on stillness, deliberation, and quiet, and these advantages promise as much benefit to church as to political and business culture. Our life together as church undoubtedly would benefit from less impulsive action (especially actions that divide Christians from one another) and more appetite for contemplation, thoughtfulness, and consideration. With specific respect to Christian community, though, silence also possesses great theological value, for the Christian tradition has consistently expected that God sometimes speaks to us in silence. In a religion centered on one who presents himself as the word of God, God nonetheless speaks to us in the absence of words as well, at the disconnect between our most eloquent expressions of profundity and the truly profound reality that is God. God may appear to us in the words we share with one another, but also at the very moment in which words fail to capture what is good or right, beautiful or comforting. As Barbara Brown Taylor has put it, perhaps "silence becomes God's final defense against our idolatry." Silence gives God distance from our hopelessly approximate attempts to give utterance to what is divine. In fact, given the ways in which our words about God can obscure the beauty of God as much as they elucidate it, Taylor wonders if it is true that "when we run out of words, then and perhaps only then can God be God."[21] One part of practicing patience is developing the art of listening to one another, seeking the word of God in the words we share with our neighbors. But surely we would do well to remember that listening for God, in the absence of human speech, is a practice worthy of the virtue of patience as well.

In the church, we listen to one another because we admit we do not know everything there is to know about God, the world, and the church's responsibility in it. We listen because we know we do not control the future, and we trust that God does. We listen as a confession of our dependence on God and as a sign of hope that God will speak words of wisdom to us, in the stillness of silence and through the convictions of those most unlike us. We listen out of respect for others in the church, fellow pilgrims in the faith. We listen because we are Christians who believe that humility and patience are often the sincerest expression of piety we can offer in the differences that most perplex us.

Practicing Patience: Persistence

Given our emphasis on listening, it is important to point out that patience does not require simple passivity in the face of real disagreement. Listening to others, and for God, is not a passive exercise. Listening requires active intention and engagement. There is also more to the practice of patience than the call for Christians to stop talking every so often. Listening is an important act of patience, but sometimes patience manifests itself in what would seem to be the opposite of listening: persistence, or the respectful unwillingness to give up the struggle for what is good.

In the Gospel of Luke, Jesus tells the parable of a woman who had a legal claim for restitution, which she takes to the local judge. The judge, whom Jesus describes as respecting neither God nor other people, dismisses her without listening, and sends her home for the day. Undeterred, the woman returns to the judge's home the next day to make her appeal. Rebuffed by the magistrate, she leaves only to return the next day, and the next day, and the next. Finally the judge is so exhausted by the woman's dogged pursuit of her claim that he throws up his hands: "Though I have no fear of God and no respect for anyone, yet because this widow keeps bothering me, I will grant her justice, so that she may not wear me out by continually coming" (Luke 18:4–5). Luke frames the story by telling us that it is a parable about the "need to pray always and not to lose heart" (18:1). If that is the moral of the story, surely a corollary is that there is virtue to be found in speaking and laboring for the things that are most meaningful to us. If this parable is any indication, Jesus considered persistence to be an admirable trait.

To my mind, persistence is not the opposite of patience, but derives from the virtue of patience. We said that patience represented the character necessary to endure hard circumstances with perseverance, a positive attitude, and a commitment to the long view of God's future. If this enduring attitude affords us the luxury of time to wait on God and better understand (and love) our fellow Christians, it also gives us the energy to sustain our commitment to our convictions. The perseverance that patient character cultivates gives us the drive to labor for what is right day after day, whether progress is clearly evident or frustratingly absent. The positive attitude that comes from a patient heart sustains us, especially through difficult times. And the long view of God's time gives us hope that God's truth and justice will prevail, despite the limited success we may experience in the present. Persistence, the dogged commitment to what we believe is right in God's eyes, clearly depends on patient hope for its energy.

Such persistence is completely compatible with the larger project of forbearance. As we have said already and will explore more deeply later, forbearance does not necessarily ask us to temper our enthusiasm for our beliefs. It does not ask us to stop pushing for what we believe to be right or true. Persistence in our convictions can be a righteous display of Christian piety, when the patient hope that animates it partners with other virtues that forbearance requires—humility, trust, courage, wisdom, and a commitment to the unity of the Body of Christ through the maintenance of friendship with others. When the persistent pursuit of our beliefs takes its shape from *all* of the virtues of forbearance, Christian conviction can be a righteous and respectful expression of patient hope.

The apostle Paul tried to embody Christian patience, but that did not mean that he shied away from calling out colleagues in the early church's leadership who he thought misunderstood some of the implications of the gospel—even Peter![22] In doing so, Paul illustrated a persistence that was completely compatible with his commendation of patience as a virtue. Sometimes when we are exercising patience, we endure what disappoints or frustrates us by peacefully maintaining community through that disappointment. Sometimes, though, we exercise patience by refusing to give up the cause, by respectfully showing up day after day to make the case for why our understanding of the gospel represents the path to righteousness for Christ's church. Sometimes patience expresses itself through the aggressive maintenance of conviction, even in an environment that shows little evidence of progress.

Some might argue, though, that persistence is precisely what is killing our churches. Within and beyond the church, people are tired of the fighting between Christians, factions forever arguing over the same issues. Persistence, however, is not the same thing as fighting without yield. The conflict fatigue that plagues our denominations and turns people off from church affiliation comes not from strong beliefs but from advocating for those beliefs in destructive ways. When persistence is embraced as part of the larger practice of forbearance, when it is exercised with respect and love for others as brothers and sisters in Christ and with a concern for the health of the Body of Christ, then persistent advocacy for what we think is right and true takes on an entirely different character than we often see in our churches, and the nature of our disagreements becomes starkly different. When done in a spirit of forbearance, persistent conviction brings with it an equally strong willingness to listen to others. It advocates for its vision with respect for others and their views. It takes seriously the responsibility to distinguish the moments to press its case from moments when the struggle needs to rest and intentional community-building needs to happen. Persistent conviction in the spirit of forbearance keeps its aim on the cultivation of Christian friendship, and in doing so contributes to, rather than threatens, the health of the church.

Admittedly, it is not always easy to know when is a good time to listen and when is the right moment to voice our sense of the right and good as we understand it. In chapters to follow, we will consider the Christian duty to speak the truth and insist on justice, and how our commitment to those ideals might be reshaped through the practice of forbearance. We will explore the Christian pursuit of wisdom, including the discernment necessary to know when silence or prophetic witness is the more virtuous course. At this point, though, I want to repeat that forbearance does not ask us to categorically stand down from our vision of what is right and good for God's church. Without debate over the things that divide us, we end up with nothing but unproductive stalemates or an unhealthy denial of conflict. Patient hope infuses health into our disagreement, but it does not ask us to pretend that there is consensus where none exists. Instead, patient hope invites us to give our differences the gift of time. Anger and disappointment do not go away with a commitment to patience, but patience makes room for everyone to share the source of their disappointment, thus making our conversations more inclusive. The cultivation of patience also increases the chance we might hear something different in the long investment in dialogue and relationship, and that in turn increases the chance we might learn something in the process.

Ultimately, a church with patient character exhibits a willingness to invest in the long-term hard labor of paving the way for God's kingdom to break through, to commit to that task and to each other. The commitment of time is counter-cultural; it flies in the face of conventional demand for quick satisfaction so prevalent in contemporary American society. When we choose to be patient instead, we honor God's time by investing in relationships and the project of community over the long haul. As an ingredient to the practice of forbearance, patient hope compels us to put in the effort to be church, even, or especially, when we encounter people or circumstances that make us uncomfortable, frustrated, or disappointed. Cultivating hopeful patience does not mean that we necessarily allow time to paralyze us. It does not eliminate hard decisions. Hopeful, patient forbearance does mean that while we are collectively pondering our responsibilities as church, while we are debating and discussing and deciding on all kinds of issues, we listen to and stick with each other. We entrust the dialogue and decisions of the present to the greater hope we have in God's future, even if with sorrow and regret over what is happening now. For by doing so, we yield the pace of the kingdom to the God who reigns.

CHAPTER 4

Wisdom

"Be careful then how you live, not as unwise people but as wise" (Eph. 5:15). If we are to take the Letter to the Ephesians seriously, the call to be communities of faith in Christ is a call to exhibit wisdom. The same epistle that implores us to practice forbearance together in the unity of the Body of Christ indicates that wisdom is part of the formula for fulfilling that duty. But what is wisdom? What does it mean to live "not as unwise people but as wise"? At first glance, it might seem that wisdom simply is the possession of knowledge, and certainly that is an aspect of wisdom. People we consider wise know things, sometimes a lot of things. The possession of knowledge, however, does not quite capture all that experience and the testament of great thinkers have suggested is true about wisdom. Following Aristotle, we usually consider wisdom to be a capacity as much as the possession of facts. Aristotle defined "theoretical wisdom" as the knowledge of scientific "first principles," what we might now call factual knowledge. But he suggested that theoretical knowledge did not exhaust the idea of wisdom. Instead, he wrote also of a "practical wisdom" that represented the knowledge of what is useful to the project of living the good life. For Aristotle, there was a moral component to wisdom, in that it represented the discovery of knowledge directed toward a proper end, a life lived well.[1]

Plato suggested that the wise person is one who lives wisely as a matter of virtue, in conjunction with other virtues, especially humility. In the *Apology*, Socrates tells of his friend Chaerephon asking an oracle if there is anyone wiser than Socrates. The oracle replies that Socrates is the wisest, which puzzles Socrates and leads him on the quest for an explanation.

Socrates does not consider himself to be the most knowledgeable person, but his account of his exploration of wisdom reveals that an important contributor to his being the wisest teacher is his humility. He knows what he knows, and he knows what he does not. He does not claim to know more than he does, and he does not celebrate his possession of knowledge. Plato suggests that this intellectual humility stems from Socrates's wisdom, and in fact makes him wiser than others.[2]

So wisdom would seem to be about knowing things in the right way, without pretension and directed toward the pursuit of the good life. The Bible's treatment of wisdom reinforces this understanding. Wisdom is celebrated as an admirable trait throughout the Bible, particularly in the Book of Proverbs. It is understood as a pursuit of knowledge in service of the good life, specifically the life of righteousness. Proverbs suggests that wisdom is rooted in the "fear of the Lord" (1:7), a reverence for God and a desire to live as God wishes us to live. Wisdom is a bequest of God to those who dedicate themselves to God's way.[3] Occasionally the Hebrew Bible personifies wisdom as the female Spirit of God, suggesting that wisdom involves being possessed by the divine.[4] As a reflection of the Spirit of God, wisdom is one dimension to living as the *imago Dei*, the image of God, in the world.

These themes continue in the New Testament, where true wisdom is contrasted with human standards of knowledge, by which allegiance to God might be regarded as "foolishness" (1 Cor. 1:25). In defiance of such human standards, Paul and the writers of other letters in the New Testament insist that followers of Christ who dedicate themselves to God's path are wise. Evoking the personification of wisdom as the Spirit in Proverbs, Paul identifies Christ as the wisdom of God, the enabler of true righteousness and holiness (1 Cor. 1:30). The Epistle of James characterizes wisdom as purity and sincerity, peacefulness, deference, consideration, mercy, and fairness (James 3:17). This letter, too, attributes wisdom to the indwelling of God's Spirit, and suggests that true wisdom that is capable of bearing moral fruit participates in the other spiritual virtues inspired by the character of Christ himself.

Like Plato and Aristotle, biblical depictions of wisdom move beyond the simple possession of knowledge to suggest that wisdom is a virtue, reflective of other virtues, and directed toward the good life—in the case of Christian witness, the life lived for God in the pattern of Christ. Protestant reformer John Calvin opened his magnum opus, the *Institutes of the Christian Religion*, with this declaration: "Nearly all the wisdom we possess, that is to say, true and sound wisdom, consists of two parts: the knowledge of God and of ourselves."[5] Calvin's point was that virtually everything it is important to know in the name of wisdom is oriented toward the life of piety, the pursuit of genuine relationship with and responsibility to God. Wisdom theologically understood is character that disposes us to thoughtful and constructive consideration of who God is, who we are, and what a right relationship between God and us includes.

The pursuit of wisdom as part of Christian character directly serves the practice of forbearance. It cultivates in us a spirit of openness and a desire for growth. As I will argue shortly, wisdom contributes to forbearance this way because true wisdom develops capacities that allow us to live productively with—and perhaps even seek out—the differences that emerge as Christians pursue growth in piety together. Before we can see clearly how wisdom contributes to the practice of forbearance, we need to spend a bit more time exploring the meaning of wisdom itself. What exactly does a capacity for wisdom—or a love of wisdom, as many have called it—involve?

Wisdom as Intelligence

Certainly it seems pretty straightforward to claim that wisdom connotes *intelligence*. In fact, in the popular usage of the terms, we often use intelligence and wisdom as synonyms to describe those whom we consider to be "smart people." People we consider wise and smart often know a lot of stuff. At the same time, we all know individuals we would consider wise who are not highly educated, so we should be careful about our association of wisdom with intelligence. Education surely can contribute to wisdom, but by this I mean education broadly construed—liberal education (like you would get from a college), vocational training, and self-teaching all can help make one wiser. But I work with a highly educated bunch of students and colleagues, and some of them I would hesitate to describe as wise. Education does not always guarantee the presence of wisdom, and I want to be clear that I am not implying a kind of intellectual elitism in my understanding of wisdom, as if only those who have had college or university education can be considered wise.

Perhaps the wisest person I have ever known in my life was a man from my hometown named Jim. As I was growing up, Jim was my father's best friend, and he had a certain warm gravitas that made him a trusted advisor in my high school and college years. Jim had nothing beyond a high school education and some training as an electrician, but he was intelligent. His practical knowledge was awe-inspiring; the man could problem-solve and fix almost anything, it seemed. He could master a misbehaving circuit, manhandle an uncooperative three-point hitch, or devise a plan to save some endangered wetlands. (Jim worked as a maintenance foreman for the Pennsylvania Game Commission.) But his wisdom consisted of more than just accumulated practical experience. He knew a lot, but he was always actively adding to his knowledge base, and he was a master at passing that knowledge on to others. He could teach you how to drive a stick shift by describing the precise feel of that moment when the clutch was engaged and it was time to give the truck a shot of gas. He could give you exact directions to a remote field on a patch of public wilderness, just by recounting the natural signposts that others would never notice. His reservoir of experiences sharpened his capacity for problem-solving, because he learned to appeal to his past experiences to anticipate solutions to analogous problems in the future.

In his book *Shop Class as Soulcraft*, Matthew Crawford writes about the kind of wisdom that comes from what he calls "manual competence." Crawford is a motorcycle mechanic with a PhD from the University of Chicago, and he argues that work with tangible objects and tasks—construction, repair, and maintenance work—makes a very real intellectual demand on those who engage in it, and in turn cultivates its own kind of intelligence in those who invest in this kind of work. Through stories of his own mechanical mentors, Crawford suggests that the manual trades make people better critical thinkers and problem-solvers by encouraging them to learn from both success and failure. They make people less passive and dependent, fostering a sense of agency and ownership in the product of their labor. They encourage habits of self-reliance and responsibility, while also awakening us to a truer sense of social solidarity—a solidarity rooted not in the obscuring of difference but the acceptance of it, revealing how our differences become moments of complementarity and thus connectedness between us. In contrast to the training of "knowledge workers" so hyped by liberal arts institutions, and the corporate culture "group think" that peddles the rhetoric of cooperation but also aggravates an increasing detachment between employees and the final product of their labor, Crawford argues that the mechanical arts develop wisdom through the intimacy of worker with work, in community with others who share investment in the trades.[6]

Wisdom includes a capacity for intelligence, and the currency of intelligence is knowledge, but that knowledge can come from the study of great books and ancient civilizations or from practical experience with real-world problems, tasks, and projects. Intelligence can be the product of extended formal education (people who are "book smart," as we say), but it also can take other forms. Experience begets intelligence in people who are open to learning from what they encounter in their lives. We can talk about emotional intelligence, people who have actively developed the capacity to understand others on an affective level. There is social intelligence, people who have an unusually keen sense of the dynamics at work in a collective or community. And there is practical intelligence, people who know how to solve problems, complete projects, and in general get things done. To describe wisdom (at least in part) as the possession of intelligence, I mean a capacity to accumulate and learn from knowledge wherever it originates, an openness—perhaps even a hunger—for knowledge and increasing understanding. Intelligent persons want to know more, and they have a knack for learning more, about whatever it is that preoccupies them.

Christian theology has always featured consistent appreciation for and incorporation of knowledge and intelligence as compatible with (often necessary to) Christian faithfulness. Christianity is an intellectual religion, as is clear to anyone who has encountered Augustine's incorporation of Platonist philosophy, Thomas Aquinas's variation on an Aristotelian theme, Jonathan Edwards's reconciliation of Puritan theology to the Enlightenment, Dorothy Day's fusion of Christianity and Marxism, or Kierkegaard's Christian existentialism. Christian thought has propelled some of the most profound philosophical, moral, social, and political movements in western intellectual history—the Renaissance, the development of human rights discourse, justifications of capitalism and democracy, and the just-war tradition, to name a few. Western intellectual history would be incomplete without the value placed on intelligence in Christian theology.

This emphasis on intelligence as a component of wisdom is a helpful reminder that Christianity is not anti-intellectual. You would not know that from the commentary of religion's many contemporary critics, for example Bill Maher and Richard Dawkins. From their perspective, religious faith is the opposite of intelligence. Bill Maher regularly depicts organized religion as "ridiculous," a regrettable human fetish that promotes closed-mindedness, stupidity, and hate. Dawkins famously wrote of religion as a "delusion," a fiction or pathology that simply makes people irrational. "Dyed-in-the-wool faith-heads are immune to argument," Dawkins categorically proclaims, "their resistance built up over years of childhood indoctrination."[7] According to these cultured despisers of religion, Christianity is the antithesis of intelligence; it squelches thinking with its adherence to anti-science dogmas and deference to church authority. Truth be told, some Christians give the charge credence by the way they represent faith as necessarily hostile to science, stunningly proud of being "folksy" and unsophisticated in their dismissal of intellectual rigor.[8] Both Christianity's critics and some of its adherents act as if being Christian requires us to be anti-intellectual.

Appreciation for intelligent wisdom is the norm in the history of Christian thought. In fact, respect for knowledge has prompted Christians to reconsider their views on a host of issues as they have confronted challenging new information. As a result of the influence of economic theory on Catholic moral theology, the Roman Catholic Church went from being suspicious of modern economies to being one of the most ardent supporters of economic freedom and the rights of workers. Similarly, the Catholic Church has shifted its teachings on the death penalty as a result of new understandings of the effectiveness of punishment and the biases inherent in criminal justice systems.[9] Mainline Protestants and Catholics alike have mitigated their support for just war principles and developed standards known as "just peacemaking" that address war through better understanding of geo-political imbalances and the nonmilitary causes and consequences of political violence.[10] American Protestants now routinely herald democracy as almost a biblically mandated form of government, when just three centuries ago it was seen as a recipe for social anarchy. Many Protestants have been influenced by the modern women's movement to reject historic gender hierarchies. The point here is that Christianity not only has given value to reason, knowledge, and intellect, it has been open to change as a result of new knowledge and understanding.

Put bluntly, Christians who represent the faith as anti-intellectual in the name of defending "traditional Christianity" do not know the tradition they presume to preserve. Progressives are prone to the same mistake, however. Many progressives seem to think that in order to be progressive one must jettison everything old, as if "intelligent" and "pre-modern" are opposites, as if everything in Christian tradition before the 1960s is misogynist, imperialist, and antiscientific. In my own progressive, highly educated part of the United States, I am amazed at the traction this assumption gets among New England Christians. The number of otherwise very educated people who remain happily ignorant of the intellectual depth of the Christian tradition, instead satisfied with peddling the easy assumption that traditional theology is ill-suited for the modern mind, is stunning to me. David Tracy, who taught for years at the University of Chicago, once wrote that religion is "the single subject about which many intellectuals can feel free to be ignorant."[11] Apparently some progressive Christians feel free to perpetuate the same ignorance of their religion too.

The truth is that there is enormous intellectual depth to the history of Christian theology, which we discover when we commit to actually studying it. Yes, a lot in this tradition also appears to us as significantly unenlightened—for instance, theological apologies for slavery and racial bigotry, religious justifications for the oppression of women, and biblically inspired oblivion to the understanding of the world that modern science opens to us. But these less attractive elements of the tradition should be understood in historical context, to illuminate the degree to which those aspects of the tradition we may be inclined to dispense with are themselves reflections (at least partially) of much different times and places. While we cannot minimize the role that power and fear have had in theological arguments that justify dominance of one race, gender, or class over others, some of these moments in Christian theology may have been products of what passed for intelligent thinking in their time. We know more now, so we are wise to move on from outdated cosmologies, race theories, and gender constructions. But as we move on, we are simply carrying on the Christian tradition of thinking intelligently about God and the cosmos in our time and place.

A historically sensitive approach to the tradition keeps us from leveling excessive judgment against Christians who have gone before us, for in imagining what it might have been like to view the world from their vantage point, we are reminded of the myopias with which they had to live. Historical sensitivity also reminds us that we are just as limited in our vantage points, just as much products of a particular moment, so that encounters with older aspects of tradition sometimes reveal blinders that a twenty-first-century perspective presents for our understandings of God and ourselves. In other words, the study of historical tradition not only gives us a chance to embrace or reject the old, it also challenges our sense of the new and improved, our equally context-dependent assumptions about what is right, true, or intelligent. For instance, one way that other historical moments in Christian thought can helpfully expose the assumptions of modern thinking is by providing alternatives to our modern embrace of individual autonomy as a supreme good. The high priority older Christian theology puts on social community, through concepts such as the common good and authority, exposes our modern idolatry of atomistic individualism, a by-product of contemporary American libertarian culture that Christians of conservative and liberal stripes often baptize with abandon. Or perhaps historical religion helpfully pushes back on the uncritical scientific reductionism that has become so characteristic of university life in our time, by lending us its relative comfort with mystery and reminding us of the real limits on human understanding, even in this ambitious (and at times self-righteous) scientific age.

Christian faith is not anti-intellectual. To be sure, Christian thinkers often have challenged the standards for what passes as intelligence, contrasting conventional knowledge with the "foolishness of God." But respect for intelligence is an enduring part of Christian wisdom. What does all of this have to do with forbearance? Insofar as Christian wisdom respects intelligence, it encourages an openness to discovery, a hunger for knowledge, and a commitment to growth that shapes the disposition with which we encounter differences. Christian wisdom that values intelligence seeks a broadening of understanding, and embraces opportunities to learn from others and to grow closer to others. Wisdom invites the opportunity to learn, to be persuaded by perspectives not yet held, to discover room for growth even in the encounter with perspectives ultimately judged unpersuasive. As a result, a spirit of forbearance informed by intelligent wisdom sees disagreement not as a problem to be solved but as an opportunity for maturation in the faith—an opportunity for the expansion of wisdom itself.

A spirit of intelligent wisdom invites self-identifying traditionalists to see that loyalty to what has come before does not require deafness to new information, because openness to new knowledge is built into the historical tradition itself. Modern scientific understandings of sexuality and reproduction, of ecological development and change, and of textual criticism need not be conversation stoppers. For the tradition is replete with thinkers who incorporated knowledge that was new in their contexts, leading them to teach something different from what came before. Many of these thinkers are heralded by traditional Christians as stalwarts of the faith: Paul's representation of the gospel was shaped by Greco-Roman intellectual culture, Augustine's by the fall of the Roman Empire, Luther's by emerging trends in German nationalism and intellectual culture, Calvin's by the end of medievalism and the advent of the European Renaissance, and Jonathan Edwards's by his encounter with the Enlightenment. Like them, contemporary traditionalists might find the engagement with new knowledge enlightening and helpful to their faith. That knowledge may confirm traditional understandings or challenge them. New information may be persuasive or ultimately rejected, but it need not be something to avoid out of hand. In fact, resistance to knowledge puts the so-called traditionalist out of touch with much of Christian tradition. Intelligence, an openness to and capacity for growing in knowledge and understanding, is a historical mark of Christian wisdom.

There is a message here for progressives, too. In acknowledging the historical importance of wisdom and intelligence to Christian theology, progressives might discover value in traditional concepts they are sometimes quick to abandon. The Christian preoccupation with sin, for instance, may not just be antiquated religious pessimism, but evocative language that still captures something self-defeating in the human condition, something we confirm as reality every time we pick up a newspaper or go on the internet. The concept of the Trinity, perhaps unconvincing to many progressives in its classical Nicene formulation, still may have use as a way of metaphorically talking about relationality as a divine and human ideal, rooted in the very being of an inherently social God. Like their traditionalist counterparts, Christian progressives do well to acknowledge that intelligent wisdom has deep roots in Christian tradition.

Wisdom as Discernment

Of course, as important as it is, there is more to wisdom than intelligence, however broadly we define the term. To be wise—not just smart—requires more than informational acquisition. People we consider wise also have a sensitivity to the moment in which they find themselves, a capacity to measure what is appropriate for a particular context. We might call this aspect of wisdom *discernment*. Discernment is knowledge with timing; it is intelligence that is aware of its surroundings in time and space.

Tom Beauchamp and James Childress, two prominent bioethicists, include discernment among the moral virtues they think are crucial to medical ethics. In their understanding, "the virtue of discernment brings sensitive insight, astute judgment, and understanding to bear on action." According to Beauchamp and Childress, discernment makes for good health care professionals because nurses, doctors, and other practitioners need more than just knowledge to treat their patients effectively. To be good at what they do, they must be able to read the needs of their patients, to treat the patients as individuals, and to understand how the specifics of personalities and circumstances might make the "right" thing to do different in different cases, despite similarities in diagnosis. Health care professionals need sound judgment. They need to know how much information a specific patient can handle, and how to communicate it in a way that maximizes understanding, promotes health, and minimizes unhelpful anxiety. They need the capacity to read each patient's situation differently, with nuance and compassion. Ultimately, Beauchamp and Childress describe discernment as the capacity to make what they call "fitting judgments" that are not unduly affected by hardened principle, irrelevant claims, or exaggerated fears and misperceptions. Discernment is an admirable virtue for health care providers because it disposes them to understand the circumstances and to judge what the proper human response ought to be in a specific moment.[12]

Building on the idea of discernment as Beauchamp and Childress describe it, we can say several things about it as a component of the broader virtue of wisdom. First, discernment is not an act so much as it is a capacity, a dimension of character, just as we have been describing wisdom more broadly. Second, discernment is concerned with determining what is right, good, and faithful in a particular moment. As such, it is necessarily attuned to the circumstances around it. Discernment implies nuance and a certain pliability. In fact, we might argue that blind allegiance to conviction with no regard for the particulars of the moment is an impediment to discernment, and thus not as virtuous as "consistency" is often characterized in, say, political media. Of course, discernment does not guarantee that we will correctly understand the right thing to do, but it does represent a commitment to trying to tease out our best estimate of what is right or good in the moral ambiguities in which we find ourselves.

From a theological perspective, we might say discernment represents an openness to God's intentions in any given moment. Elizabeth Liebert defines this aspect of wisdom as "the Christian practice of seeking God's call in the midst of decisions that mark one's life."[13] For Liebert, discernment is essential for determining how "to live our lives thoughtfully and faithfully in the midst of all the forces, options, and decisions that characterize modern life." Discernment, she says, is a "discriminating way of life, in which we come to notice with increasing ease and accuracy how our inner and outer actions affect our identity in God."[14]

Liebert points out that the Christian practice of discernment has deep biblical roots. She reads the Old Testament story of Samuel as one such example; in his encouragement to Samuel to listen quietly for God's prophetic call, the priest Eli trains his protégé in the virtue of discernment.[15] The opaqueness of Jesus's parables was an invitation to his disciples to tease out their meaning in the new moment in which they were seeking the word of God. In his illustrative celebration of the cleverness of serpents, economical maidens, and the opportunistic servant, Jesus directly commended discernment, a wisdom finely attuned to its time and place. Similarly, in various epistles in the New Testament, Christians are explicitly encouraged to read the "signs of the times" to discern God's intention.[16]

When I think of wisdom as discernment, I am reminded of Thomas Aquinas's teachings on what he called prudence, or "practical wisdom," which he identified as one of the cardinal virtues of human flourishing. Indebted to Aristotle's understanding of wisdom, Thomas defined prudence as "right reason of things to be done."[17] According to Thomas, prudence guides us in knowing not only what we should do but how we should do it, in a way that furthers the end of human flourishing.[18] Prudence takes into account not only principles but also the circumstances in which we must decide or act.[19] It provides us a moral compass and the capacity to deliberate and determine the best way to pursue the good and the right in a particular moment.[20] Quoting Augustine, Thomas insisted that "prudence is love discerning aright that which helps from that which hinders us in tending to God."[21]

For Thomas, prudence enables calculation in the immediacy of a moral moment, but it also has a "unitive function," meaning that it helps a person be morally consistent with herself in a couple of ways.[22] Prudence matches the aspirations of the religious and moral life to the needs of a particular circumstance, so that a person can balance various, even competing, moral obligations. It helps to align rational deliberation, intuitive judgment, and emotional response, so that all of these aspects of responding morally to a situation are in tune with and mutually informing one another. Prudence reconciles the three temporal dimensions, utilizing memories of the past, present understanding, and future predictions—what Elizabeth Liebert calls "accumulated learning"—to inform its estimate of the right and good at that moment.[23] In all of these ways, says Thomas, prudential wisdom helps us to think holistically about the moral moments we encounter.

If Thomas elucidates the role of discernment in maintaining a sense of moral consistency within our whole selves, then H. Richard Niebuhr reminds us that discernment takes into account the complexities of our social ethical responsibilities. Writing in his classic book *The Responsible Self,* Niebuhr explored various images through which western morality has described the moral life.[24] Some thinkers have depicted human beings as basically law-abiders, so that the fundamental moral question becomes "what is the law, principle, or rule that is relevant to me" in any particular moral moment. Other thinkers have described moral agency as the pursuit of "the good life," so that the ultimate moral question becomes "what is the great end of life that all of my actions ought to serve?" Niebuhr found both of these classical symbols helpful but ultimately unsatisfying, particularly in the modern age. Appealing to the unprecedented awareness of human connectedness disclosed to us by what he calls modern "psychology of interaction," Niebuhr offered the image of "the responsible self" as a summary of moral agency. None of us decides or acts in a vacuum, Niebuhr observed. We know that our actions are often reactions to things that have happened in the past; we interpret what has gone on before us, and then we respond to that understanding of the past, with the realization that our actions will become stimuli for others' subsequent responses. Moral agency, then, is fundamentally social and contextual, not theoretical, so that the most basic moral question we must always ask ourselves in our web of interactions is not "what is the right principle?" or "what is the good I am pursuing?" but instead "what is going on?"

Though he did not use the term, this interpretation of moral agency puts discernment at its center. Being a moral agent means deciding and acting in the context of others' actions and decisions, and moral responsibility requires that we read our obligations in the context of these circumstances. Consequently Niebuhr argued that intentional moral activity is ultimately geared not toward discovering what is right or good, but toward determining what is *fitting* for our particular moment and *responsible* to the specific relationships in which we find ourselves:

> The idea or pattern of responsibility, then, may summarily and abstractly be defined as the idea of an agent's action as response to an action upon him in accordance with his interpretation of the latter action and with his expectation of response to his response; and all of this in a continuing community of agents.[25]

Responsibility requires discernment. We make moral choices in relationships and circumstances in time, and much of our evaluation of what is right or true requires that we discern where we fall in the story of those relationships and circumstances. What has happened before this moment, how is my choice a response to what has gone on before, and how might I anticipate that my act will itself elicit a response? Moral wisdom is social and contextual, and it requires discernment of the social circumstances in which we find ourselves. Christians understand this ethic of responsibility to include our need to respond to God's responsiveness, as well as to other people.

Both Thomas's understanding of prudence and Niebuhr's image of responsibility reveal discernment's importance to the project of forbearance. The wisdom that comes from discernment represents a challenge to unbending allegiance to principle, for discernment demands awareness of the ways in which context can shape or re-shape our sense of what is "fitting." Loyalty to theological or moral principle may not always compel us to act on it, or act in the same way, once we take into account the lessons we have learned from the past, the anticipated outcomes of different choices in the future, and the complicated circumstances involved in the webs of relationship in which we live. Seen through Niebuhr's notion of responsibility, discernment may prompt us to distinguish between the right thing to do in theory and the fitting thing to do in the moment that confronts us. Seen through Thomas's teachings on prudence, discernment may encourage us to distinguish between determining the right thing to do and figuring out the proper way (and moment) to go about doing it. Appreciating these moral nuances creates room for negotiating differences in the church, in ways that take better account of the effect of our convictions on others. For the project of maintaining the unity of the Body of Christ, the fine tuning that comes with the exercise of discernment is a welcome skill set. Wisdom as discernment is absolutely essential to the practice of forbearance.

Wisdom as Empathy

The gift of discernment, to read a moment and know what is right to say and do, is aided by the capacity to see things from a number of angles, from perspectives other than our own. Attempting to see things from others' points of view gives us a more complicated understanding of our circumstances, as Thomas Aquinas encouraged for the sake of prudence. Seeing from others' perspectives allows us to better understand the web of responsiveness in which Niebuhr claimed all moral beings live. When we step outside of ourselves and try to see the world from others' points of view, to imagine the ways they are invested in the issues that divide us, we practice another aspect of wisdom, *empathy*.

Empathy is a scarce gift, and the understanding it yields is an important part of true wisdom. Contrary to the way we sometimes use the word, though, I do not believe that the ability to empathize with others is entirely natural or intuitive. To be sure, some empathy seems to be hardwired; natural and social scientists have been preoccupied of late with tracing the biological and evolutionary roots of human empathy. However, Leslie Jamison is right that empathy is as much intentional exercise as it is natural inclination.[26] Clearly some of us are more successfully empathic than others, and some of that difference is the result of different levels of attention and effort. Empathy is at least in part a disposition we choose to develop, and in this way we rightly think of it as moral virtue as much as human instinct.

The complexity of empathy is consistently on display in my home. My son Jae is on the autism spectrum, and one of the common manifestations of autism is a struggle to empathize with other persons, to imagine what they might be thinking or feeling. It does not come naturally to Jae to step outside of himself and picture how others may react to his actions or words, especially in highly emotional situations. He struggles, therefore, to respond appropriately. Jae's challenges are a result of the way his brain functions, but I am encouraged by how hard Jae works sometimes to create artificial constructs that allow him to compensate for the deficiencies in his natural empathy. Where natural empathic imagination fails him, he relies on external signposts (e.g., his mother or father pointing out the way his comments might hurt his little brother) or data from past events (e.g., the last time I did this, Kisung cried and Mommy told me I hurt his feelings), or compatible motivations (e.g., responding this way gets me "points" in the family "good attitude" game). In doing so, Jae experiences an extreme version of how we all experience empathy, as a mixture of effort and natural inclination.

Of course, all of us are limited in our ability to walk in someone else's shoes, to understand how our views or actions might affect others. Despite my intellectual understanding of the relevant issues and my professional preoccupation with them, I cannot truly understand how my students of color experience being at a college that is in many ways a bastion of white privilege. I can make a sincere attempt to see things from their perspective, and I can appeal to some similarities between my experience as a first-generation college student from an economically disadvantaged environment, but at the end of the day I am white and male and have limited perspective on how my color and gender have removed obstacles from my path that are significant impediments to educational and social success for some of my students.

For all of us, the ability to be empathic has its limits. True wisdom, however, invites us to push against those limits, to work aggressively to move the boundaries of our attentiveness to perspectives different from our own. Empathy extends from the humility that we explored earlier; when we recognize that we do not know everything there is to know about the issues between us and others, and we acknowledge that our perspective is not paramount or objective, then we more ably see that there is something important to be gained from viewing the world from others' points of view. Empathy depends on the exercise of patience, because it is only through the investment of time and effort to listen to others that we expand our capacity to de-center ourselves and imagine the world with different eyes. Christian empathy builds on the idea of faithfulness that we explore in the next chapter, calling us to engender a spirit of trust—in God and one another—that allows us to be open to the critical reform of our own perspectives. Developing moral empathy ultimately requires us to marshal all of the other virtues of forbearance in the pursuit of wisdom.

Cultural critic Paul Bloom thinks empathy is overrated, even dangerous, as a moral guide. Writing for *The New Yorker*, Bloom acknowledges that "empathy is what makes us human; it's what makes us both subjects and objects of moral concern." But he thinks it often leads us astray as a guide for moral choices. "Moral judgment entails more than putting oneself in another's shoes," he writes. Making moral choices on empathy leads us to give unjustified preference to the people we know or have heard of, for their perspectives are the ones to which we have immediate access and which play upon our emotions most successfully. As a result, empathy can lead us to prefer the concerns of the nearby few over the millions of nameless victims of injustice whose moral claims might reasonably be considered stronger. Because of its preference for the local and the tangible, empathy tempts us to identify with the sensationalized story at the expense of less titillating but equally outrageous cases of harm or unfairness. It also allows us to prioritize our contemporaries over the unknown persons in the future who will be affected by economic and environmental decisions we make. "Eight deaths are worse than one, even if you know the name of the one; humanitarian aid can, if poorly targeted, be counterproductive; the threat posed by climate change warrants the sacrifices entailed by efforts to ameliorate it. . . . A reasoned, even counter-empathetic analysis of moral obligation and likely consequences is a better guide to planning for the future than the gut wrench of empathy."[27]

Bloom is right that emotional impulse is seldom a sufficient base for wise moral decision making, for individuals or communities. His dismissal of empathy, however, is rooted in a common but misleading opposition between reason and emotion. He insists that "empathy will have to yield to reason if humanity is to have a future," but he is mistaken to characterize empathy as predominantly emotional and therefore irrational. Empathy contributes to wisdom precisely because it is *both* emotional and rational, and provides a linkage between intellectual and affective reason. When experienced well, empathy requires an essential connection with another person, real or imagined, in order to compel us to understand their perspective. But the moral knowledge that empathy draws from that connection is entirely rational. The emotional connection in empathy allows us to see things we would not otherwise see, to understand things that otherwise would escape us. It therefore contributes to reason; it does not distract from or compete with it.

Bloom is also right that empathy alone does not tell us what is right, true, or appropriate, and in fact we sometimes should conclude that the proper response to a particular situation is justified despite our empathic inclinations. But empathy often contributes constructively to our rational analysis of moral problems, and in fact "reason" without empathy is deficient. Appeal to reason with no concern for empathic extension of ourselves renders our understanding of moral obligation myopic, for the abandonment of empathy allows us to remain unjustifiably confident that our perspective exhausts what is rational.[28] Empathy broadens our deliberation with the partially emotional incorporation of perspectives beyond our own, and by doing so makes us more reasonable, not less. Empathy makes us wiser.

In their best-selling book *American Grace: How Religion Divides Us and Unites Us*, Robert Putnam and David Campbell suggest that moral empathy might be transforming the landscape of religion in the United States. Based in one of the most thorough survey studies of American religion ever conducted, the Faith Matters Survey, their book shows how religion since the 1990s has contributed simultaneously to an entrenched polarization and an increase in tolerance in American culture. The rise of the Religious Right and the exodus of young people to secular liberalism, they argue, has led to expansion of ideological fragmentation in the United States, as these two groups increasingly define themselves against each other. At the same time, the increased frequency with which Americans experience intimate interfaith commitments—especially exemplified in friendships and marriages—has led to an unprecedented level of interreligious tolerance and understanding, especially among young people. Their conclusion is that intimacy with people of other religious convictions has led to greater understanding across differences, despite the ideological polarization characteristic of the larger political camps. Although they do not use precisely this language, we might say that Putnam and Campbell have detected a growth in empathic wisdom among younger generations of religious persons, including Christians. Intimacy with difference makes it more difficult to demonize the other, and enables identification with those on the other side of the divide. Empathy empowers our moral imagination to consider conversation and coexistence in ways that are inconceivable when we interact with difference on the level of straw men.

Wendy VanderWal-Gritter provides another illustration of empathic wisdom, this time from an evangelical perspective, in her book *Generous Spaciousness: Responding to Gay Christians in the Church*. VanderWal-Gritter tells the poignant story of her journey from ideological certainty to what she calls "generous spaciousness" on the issue of gay persons in the church. VanderWal-Gritter is executive director of New Directions Ministries of Canada, an organization that upon her arrival was dedicated to an "ex-gay" mission, encouraging gay and lesbian persons to live celibate or heteronormative lives. Many of the evangelical ministries associated with New Directions confidently asserted that homosexuality was a sinful "lifestyle choice" from which a person could and should choose to change. After years of dialogue and close relationships with gay and lesbian persons, however, VanderWal-Gritter found herself increasingly uncomfortable with her organization's assumptions and associations. She began to see the injury her perspective inflicted on persons who identify as gay and to appreciate the complexities surrounding sexual identity and Christian conviction. More to the point, she began to learn, from friends with much different perspectives, the shortcomings of her own: "My new experience with the wideness of God's mercy was not so much about learning that my gay Christian friends experienced God's mercy but that I came face to face with the limitations I imposed on *how* to experience God's mercy."[29]

Over time VanderWal-Gritter steered her organization away from the "ex-gay" paradigm and toward the facilitation of gay and lesbian persons' nonjudgmental inclusion in the church. For VanderWal-Gritter, this move toward inclusion was not a retreat from faith conviction, but an acknowledgment of moral ambiguity and the inevitability of disagreement among equally faithful and equally fallible Christians. The change in her stance was an embrace of the importance of maintaining the church's unity even in the face of such difference and disagreement, and a reflection of her willingness to learn from the perspectives of those with whom she disagreed. The change marked a preference for forbearance and friendship over exclusion and division. A theology of "generous spaciousness," so movingly articulated in her book, was the product of empathic wisdom, insight gained from the faithful engagement of people not like her.

Another example of the growth of empathic wisdom that comes to mind is more local to me. As I have mentioned already, my home congregation is a UCC church that constantly flirts with an identity complex. We are home to traditional Nicene Protestants, de facto secular humanists, longstanding Congregationalists, dedicated Presbyterians, functional Unitarians, religious pluralists, and skeptics who find in our congregation room to question and wonder. This diversity is rich, but it is not without its challenges. At times the language we use for worship becomes a matter of debate, with some of us preferring the aesthetics and theological profundity of traditional Christian prayers and hymns, while others prefer more contemporary and inclusive sources of wisdom and poetry. Some of us miss the recitation of classical Protestant confessions and psalm-based calls to worship, while others think our services are still too beholden to traditional Christian language, preferring instead words taken from the likes of Gandhi and Mary Oliver. Given that worship is the central act of congregational life, these differences can become intense; there is a lot riding on them—questions of collective identity, welcome, and mission.

As we discuss our differences, one challenge we have had to overcome is the temptation for caucuses within the church to claim to speak for the majority. Both the traditionalists and the most radical progressives at times have been inclined to locate themselves at the center of the congregation, which has the effect of minimizing the diversity we actually host and marginalizing others as an apparently small minority. To help counter this tendency, we have dedicated many of our adult education offerings lately to explicitly theological discourse. What do we believe, individually and collectively, and what are the implications of our use (and abandonment) of particular kinds of theological language? One of the outcomes of this long-term exercise, I think, has been a wider appreciation for the depth and complexity to our theological disagreement. These intentional conversations also have resulted in the empowerment of members who felt heretofore squelched by members perceived to be more knowledgeable or powerful. Most fundamentally, the deliberate engagement—talking and listening—with perspectives much different than our own has helped many of us to better appreciate the convictions of others, why they believe the way they do, and how our own convictions fail to resonate with them, and sometimes even hurt them.

In other words, the intimacy of honest conversation has made us, as a church, more empathic regarding the theological needs of others in our fellowship. The culmination of all of that intentional conversation was the construction of a new statement of faith, in which we tried to capture the wonderful diversity we host and the forbearance we try to practice. (I have included the statement of faith as an appendix at the end of the book.) All of this talking has not necessarily brought us to closer theological agreement, but if the gracious reception the statement of faith received in the congregation is any indication, I think we understand one another better. We empathize more successfully with one another, and we are wiser for the exercise.

One more example of empathy begetting wisdom: as I worked on this chapter, the country observed the one-year anniversary of the horrible racially motivated execution of members of the Immanuel Baptist Church in Charleston, South Carolina. Nine people were gunned down in the name of one man's racial hatred. There is nothing redeeming in a tragedy like this, but in the aftermath of the shooting, one development was surprising. Calls erupted for the removal of the Confederate flag from public places in South Carolina and other southern states. For many people, the Confederate flag symbolizes the "southern cause" for slavery more than a century and a half ago, but to others it represents benign southern culture. Opponents of the flag have called for its removal before, with no success, but this time was different. Whether it was the suddenness of the attack, its perpetration in a church, or the heart-wrenching public mourning (covered by CNN and other outlets), more Americans made the connection between racial hatred and the flag's symbolism. Empathic wisdom led South Carolina Governor Nikki Haley and others to call for the removal of the flag, and the calls gained a momentum they never had before. Ultimately, South Carolina removed the flag from its statehouse, Virginia outlawed the flag from its specialty license plates, and throughout the southern states leaders and citizens began to see with new eyes the implications of their allegiance to this symbol. Empathy with innocent victims of hate yielded wisdom, albeit generations overdue.

Wisdom as Imagination

The shadow of Charleston naturally brings to mind Martin Luther King's unrealized vision for an America devoid of racial injustice. More than a half century ago, King dreamed of a country in which people of different races could join together "at the table of brotherhood," where citizens would "not be judged by the color of their skin but by the content of their character."[30] The killings in Charleston and other cases of racial tension in the last several years—Ferguson, Baltimore, New York, North Carolina, Baton Rouge, St. Paul—cure us of any illusion that the work King inspired is done. We do not live in a "post-racial America," as pundits were fond of saying after the election of our first African American president. Though King's aspirations remain unfulfilled, his prophetic vision remains an essential part of our national conscience. We are not the same country we were before the summer of 1963. King, along with many other leaders of the Civil Rights movement, inspired great improvements in racial justice in the United States over the last half-century, and that cloud of witnesses continues to speak a word of indictment on us today, reminding us we have much more to do.

But why has King's voice and vision stuck with us? What is it that continues to draw us to King's dream of a new America? Was the progress of the Civil Rights movement a matter of good timing? Perhaps it was in part; historians have pointed out that what we consider the Civil Rights movement of the 1950s and 60s was the culmination of struggles for justice since the Civil War. Was it the strategy of nonviolence? Surely this was important for how King was able to move white sentiment from fear of black Americans to disgust over the violent treatment of protestors who refused to respond in kind. The explanations for the (relative) successes of the Civil Rights movement are complex, but surely one factor was King himself, or more specifically, his command of language and ideas through which he invited all Americans to imagine a different national character.

In the "sweltering heat" of racial apartheid, King painted a vivid picture of the indignities and brutalities of Jim Crow and the KKK, laying bare those realities to a larger national audience. By invoking both biblical texts and the canon of American political history, he also helped us to imagine a future characterized by cooperation, solidarity, fairness, and the "symphony of brotherhood." He helped us imagine a more just tomorrow, and he did it in a way that stirred our affections as much as it resonated with our intellects.

In the midst of brutality, King emerged as a voice of wisdom, one of the wisest American leaders of any generation. His was a particular kind of wisdom—it was a wisdom born of moral and theological imagination. People whom we consider wise like King often have an unusual ability to see what is not there, to imagine a future starkly different than the present in which we live. Imaginative wisdom sees beyond reified conventions, and it appeals to the aesthetics of our souls to paint a prophetic portrait of a creative future. It helps us to yearn and strive for things yet unseen.

In a Christian community that sometimes seems paralyzed by intractable debate and division, we could use more imaginative forecast, more creative solutions for how to navigate the balance between conviction and unity. One way that imaginative wisdom helps the practice of forbearance is by equipping us to see past the binaries in which most of our ecclesial and civic debates are stuck. At least as it is represented on cable television, talk radio, and the internet, public debate over social and moral issues tends to come to us in the metaphorical categories of black and white—normally articulated as an either-or. You either hate women or like to kill babies. You are either a hawk or a peacenik. You are either homophobic or a fan of bestiality. You either prefer owls to people or condone raping the environment. You are either a socialist or a one-percent. You are either for law enforcement or for African-American rights. This is what most of our public debate looks like these days.

Sadly, church debate increasingly resembles this binary tendency. Whether over abortion, marriage, the Middle East, or immigration, we Christians tend to categorize our disagreements in stereotypical conservative and liberal positions. Many of these binaries are rooted in unimaginative assumptions about the authority of Scripture. Ultra-conservatives so simplify the meaning of the "authority of Scripture" that almost anything beyond a near-literal reading of the Bible does not count as sufficient respect for that authority. For their part, ultra-liberals have become so suspicious of appeals to biblical authority that some regard anyone who takes the Bible seriously as a "fundamentalist"—whether or not they actually take Scripture as literally true and inerrant. Once factions in the church are defining themselves and others in these easy categories, it becomes difficult to imagine what there is to talk about.

Imaginative wisdom invites us to picture a church in which we have more than two options on the issues that divide us. It equips us to see possibilities where popular rhetoric suggests there are none. Perhaps supporters of abortion rights are not cavalier about the destruction of fetal life, even if they ultimately make the tragic choice between the best interests of a woman and the potential represented in a fetus in favor of the former. Perhaps opponents of marriage between gay or lesbian partners are not necessarily afraid of gay people, but instead are concerned that religious endorsement of such a radical deviation from the historical definition of marriage risks the loss of definition altogether, to the detriment of an institutional pillar and insurer of stable society. More broadly, perhaps tolerance and strong conviction are not mutually exclusive. Perhaps theological integrity can be maintained in ways other than leaving. Perhaps there is a future for the church beyond the seemingly contradictory allegiances to "orthodoxy" or "social justice." Perhaps there is an opportunity for the church to respond to its differences in new ways.

To enlarge the possibilities before us requires imaginative wisdom, and cultivating this kind of wisdom in the church would make the Body of Christ healthier. Certainly we ought to encourage it among our leaders. In my denomination, the Presbyterian Church (USA), our leaders are in fact charged with incorporating imaginative wisdom in their service to the church. The ordination vows that our elders and ministers take include the commitment to lead and serve "with energy, intelligence, *imagination*, and love," a promise that immediately follows the pledge to "further the peace, unity, and purity of the church."[31] The tandem implies that the two promises depend on one another. We do not have a chance at holding together peace, unity, and purity in the church unless we put some energy, intelligence, and imagination into it, motivated by love for God and one another. The capacity to wisely imagine a new future beyond tired ideological paralysis is a remarkable gift of the Spirit, necessary but frustratingly rare these days.

Kathleen Norris wonders if our sixteenth-century Protestant ancestors are responsible for our current lack of imaginative wisdom. She writes that their singular focus on the word—captured in the mantra "Scripture alone"—dispensed too stridently with aspects of Christian faith and practice that cultivate imagination. The evocative aesthetics of images, music, and poetry that were met with such disdain from classical Protestant thinkers appealed to and exercised the imagination. Without them, Protestant Christians arguably have become excessively rational in their faith, a tendency on display in the kind of literalism often at work among both fundamentalists and many liberals.[32] Perhaps then what we need is a new reformation in the church, a new great awakening, this time of the imaginative capacity of Christians to envision new ways of being church. With God's help, part of this new awakening will be a rediscovery of the poetic qualities of Christian theology, which provide the "play in the joints" we need to live more comfortably with people who do not believe exactly what we believe.[33]

Imagination, empathy, discernment, and intelligence—this is wisdom, as I understand it, the capacity and eagerness to grow in understanding of God, ourselves, and the world in which we live. Wisdom serves forbearance by opening us to the possibility of real growth and to the potential for learning from one another in a context of difference. Wisdom also contributes to a forbearing church by equipping us with the ability to imagine different ways to respond to disagreement—indeed, to imagine a different standard for faithfulness, one that prioritizes unity and friendship over ideological victory.

CHAPTER 5

Faithfulness

How many times have you heard forms of these accusations in Christian dust-ups over gay marriage and ordination?

"Christians who want to be faithful to God's Word in the Bible cannot support gay marriage."

"A church that excludes LGBTQ people from ordained service or the blessing of Christian marriage cannot be faithful to the spirit of Jesus."

For many Christians, the issues surrounding homosexuality and the church boil down to a matter of faithfulness. Are we willing to be faithful to the gospel of Jesus Christ? Both sides ask the same question, but of course what they mean by faithfulness to the gospel differs. Some Christians think that it means honoring the authority of the Bible and its apparent affirmation of heteronormativity. Other Christians insist it means extending hospitality and working for fairness for LGBTQ individuals, as they believe Jesus would do. Both sides consider their convictions on gay marriage or ordination to be the barometer for Christian faithfulness, and both sides charge their opposites with abandoning the faith. In fact, many folks feel that to even coexist in a church with people who believe something contrary impinges on their own faithfulness. The church's response to questions around sexual norms is apparently a measure of our faithfulness, but unfortunately we do not agree on what faithfulness requires us to do.

These days the Christian tendency to view our convictions as the measure of faithfulness is most clearly on display in debates about sexual identity, but we have engaged in the same habit with other matters as well. Abortion, evolution, and economic justice are just a few examples of issues that Christians have used as litmus tests for the church's fidelity to the God of the Bible. In this chapter, I want to look at this question of faithfulness and how it relates to the practice of forbearance. As you will soon see, the relationship between faithfulness and forbearance depends a lot on what we think "faith" means. I do not think that "faith" is best understood as an executive summary of what Christians should believe, a doctrinally specific measure of conformity with what it should mean to be a "true" Christian. Instead, I approach faith as I think the Bible does, as a virtue, the habit of trusting and relying on God, and by extension of this trust in God, the practice of trusting other Christians as well. The virtue of faithfulness also includes a commitment to being trustworthy ourselves. To be faithful, then, describes the character of our relationships, not the specific content of our creed. Understanding faithfulness this way, we see that the church's faithfulness is not threatened by theological error as much as it is by the division that results from our disagreements. By the same token, we discover that the practice of forbearance actually gives us profound opportunity to improve our faithfulness, to God and one another, even in the midst of disagreements about how we should respond to the theological and moral issues that perplex us.

Faith in God

To begin, we need to clarify what we mean by faithfulness. In Christian circles, to have faith is commonly treated as a synonym for "believing," as if faith is primarily about believing in the reality of God, the divinity of Christ, the authority of the Bible, and so on. On this account, to be a person of faith means that I believe that God exists and possesses the attributes Christianity tells me belong to God. Having faith means that I assent to what Scripture tells me is true about God, God's activity in the world, Jesus, and the Bible. In fact, through much of our history, particular groups have assumed that to "have faith" meant something even more specific, subscription to a precise list of Christian theological claims. The virgin birth, the primacy of the Roman papacy, justification by faith, and the inerrancy of Scripture have all appeared on one list or another of essential dogmas that authentic Christians must believe. Whether the summary of those propositional truths is the Nicene Creed, the Westminster Confession, or the Five Points of Fundamentalism, Christians have regularly lifted up convenient bullet summaries of doctrinal affirmations that serve as the litmus test for who has faith and who does not. Christian conservatives are especially fond of such lists, but even liberals grant this understanding of faith by debating conservatives over the content of the essential list while rarely contesting the idea that faith requires subscription to a list in the first place. Similarly, skeptics outside the church define themselves—and their intellectual superiority over religious persons—by pointing out the absurdity of a particular summary list of truth claims, thus implicitly reinforcing the idea that this is what faith is, adherence to a list of propositional claims about God.

These assumptions about "having faith," though, are a particularly modern interpretation of religious experience, and a rather unbiblical one. They come to us chiefly as a by-product of the title fight between Christian modernists and fundamentalists in the early twentieth century. At that time, the rapid pace of scientific discoveries was challenging many of the beliefs that Christians historically had taken to be true, most notably the biblical narrative of creation and the reality of miracles. In addition, the maturation of the Enlightenment's priority on reason contributed to religious skepticism, as intellectuals subjected the claims of Scripture to rational verification, and questioned the authority of the Bible as a source of empirical truth. Even within biblical scholarship, growing reliance on historical-critical methods revealed the complexities of authorship in the Bible, making clear the ways in which the Bible is as much a product of human beings writing in particular times and places as it is a reflection of divine intent.

As a result of this confrontation between biblical authority and modern intellectual discovery, people inside and beyond the church began to call into question many ideas rooted in Scripture and heretofore taken as literal truth. Was the world really created in six days, or did it evolve over millions of years? Could Jesus really have been the product of a virgin birth, or does that dogma result from a misreading of prophetic texts and an unsophisticated understanding of human sexuality? Could Jesus really have been raised from the dead after three days, or does human biology require us to understand that traditional affirmation in non-literal terms? Skeptics beyond the church and modernists within it took these questions as indications that radical revision of Christian theology and its assumptions about biblical authority were in order. Traditionalists responded to these kinds of questions with outrage, as if questioning the empirical truth of these doctrines was to undermine the viability of Christianity itself. They reasserted the classic propositional truths of Christian orthodoxy, and the biblical authority on which they rested. And with that, the century-long fight for the soul of American Protestantism was on—all predicated on the assumption that "faith" means believing certain things are "true."

Interestingly, both modern liberalism and contemporary fundamentalism are products of modernity, because the assertions both camps make are reflections of this confrontation between traditional notions of scriptural authority, modern scientific discovery, and empirical definitions of truth. For our purposes, what is most important to see is that, in responding to modernism, fundamentalism actually shifted the historical meaning of faith and faithfulness. The Bible does not depict faith as primarily the affirmation of certain tenets, as fundamentalists would have us believe. In the Bible, to have faith is to display supreme confidence in God. Biblical faith is not cerebral subscription to specific theological propositions; it is wholehearted trust in God. From a biblical perspective, then, it follows that the opposite of faith is not rational skepticism; it is doubt in God's reliability. The best synonym for biblical faith is not *assent*, but *trust*.

Faith is the cultivation of radical trust in the sovereign God. God sent Moses down from Sinai with Ten Commandments that demanded the Israelites acknowledge God as God. In disobeying those commands, which the Israelites soon would do, the people did not wake up one day and regard God as a fiction. Their sin was that they shifted their allegiances to other gods they considered more reliable than I AM. "I am the LORD your God," said God. I am the one "who brought you out of the house of slavery." I am the one who shows "steadfast love to the thousandth generation of those who love me and keep my commandments" (Exod. 20:1–6). I am the reliable one, says God, as I have demonstrated in the past. Trust and loyalty are the concerns that underwrite the first commandments against idolatry and taking God's name in vain. Similarly the requirement of a Sabbath Day was meant as a ritualistic reminder to the Israelites that it was God who created and protected them, and thus it was God who should be relied on for their every need. Sabbath was a weekly celebration of the people's dependence on the reliable God.[1] When we understand trust and loyalty as the central theme of the commandments, it makes the later transgression of the Israelites even more poignant, for when they constructed the golden calf, their cardinal sin was not ceasing to believe in God's existence. Their sin was infidelity, the abandonment of God as the one whom they trusted to get them to the Promised Land.

Reliance on the God who first pledged loyalty to them was the central obligation that defined the Hebrew people and their relationship with God in the Old Testament. It was the heart of the covenant between Israel and God's people, and that radical trust was tested in the subsequent political trials Israel was forced to endure. We see the crests and falls of faith in God poignantly displayed in the Book of Psalms. Some of the psalms are poetic affirmations of faith as trust, as when Psalm 23 melodically celebrates, "The LORD is my shepherd, I shall not want" (v. 1). Trust is not easy to maintain in the face of hardship, however, and some of the psalms, for example Psalm 22, seem to question God's reliability: "My God, my God, why have you forsaken me?" (v. 1). In the waxing and waning of the psalmist's confidence in God, in the oscillation between the celebration of God's presence and open questions about God's willingness to secure the future, we see the true meaning of a life of faith. Faith in the Psalms is not about intellectual assent. It is about the joys of trusting God, and the challenges of doing so as well.

Similarly the sins against which the prophets railed were sins of betrayal, not modern rational skepticism. The prophets charged the people with abandoning God in favor of allegedly more trustworthy sources of power and security, whether those objects be foreign gods or material wealth:

> Hear the word of the LORD, O people of Israel;
> > for the LORD has an indictment against the inhabitants of the land.
> There is no faithfulness or loyalty,
> > and no knowledge of God in the land.
> Swearing, lying, and murder, and stealing and adultery break out;
> > bloodshed follows bloodshed. . . .
> My people consult a piece of wood,
> > and their divining rod gives them oracles.
> For a spirit of whoredom has led them astray,
> > and they have played the whore, forsaking their God.
> > > > > > (Hos. 4:1–2, 12)

The prophets accused the people of cheating on God, of retreating from the pledge of fidelity God and Israel made with one another.[2] Yet

93

time and again, the prophets assured the people that God will prove trustworthy:

> But now thus says the LORD, he who created you, O Jacob,
>   he who formed you, O Israel:
> Do not fear, for I have redeemed you;
>   I have called you by name, you are mine.
> When you pass through the waters, I will be with you;
>   and through the rivers, they shall not overwhelm you;
> when you walk through fire you shall not be burned,
>   and the flame shall not consume you.
> For I am the LORD your God, the Holy One of Israel, your Savior.
>
> (Isa. 43:1–3a)

The prophets invoked the people's trust by reminding them of what God had done for them in the past. They called them to return to faithfulness, which required restoring their trust in the God who delivered them in ages past, and pledged to them a future.

When Jesus spoke of faith in the Gospels, his depiction maintained the Old Testament emphasis on trust. When he praised the bleeding woman who had enough faith in him to be healed, it was her trust in him that he celebrated, not her intellectual assent to a two-natures Christology. When he chastised Peter for being of too little faith to walk on water with him, the test was clearly an exercise in trust in which the disciple came up short. Even in the exchange with Thomas after the crucifixion, when Jesus praised those (unlike Thomas) who would believe in the risen Christ without seeing, the foreshadowing of good faith was not about intellectual belief in certain theories of resurrection. It was about the acceptance of God's guarantee that the light would shine in the darkness and the darkness would not overcome it, a guarantee for which the resurrection stands as the paramount signal.[3]

Nowhere did Jesus make more explicit the importance of trust to the life of faithfulness than in the Sermon on the Mount. The teachings captured in the Sermon represent a dissertation on fundamental trust in God. We routinely read the Beatitudes as commendations of certain virtues—meekness, mercy, purity—but the real power behind those virtues is the trust in God from which they derive. Blessed are the poor, those who face tragedy, those who hunger for fulfillment, and those who are persecuted, because they refuse to allow their present circumstances to divert their trust from God. Later in the Sermon on the Mount, Jesus famously taught his disciples not to worry about food, clothing, and their future. He instructed them this way, not because these things are unimportant, but because he was inviting them to trust in God to provide the future:

> Therefore I tell you, do not worry about your life, what you will eat or what you will drink, or about your body, what you will wear. Is not life more than food, and the body more than clothing? Look at the birds of the air; they neither sow nor reap nor gather into barns, and yet your heavenly Father feeds them. Are you not of more value than they? And can any of you by worrying add a single hour to your span of life? And why do you worry about clothing? Consider the lilies of the field, how they grow; they neither toil nor spin, yet I tell you, even Solomon in all his glory was not clothed like one of these. But if God so clothes the grass of the field, which is alive today and tomorrow is thrown into the oven, will he not much more clothe you—you of little faith? (Matt. 6:25–30)

As he is portrayed in the Gospels, Jesus's whole reason for being—his teaching ministry, his crucifixion, and his resurrection—was to make clear the reliability and durability of God's love. In light of God's trustworthiness, Jesus invites disciples to join his clan, not by simple intellectual assent to doctrinal tenets, but by wholehearted confidence in the ultimate goodness of God.

It is perhaps an unsurprising consequence of human nature that as the church transformed from a network of communities into an institution, its understanding of faith also morphed from one of intimate trust in God to propositional uniformity. The shift to a preoccupation with doctrinal tenets was partly a reaction to growing pluralism in the church, and the sense that (as we saw in chapter 2) it would be theologically and politically advantageous to define who was in and who was out. But the concern for doctrinal assent never overcame the fundamental understanding of faith as trust in reliable grace. It could not, since the trustworthiness of God's grace was the heart of Jesus's message. The rediscovery of faith as radical trust in divine grace was at the heart of Martin Luther's theological epiphany, which gave us the Protestant Reformation. Weighed down with the reality of his own sinfulness and the despair he experienced as he futilely tried to live up to the majestic expectations of a righteous God, Luther discovered that true faith is not found in our imperfect efforts to be good, but instead abides in the radical trust that God will make us good. Faith is the assurance that God will love us despite our unworthiness, and make us worthy through Christ's love, as Luther beautifully put it in his classic hymn: "And though this world, with devils filled, / Should threaten to undo us, / We will not fear, for God hath willed / His truth to triumph through us."[4] Faith saves us, not works, concluded Luther. Faith in "the mighty fortress" who is our God is all that will deliver us from evil.

More recently, as those tussles between skeptics and fundamentalists tempted Christians to dissolve the question of faithfulness into matters of propositional consensus, theologians still asserted the importance of trust to the heart of faith. The nineteenth-century German theologian Friedrich Schleiermacher described the foundation of piety as a feeling of utter dependence.[5] Paul Tillich described religion as the experience of our Ultimate Concern in response to an awareness of our own contingency.[6] Karl Barth, who taught a theology in many ways more traditional than these two thinkers, was equally adamant that faith fundamentally "does not have reference to any creed or dogma formulated and championed by the community, not even the most ancient and universal."[7] Barth was far from hostile to traditional Christian theology; considered a father of the "neo-orthodoxy" movement of the twentieth century, his magnum opus was a fourteen-volume reassertion of Christian theology called *Church Dogmatics*! But Barth was clear that, at its heart, Christian faith is not assent to this or that theological formula. Faith is the "acknowledgment, recognition, and confession" of Jesus Christ, God's fundamental act of love, meant to reconcile us to God. Faith is the experience of the Holy Spirit, "the awakening power" by which we are summoned to affirm what God has done for us in Christ, and to count ourselves among those who proclaim the triumph of grace over sin. Faith is a response to God's gracious reliability embodied in Christ, and Barth argued that "this truth is either denied or hopelessly obscured in a conception of faith which involves as its basic act the acceptance of certain statements which attest and proclaim Him, which does not, therefore, consist in simple obedience to Himself."[8] For the Christian gospel, faith is testament to God's loving reliability. Trust is the central ingredient to faith.

Christian faith, then, is an attitude, and this is what makes it appropriate for us to talk about faith as a virtue, rather than as an act of simple assent to doctrinal short-lists. The apostle Paul included faith in his triad of Christian virtues. "Faith, hope, and love abide, these three," he wrote in 1 Corinthians 13, marking faith as one of the most basic virtues in the

Christian life. Faith is a capacity, a trait of character that shapes how we live the Christian life. To be faithful is to develop an openness to trust that runs through our relationship with God, that helps to define what and how we think about God, and that (by extension) colors how we relate to other people. Faithfulness makes trust and trustworthiness a part of who we are as Christians.

To talk of faithfulness as a virtue fits well with the way we have been thinking of forbearance as the practice of virtues. In fact, faith is an essential part of the constellation of virtues we have considered so far. In chapter 2, we considered how the practice of forbearance depends on adopting a spirit of humility, a virtue that itself is rooted in the classical Christian confession that God is God and we are not. Humble acknowledgment of our limitations as human beings prompts us to temper our confidence in our truth claims, not in a way that undercuts the pursuit of truth, but in a way that acknowledges that our perspective on truth always will be partial and incomplete. Humility also invites us to recognize that God may be disclosing some of that truth in the perspectives of those who are in a different ideological place than we are. Given the recognition of our limited vantage point, we also explored the importance of patience to the practice of forbearance. When we exercise patience with God and with others in the Christian community, we testify to our hope that God will reveal the "big picture" of God's reign in God's time. In the meantime, we struggle with our fellow travelers on the pilgrimage of faith to look for the signs of God's reign bursting through in our midst, and our hope in God's future tempers the frustration that present uncertainty or conflict—in and beyond the church—brings us.

The path from acknowledgment of our limitations to hope for God's future runs through the virtue of faithfulness. In other words, faith in the power and goodness of God is what frees us to humbly and patiently seek truth, practicing forbearance in the meantime. But forbearance requires that we understand faith in this way, as a shared trust in God. Faith as assent to propositions implies that what is important to being Christian is believing the right things, but faith as trust suggests that what binds us together is the one in whom we Christians place our confidence. This difference is crucial to the practice of forbearance. If good faith means believing the right things, then it creates very little room for—and a whole lot of anxiety about—being wrong. Faith as assent implies that certainty, not humility, constitutes good virtue. Faith as assent implies that getting things right as completely and quickly as possible is the mark of a righteous church. Faith as trust in God, though, gives us permission to admit the limits of our understanding and to seek God's wisdom in all kinds of surprising places, even the encounter with others. Recognizing faithfulness as shared trust in God invites us to affirm and learn from the exercise of faithfulness in people with whom we have deep theological differences. In doing so, we may discover that radical trust in the grace of a good God can be expressed in surprisingly different ways. Faith as reliance on God grants us the time to find our way to greater understanding together, and to exhibit patience, even with those who seem to understand more slowly what God desires.

Shifting the focus of faith from doctrinal conformity to trust in God clarifies the kind of faith that draws a diverse church together, namely their shared reliance on the God of Jesus Christ. Accepting the invitation to adopt this attitude of trust in God to secure the future changes how we approach our lives in this age of anxiety, including how we think about the life and future of the church. Trusting in God to secure the future frees us from the illusion that the church's success and failure rest on our ability to get our life together exactly right; that is, it frees us from the pressure of perfection. This is not to say that we do not take seriously our responsibility to pursue truth and labor for justice. As we saw with our exploration of hope, reliance on God is not necessarily passive, for we know that God works out God's future through secondary causes, forces and actors in the world that include us. But by practicing faith as radical trust, we are reminded that our responsibility as Christians is not to secure that future ourselves. God is doing that, often through us, but sometimes around and despite us. In moments of uncertainty, confusion, and conflict in the church, our responsibility is to look for the signs of God working out that future, in confidence that it is God's to assure.

Faith in One Another

What binds us to one other and makes us Christians, then, is not a short list of shared dogmas, but this common reliance on the God revealed to us in Christ as our axis of meaning, and our shared trust in God to secure the future with grace and love. That attitude of trust marks us as the community of Christ in the world. We do not all share an identical understanding of God or God's wishes, we do not always see God's future with the same eyes, but presumably we share the conviction that "the LORD is good; his steadfast love endures forever; and his faithfulness to all generations" (Ps. 100:5). To believe in the church as the fellowship of Christ's disciples, who have accepted his calling to entrust the future to God, makes us one in the end that we pursue—the kingdom of God—even if we see the way to that end very differently.

Our shared confidence in the God of Jesus Christ also binds us together and gives us reason to trust one another, even in those moments when our varied theological interpretations threaten to separate us. Even then, we can assume the best intentions in one another because of our shared profession in the God disclosed to us in Christ. And trusting one another is another exercise of faithfulness that is essential to the practice of forbearance. In the Letter to the Ephesians, the basis for our obligation to bear with one another through our disagreements is precisely our common confession of the one God: "There is one body and one Spirit, just as you were called to the one hope of your calling, one Lord, one faith, one baptism, one God and Father of all, who is above all and through all and in all" (Eph. 4:4–6). Our common calling in Christ to a life reliant on God reminds us that we are family. Faith in that one God and one Lord becomes the basis on which we extend faith in one another.

What does this mean in practice? It means that when we are in the midst of intractable disagreements over remarkably divergent interpretations of Scripture and its meaning in the world today, a healthy church is one in which Christians assume that sisters and brothers share a fundamental commitment to the God revealed in Jesus Christ, and therefore give one another the benefit of the doubt. To have faith in one another means that, despite our differences, we recognize that others in the church are after the same thing we are, which is to live in God's ways. We might disagree on important theological matters. Those disagreements might be profound and deep, and we might sincerely believe that others in the church are tragically mistaken in their understanding of Christian responsibility in this hour. But to live faithfully with each other requires a certain presumption of good will. Christians with whom we disagree are not trying to undermine the church. They simply understand the implications of faith differently than we do. With confidence in our one calling, we resist the temptation to question the commitment to the gospel of those with whom we disagree.

Call this the "refusing to see the devil where he ain't" rule of Christian forbearance. In a forbearing church, Christians refuse to demonize their theological opponents, no matter how deep their disagreements lie. We extend the benefit of the doubt to each other, understanding our differences not as the encroachment of demonic forces on the integrity of the church but as the inevitable disagreements that emerge when fallible, sinful human beings embark on the journey of faithfulness together. As we pursue God's truth together, therefore, we are free to question our fellow Christians' interpretations of the faith, and in fact the pursuit of wisdom encourages us to question each other's convictions, as well as our own. Among Christians who profess trust in God through Christ, however, we should be reluctant to judge other Christians' spiritual credentials on the basis of our disagreement with their theology. As a norm, forbearing Christians refuse to ask whether fellow Christians are "worthy" to remain in fellowship with us. Of course they are worthy of our fellowship, because they are sisters and brothers in Christ, with whom we are united as the Body of Christ. As Richard Gillard's hymn reminds us, they are not antagonists, but fellow travelers on the pilgrimage of faith:

> We are pilgrims on a journey, fellow trav'lers on the road.
> We are here to help each other walk the mile and bear the load. . . .
> I will weep when you are weeping, when you laugh I'll laugh
>   with you.
> I will share your joy and sorrow till we've seen this journey through.[9]

Christians with whom we disagree still walk with us on the journey to discern God's intentions for us in our time and place. They are not opponents; they are kin in the family of God, even when they see Christian responsibility in remarkably different ways than we do.

Forbearance invites us to trust each other, to risk reaching out to others in the name of seeking truth and strengthening the Body of Christ. It involves relying on our shared trust in the goodness of God and refusing to question other Christians' faithfulness. Frances Taylor Gench is a biblical scholar who several years ago participated in a group I mentioned in chapter 3, the Theological Task Force on Peace, Unity, and Purity in the Presbyterian Church (USA). This task force, made up of folks across the theological spectrum, was commissioned to chart a way forward for the denomination around issues of sexuality, ordination, and marriage. In her book, *Faithful Disagreement: Wrestling with Scripture in the Midst of Church Conflict*, she honestly describes her initial involvement with the group as a *fearful* experience. She and the rest of the group feared the intimate encounter with polarized views, with conflict, and with failure to live up to the task they had been given. But as the group spent some time studying together Jesus's invitation to Peter to walk on water with him, they realized the importance of *risk* to drawing close to Jesus and following him. Sometimes following Jesus requires that we step out into the storm, that we risk living with conflict, difference, doubt, and fear. What we often discover is that the middle of the storm is where we encounter the presence of Christ. "He was really there," Gench proclaims, whenever they got together to study, pray, and discuss hard issues. And in walking together through the storm, the members of the group discovered something else, a reminder of the baptismal bond they shared:

> And when [Jesus] came, what we discovered about our fellow travelers, much to our surprise, was that every one of us really did love him and that every one of us was striving as best we could to be his faithful disciples. And so, like Peter, we decided to take some risks, to try to draw closer to him through new ways of discerning and learning together.[10]

Sharing faith in a loving God made having faith in one another easier, for in the eyes of the other—even the one on the other side of the theological universe—they encountered the Christ who bound them together.

Sharing faith in God enables us to have faith in each other. What I am imagining was graciously on display in my home congregation recently, when we faced a vote on whether or not to proceed with a $3.5 million campaign to build an addition on to our historic building. We raised a substantial percentage of the funds before the vote, but the budget that remained was daunting, and some opponents of the addition felt it was too extravagant for our means, unnecessarily diverting funds away from other ministries and threatening the fiscal future of the congregation. Some members also raised concerns about the addition's aesthetic effect on what is widely considered the most beautiful architectural specimen in the entire state of Vermont. Supporters of the addition cited the very real danger our children face each week as they have to cross a busy street to get to the building where our Sunday school classes currently reside. They pointed out that the new addition will provide a safer and more modern environment for our Christian education program, expand facilities for our community service programs, and increase our capacity to host meetings for other local organizations in a spirit of neighborliness.

Eventually the congregation voted and decided to proceed with the addition. A part of the congregation was disappointed in that vote. But at no moment in the extensive debate over that addition—at numerous congregational meetings and online—did the dialogue dissolve into personal attacks on motives or perspectives. Quite the contrary: congregation members regularly reminded each other that we were after the same goal of seeking what is best for the church's future ministries, even if we understood that future differently. They thanked one another for their dedication to the process, even as they offered contrary perspectives. And before the vote, at church members' prompting, we held a prayer vigil, a liturgical reminder of the bond we have with one another in our desire to entrust the future of our congregation to God. To my mind, that entire exercise reflected the virtue of faithfulness in action.

Many of us enjoy the blessing of worshipping and serving with Christians capable of this kind of faith in each other. Truth be told, however, many other congregations suffer from hostility, resentment, and mutual suspicion in difficult moments like these. Of course our denominations also are plagued by conflict that is propelled by a lack of trust in one another. Faith in one another, as sisters and brothers of the community called together to trust God, reminds us of our common bond at the very moment in which our disagreements threaten to divide us. That common bond reminds us that the others with whom we share church are relying on God just as we are, and in fact may very well be the "secondary causes" through which God is trying to provide us a glimpse of the future. Even those we think are quite mistaken in their understanding of the gospel may be vehicles through which God is speaking—speaking to the world, to others in the church, to us. Chastened by theological humility and emboldened by faith, we remain committed to the idea that, in their difference, those with whom we most disagree still deserve our faith. In our solidarity as church and through our differences within it, we members of the Body of Christ maintain faith in one another, as a reflection of the faith in God we hold in common.

This commitment to trusting one another is symbolically captured in the covenant we forge with new members joining our congregations. Often we think of those moments in our church life as flowing primarily in one direction; in sharing a statement or creed or responding affirmatively to a set of questions, a prospective member commits to a congregation and perhaps to the larger denomination to which that congregation belongs. In reality, though, those ceremonies commemorate a *mutual* commitment. Prospective members commit to the church, but in receiving their pledges of faith, we as church community affirm them as fellow travelers on the journey of faith and pledge to remain in community with them. The membership liturgy used in the United Methodist Church captures the bidirectional nature of church membership particularly well. After candidates for membership have affirmed their faith in God and have promised faithfulness to the church, the congregation answers in kind:

> We rejoice to recognize you as [a member] of Christ's holy church,
> and bid you welcome to this congregation of The United Methodist
>   Church.
> With you we renew our vows to uphold it by our prayers, our pres-
>   ence, our gifts, and our service.
> With God's help we will so order our lives after the example of Christ
> that, surrounded by steadfast love, you may be established in the
>   faith,
> and confirmed and strengthened in the way that leads to life
>   eternal.[11]

Upon joining the fellowship of faith, prospective members join in a mutual covenant of faithfulness between them, us, and God. Together we are joined in our faith in God, and we extend faith to the newest among us, just as they invest faith in us. They are one with us, even if their convictions develop in ways different than ours, even if disagreements emerge between us. In these moments when individuals "join the church," we say to them: we value and trust you, and so we will remain committed to you through our common life together. That includes extending the benefit of the doubt to you, as we hope you will to us, when we find ourselves not seeing things eye to eye.[12]

Faithful to One Another

Commitment to maintaining community in difference leads to a distinct standard of behavior within the community. First, if we are committed to one another in a covenant of faithfulness, then it seems obvious that we ought to deal with one another with *honesty* and *integrity*. If we trust one another, we will engage our disagreements with a commitment to truthfulness and openness. We will be honest about our differences, communicating them in love and patience, and representing ourselves, others, and the issues that stand between us accurately. We will commit to a certain amount of self-criticism as a measure of honesty with ourselves, so we can understand and represent our own motives and biases transparently. And, of course, we will represent the convictions of others with as much accuracy and understanding as possible.

You might think that this call to honesty and integrity would be obviously important for a community like the church. The trends in our national discourse stridently lean in the opposite direction, however, so powerfully affecting how we think about communication in our culture, that it is no longer a given that Christians will know how to engage hard conversation in a healthy way. In fact, evidence suggests that the pollution of incivility from our political culture has infiltrated ecclesial discourse, to the point that many of our church debates resemble what we see from politicians more than the virtues commended to us by Scripture. Public "discourse" in America routinely features hostility, misrepresentation, duplicity, and unapologetic lies for political gain. Debates and town hall meetings once aimed for an exchange of ideas, but they have become superficial rhetorical contests to be won by any means effective. And those means tend toward the vitriol, stupidity, and character assassination that apparently still win points for cable television shows. The 2016 presidential election cycle taught us nothing if not that meanness works in contemporary political debate.

Similarly, church gatherings these days exhibit a sad display of vices that betray a lack of trust among Christians. Congregants transform pastoral missteps or disagreements into intentional affronts, conspiracies, or evidence of incompetence. Ministers attribute congregational resistance to the ignorance or willful malice of their parishioners. Conservatives accuse liberal Christians of abandoning historical Christianity out of embarrassment or because of the seduction of secular priorities. Liberals accuse conservative Christians of abandoning Christian morality for the platform of the GOP. In the face of all this distrust and mutual accusation, productive strategies for working through our disagreements quickly disintegrate, or themselves become the object of suspicion. Instead we gather into our ideological camps, and we lob our rhetorical grenades. Too many congregational and denominational meetings validate the suspicion that Christians have learned well from the distrust that reigns in contemporary politics.

By contrast, a Christian community dedicated to biblical forbearance, and specifically to the task of maintaining community around the shared commitment to faithfulness, engages its differences in ways that are distinct from the culture around us. Christians negotiate disagreements with honesty and integrity, disavowing character attacks and misrepresentation in favor of understanding the differences between fellow members of the community of faith as accurately as possible. Toward that end, the art of listening that we explored previously becomes monumentally important. To represent another with integrity and accuracy, and to respond to what another Christian is actually saying rather than a convenient misapplication of what she is saying, requires the commitment to listen with openness. Faithful conversation depends on the art of listening, and any hope for movement through our differences requires it as well.[13]

Another specific implication of Christian faithfulness to one another is a pledge of *fidelity*. Faithfulness encourages us to commit to one another, to stay with one another through the long haul of seeking God's truth. Fidelity as an act of faithfulness to one another is, of course, a reflection of God's fidelity, which each of us experiences by God's grace. The Christian story *is* the narrative of God's fidelity through all kinds of estrangement. The Old Testament tells the story of God's loyalty, despite the people's persistent inclination to abandon God for other gods. Christians profess Jesus Christ to be the embodiment of God's fidelity; "For God so loved the world," declares the Gospel of John, "that he gave his only beloved son, that whosoever believes in him shall not perish, but have eternal life" (John 3:16). The incarnation of divine grace in the person of Christ is the ultimate expression of the insatiability of God's fidelity, God's refusal to take humanity's "no" as the final answer. God insists on being with humanity and for humanity, even in the face of our shortcomings and disloyalties. As Karl Barth put it, Jesus Christ is God's response of "nevertheless" to human beings' prideful attempt to evade God's love. When we wandered from God and God's ways, God in Christ "nevertheless" insisted on traveling the far country of our sin to bring us back to God.[14]

By pledging to remain with one another through our differences and disagreements, we seize the chance to witness to God's essential faithfulness through our own faithfulness to one another. In other words, fidelity presents us with an opportunity to be the *imago Dei*, the image of God, to one another. Even in the context of important differences that we are tempted to interpret as irreparable breaches in our fellowship, forbearance asks us to resist the temptation to abandon one another. Forbearance asks us to choose instead to remain with those Christians with whom we most disagree as a model of the fidelity of God. Let me put it bluntly: I believe that, more often than not, responding to conflict in the church with a cut and run, retreating to like-minded enclaves or leaving church altogether, betrays a profound lack of faithfulness to our fellow Christians and to the God who calls us together. In moments when we think fellow Christians are terribly mistaken in their read of Christian truth or obligation, we ought to commit even more to one another, in the name of the God who refused to abandon us when we had strayed. Our fidelity in the face of difference offers us a chance to witness to God's fidelity. In our most difficult moments, our faithfulness to one another offers us a chance to be the reflection of God's faithfulness to us.

Faithful to God

The extension of faithfulness to one another in the church is, in turn, an exercise of faithfulness to God as well, because it actively serves the unity of God's church. When we refuse to give in to division, our faithfulness to one another becomes an act of faithfulness to God. What we say in our commitment to staying together in disagreement is that we will not sabotage the unity of Christ's church in our pursuit of our vision of the right, as compelling as our vision might be. For we understand that an important part of what is right and good in the eyes of God *is* the unity of God's church. The commitment to the virtues of forbearance is an important part of our obligation to God's future, so we commit to forbearance even as we struggle to better understand together the future God intends for us and for the world.

As the pastoral letters in the New Testament abundantly illustrate, to be invested in the unity of the church does not require that we ignore our differences or strive for an artificial (or impossible) theological uniformity. The unity of the church never has depended on singular agreement. Instead, the church's unity rests in its collective confession of Jesus as Lord, and the living out of that confession in what we might call a "moral unity"—the preservation of community, the cultivation of character, and the maintenance of trust in the church, all motivated by our bond in Christ. This is a vision of unity reflected in Paul's letters to the first Christian congregations, but one too rarely embraced in the church since.

In a lot of ways, it is so much easier to divide into ideologically distinguished enclaves, to practice community with people who believe and understand the world the same way we do. Just removing ourselves from disagreement saves us from the constant frustration that conflict can bring us, when serious convictions are at stake. Leaving does not require us to compromise the intensity of our convictions. If we stay, we risk being wrong. Worse yet, we risk being outvoted. Cutting and running from ecclesial disagreements is the easier path, for it allows us to just keep thinking as we always have, without the bother of growing in wisdom and piety. It is a much riskier proposition to stay in community with neighbors who we think profoundly misunderstand the gospel, or who fear the convictions we pursue as wrong for the church and bad for the world. Turning over the church's future to God seems a dodgy proposition when we risk losing the contest for the ideological soul or the strategic direction of the church we love.

To struggle for what we believe is right and good while remaining in community with those who do not share our understanding requires more than a little bit of *courage*, a virtue that serves as a direct corollary from the virtue of faith and faithfulness. It takes courage to live in the messiness of disagreement, to remain with others with whom at times we are tempted to conclude we have little in common. It takes courage to persist in our labors for righteousness, while willingly turning over the future to God. It takes courage to win some disagreements and accommodate the continuing presence of persons holding on to the minority perspective. It takes courage to lose the battle for what we consider right for the church, and to stay with that church anyway. The courage to risk living with difference is an essential part of faithfulness, and the practice of forbearance more broadly. Courageous faith helps us to take a chance in reaching out to those with whom we most energetically disagree, to build bonds rather than burning bridges, trusting that it is our loving God and not we ourselves who will determine the future of the church.

If risking the messy road of maintaining community in the face of strident disagreement requires courage, then courage depends on trust in something greater to sustain us. In his commentary on the Book of Joshua, John Calvin reminds us that the recipe for courage includes fortitude and faith. With reference to the beginning verses of that biblical book, where Joshua assumes the mantle as Moses's successor with the instruction to "be strong and courageous," Calvin insists that true Christian courage can only be maintained when we are rooted firmly in the rehearsal of God's past promises fulfilled.[15] When we exaggerate the importance of our own rightness, we are tempted to conclude that the future of the church depends on whether or not our side of the battles we wage in church wins.

When we remember that the church's hope lies in One beyond us, however, faith as radical trust in God makes it easier for us to settle into the hard work of being church together through our conflict.

Sometimes courageous faith will prompt us to maintain bridges while we persistently labor to bring about change we think is needed for the church to reflect the wishes of God more obediently. Martin Luther King Jr. talked about courage as an antidote for the fear that naturally comes with the struggle for justice in church and society. As high as the stakes were in the fight for civil rights, King could talk of a courage that sustains our commitment to the good, rooted in the trustworthiness of God. To persistently struggle for what we think is right with courage is not necessarily selfish (if we also practice the other virtues of forbearance), nor does it depend on a naïve underestimation of the risks or stakes involved. Instead, King said, courage is righteous "self-affirmation," a positive self-love and self-respect rooted in faith and love. Courage "does not offer an illusion that we shall be exempt from pain and suffering," he wrote, but "it instills us with the inner equilibrium needed to face strains, burdens, and fears that inevitably come, and assures us that the universe is trustworthy and that God is concerned." For "beneath and above the shifting sands of time, the uncertainties that darken our days, and vicissitudes that cloud our nights is a wise and loving God."[16] Sometimes courageous faith provides us the will to fight the good fight in the right way.

Surrounded by shrill calls for congregational divorces and denominational anarchy, however, sometimes courageous faith calls us to stand down and see the "grace in doing nothing," as H. Richard Niebuhr once put it.[17] In some moments, we may discern that our struggle for "victory" in our congregational and denominational battles may not be the best vehicle for the emergence of God's grace in Christian community. God's grace might be better served in our refusal to sacrifice community for the sake of triumph. God's love might be better shown by our commitment to living with precisely those who disagree with us the most. Having the strength *not* to act sometimes can be a sign of faithfulness, too, not to mention wisdom, patience, and humility. To commit to this kind of faithfulness—to God, to God's church, and to each other—is to trust the future to God, and to confess with Paul that "all things work together for good, for those who love God" (Rom. 8:28).

Whether faith gives us the courage to wait or the strength to work tirelessly for the right and the good, it represents in either case a commitment to our fellow Christians, rooted in confession of God's commitment to us, that ultimately testifies to our commitment to God and God's church. Our steadfastness to others derives from the reliability of God's love for us, and it returns to God as proclamation of our trust in God to provide in the present and to command the future.

As a result of faithfulness to one another, our commitment to remain together in our differences, sometimes it will feel like the church sentences itself to perpetual uncertainty or inaction on a variety of theological and moral matters. Faithfulness in difference often will lead the Christian community to say more than one thing at once. At times we will not be on the right side of history, because we will harbor too much disagreement on some issues to provide a clear prophetic witness. Unfortunately, this occasional confusion is part of the project of being a diverse human community; but as frustrating as that might be, we offer even greater witness to the world by modeling how human community can negotiate ideological difference, the preservation of the good, and the march of history with character, respect, and integrity. In this way, our differences themselves testify to God's faithful endurance, and thus become our most important witness. Perfecting the virtue of faithfulness in all its varied layers of meaning—faith in God, faith in one another, faithfulness to one another, and faithfulness to God—requires that we trust in God to preserve, bless, and guide the church through our disagreements, differences, mistakes, and misunderstandings. Ultimately that trust is grounded in the Christian confession that, as John Calvin elegantly put it, "we are not our own":

> We are not our own: let not our reason nor our will, therefore, sway our plans and deeds. We are not our own: let us therefore not set it as our goal to seek what is expedient for us according to the flesh. We are not our own: in so far as we can, let us therefore forget ourselves and all that is ours.
>
> Conversely, we are God's: let us therefore live for him and die for him. We are God's: let his wisdom and will therefore rule all our actions. We are God's: let all the parts of our life accordingly strive toward him as our only lawful goal.[18]

CHAPTER 6

Friendship

Difference, disagreement, and conflict are inevitable experiences for the church. As long as the church is made up of human beings who are not all exactly the same, we will disagree about what it means to be church in our time and place. We will highlight different priorities and convictions. We will interpret and understand the values of Christian faith in various ways. We will subscribe to different visions of Christian living. To be faithful, we Christians do not have to minimize our disagreements or pretend that we do not have conflict. In fact, to deny the reality of conflict in the church simply buries difference in an unhealthy way. But to allow our discord to threaten our fellowship is also not an option for faithfulness, because it risks the unity of Christ's church. Instead, we are called to acknowledge the difference that Christian community—like all other human community—harbors, and to commit to live together in that difference, in a way that reflects the ways and intention of the One who calls us together.

I have been suggesting that we might capture that practice of living faithfully in difference in the biblical idea of forbearance. We have isolated some of the virtues that make forbearance a faithful reflection of the way of Christ and a distinct way of living with difference in Christian community. One virtuous ingredient of forbearance remains, however, and it is, as the apostle Paul suggested long ago, the "greatest" of the virtues: love. Love sets the context that makes forbearance possible. But Christians who are bound together in the community of faith experience and practice love in a particular way. Forbearance makes sense as an imperative for Christian community because, in that community, we Christians live and love together as friends.

The Meaning of True Friendship

Many of us use the term "friend" to describe a wide circle of people we know. We include people we see several times a week and those we are lucky to talk to once or twice a year. We include in our circle of friends those with whom we share common interests, including hobbies or sports allegiances. We include as friends people with whom we get together only because our children play with theirs. People we know from work are our friends, as well as neighbors, club affiliates, and the folks we see at PTA events. I once had a graduate school teacher who referred to every fellow scholar with whom he had had an intellectual conversation as "my good friend" so-and-so. For many of us, the circle of people we casually refer to as friends is wide.

For our purposes, though, I would like to define friendship more precisely. Friendship is a cultural experience and a social term, but it is also a moral concept and (as we shall see) a theological good. So let's start with a definition for this moral ideal: *friendship is a relationship of mutuality and intimacy rooted in shared interests, loves, or goals and characterized by genuine interest in the other person as a particular other.* Allow me to unpack this definition a bit. To suggest that friendship is a relationship of mutuality is to say that it is bidirectional. Another person is not your friend if your affection for him is unrequited. Without return of your feelings, that person may be someone of whom you are quite fond, someone you admire or desire to know, but there is no relationship that can be described as friendship. Similarly, for a relationship to aspire to friendship in a substantial way, there must be a significant level of intimacy in the relationship. You know your friend's tendencies, strengths, shortcomings, loves, concerns, and pet peeves—and she knows yours. Finally, friendship is more than a relationship of mutual satisfaction or convenience. We are invested in our friends as persons; we care for them as specific others, well beyond the circumstances or commonalities that bring us together. At least as a moral experience, friendship requires this mutuality, intimacy, and other-regard to live up to the term.

Perhaps it would help to compare friendship with other kinds of relationships that might resemble it. A friend is different from an *acquaintance*, because we normally do not know an acquaintance as deeply as we do a friend. We might share interests and goals, we might respect him as a person, but we do not share the level of mutual investment with acquaintances that we do with friends. Similarly, a *colleague* might be someone with whom we are significantly invested in shared tasks or objectives, especially around work, but without a mutual investment in one another as persons. If the main thing we share is the work that we do together, then that relationship lacks the intimacy and genuine mutuality of a friendship. Finally, friends are more than *allies*; without denying the emotional, intellectual, or recreational benefit we get from our friendships, at the end of the day I value my friend not simply for what the friend does for me. True friendship—*moral* friendship—runs deep, in both directions, and is valued beyond its utility. We value friends ultimately not for what they do for us, but for the persons they are and the persons they help us to become.[1]

Aristotle once described three types of friendship, of varying degrees of moral worth and distinguished by what brings the friends together. The first two types of friendship are bonds based in pleasure and utility respectively. These kinds of friends value one another primarily because they derive some enjoyment or advantage from the relationship. Many of us have relationships like the ones Aristotle is describing here. The guys with whom I ride my motorcycle might not be people I am deeply invested in as individuals; my main reason for hanging out with them might be because it gives me a group to ride with, and riding brings me happiness. Or perhaps I am friends with a group of fellow parents, from whom I get a forum in which to complain about my children, as well as the occasional babysitter. To describe these relationships as based on pleasure or mutual advantage is not to say that I care nothing for the others in the relationship, but it is to admit that the primary connection is the recreation or usefulness I derive from the relationship.

For Aristotle, relationships built primarily on pleasure or usefulness can be considered friendships, and quite common ones at that, but they are not the highest order of friendship. The most desirable friendships, says Aristotle, are those which are based not only on utility but on character. The highest order of friendship is built on a deeply shared sense of "the good" and a mutual concern for one another as persons. According to Aristotle, in a truly virtuous friendship, pursuit of our shared vision of what is good binds us together, and I am motivated to maintain the relationship out of genuine concern for the other and the other's pursuit of the good with me. Truly virtuous friendships likely bring us pleasure as well, and they often can be mutually advantageous, but that is not all there is to the relationship, as if we would cease to be friends when our children were grown or if one of us could no longer ride his motorcycle. We are friends because we are mutually invested in each other as persons, and we share a deeper sense of what is right, true, and good that binds us to one another.[2]

For our purposes, I have in mind something of Aristotle's third type when I talk of moral friendship. Relationships built primarily on mutual recreation or advantage are not unimportant or dubious. Our lives are filled with such relationships; but as common and important as they are, their lack of intimacy and mutuality fails to rise to the ideal of moral friendship. Philosophers, poets, and the best cases in our own lives testify that moral friendship runs deeper. Moral friendships rarely exhibit perfection; like most other dimensions of the moral life, our friendships are works in progress, providing us regular opportunities to succeed and fail at exhibiting the other-regard that they demand. Despite their imperfections, however, they distinguish themselves from other relationships in our lives by their foundation in character and mutual concern.

With this understanding of moral friendship in mind, I think it makes good sense to think of our relationships in Christian community as moral friendships. What might it mean to talk about the church (local and universal) as a community of friends? What is the vision of "the good" and the mandate of character that binds us to others in Christian community, and what are the consequences of describing relationships in church this way? What might an appreciation for Christian friendship contribute to forbearance, a theological ethic for a disagreeable church?

Is Friendship Unchristian?

In much of Christian theology, there exists a strange but persistent resistance to the idea that friendship could be an accurate reflection of the requirements of Christian love. The alleged opposition between friendship and Christian love is often rooted in the words themselves. In classical Greek, the word *philia* is normally translated "friendship," "mutual regard," or "brotherly love"—which is where the city of Philadelphia gets its name. By contrast, expositions of love in ancient Christian texts normally used the term *agape*. For much of Christian theology, *philia* has been understood to be quite different from *agape*. *Philia* friendships are relationships based on mutual satisfaction. In other words, we are friends because it makes us both happy to hang out together, to share similar interests, and to meld complementary personalities. But when a relationship ceases to satisfy those interests, personalities, and need for happiness—either by changes in one or both friends or an alteration of the circumstances that bring them together—friendship erodes and dies. In the meantime, the experience of friendship is an exclusive one, in that our circle of friends is usually limited and defined. There are people inside our circle of friends, and there is a world of humanity outside of it, and we tend to show preference to those in our community of friends. Friendship is a relationship of a certain exclusivity and mutual satisfaction that depends on the continuation of that satisfaction to maintain it.

By contrast, theologians tell us that Christian love is disinterested love, an affection for people that does not depend on how they satisfy our needs and interests. Christian love shows no special regard for the personalities of others, for what they do for us, or how they satisfy us. It is Good Samaritan love, a love that responds to the needs of a stranger without regard for something in return. Christian love is also inclusive; it loves people as people. Rather than drawing boundaries around our obligations, as friendship does, Christian love compels us to love abundantly. Christian love binds us in obligation to neighbors, strangers, and enemies alike. *Agape* compels a love that is universal, extended to human beings qua human beings, without concern for reciprocation.

Philia, then, represents relationships of mutual investment, while *agape* obligates Christians to love beyond their friends and "brethren," to show other-regard to strangers and even enemies. For classical Greek writers, *philia* admirably captured the morally and civically important bond between two friends, but for early Christians, *agape* was a superior obligation to embrace all human beings in selfless love. The Christian ethicist Gilbert Meilaender reflects this common distinction in his important book on friendship. He begins his exploration of friendship from a Christian perspective by granting the premise that there is a qualitative difference between *agape* and *philia*. The distinction, he says, is that friendship "is clearly a preferential bond in which we are drawn by what is attractive or choiceworthy in the friend."[3] Friendship is a relationship of mutual advantage and attraction; what binds us to another might be relatively superficial or quite noble, but our friendship is based on the satisfaction of our preferences in the friend—I am friends with another because of what I get from that relationship. Because friendship is based on preferences, and both our preferences and their satisfaction are subject to change, friendships themselves are necessarily finite, subject to change or even dissolution "when the characteristics which gave rise to such preference are no longer present."[4] By contrast, Christian love (*agape*) "is to be nonpreferential, like the love of the Father in heaven who makes his sun rise on the evil and the good and sends rain on the just and the unjust."[5]

Meilaender clearly states that it is not his intention to denigrate friendship in order to build up the concept of Christian love. Nonetheless, he accepts the common distinction between the two. Precisely because friendship requires us to gravitate toward particular relationships at the expense of others, friendship stands in tension with the universal, nonpreferential expectations of Christian love. Furthermore, the impermanence of friendship is at odds with the fidelity that characterizes Christian love; in fact, he declares as "harsh truth" that in reality, "friendship and fidelity are incompatible."[6] As a result of disparate characters, says Meilaender,

> The tension between philia and agape must be permitted to stand. Friendship, in order to be preferential and reciprocal, must be subject to change. Yet, a friendship which lacks permanence seems less than perfect. Agape, in order to be faithful, must be nonpreferential and unconcerned with reciprocity. Yet, a love which lacks these marks of philia—its deep intimacy, mutuality, and preference— seems too impersonal and cold to satisfy the need of our nature.[7]

Friendship is a species of interpersonal bond with substantial natural and civic benefit, but Christian love's expectations are broader and necessarily unrequited.

The great Christian philosopher Søren Kierkegaard sharpens the distinction Meilaender exposes. Kierkegaard claims that friendship is a concept foreign to the New Testament, the "opposite" of *agape* love. Any attempt to synthesize Christian love and friendship does injury to both ideas. To claim that Christianity teaches a higher love that supplements but does not contradict friendship represents "a double betrayal—inasmuch as the speaker has neither the spirit of the poet nor the spirit of Christianity."[8] For Kierkegaard, the defining characteristic of Christian love is that it is rooted not in passion but in duty. To love as a Christian is to heed the command, "You shall love your neighbor as yourself." It is not an expression of desire, but stems from self-renunciation and is a discharge of an ethical task.[9] By contrast, friendship as the "poet" and the "pagan" celebrate it is an inclination of passion, an attraction to a "beloved" rooted in our desire for the traits of the other as an extension of our love of self. Friendship is exclusive in its claims and expression, focused on the "beloved," while Christians are advised that "all men are your neighbor" and their obligations to love are governed by proximity, not preference (that is, I love and serve whom I can, not whom I want).[10] To be satisfied with friendship is "the very height of self-feeling, the I intoxicated in the other-I."[11] Friendship is "essentially idolatry," says Kierkegaard, for in friendship "preference is the middle term." From a Christian perspective, however, "love to one's neighbor" requires that "God is the middle term."[12]

Kierkegaard's assumption of an oppositional relationship between friendship and Christian love plays into a tendency within the faith tradition, one that interprets Christian teachings as necessarily against prominent values and ideals of human culture. Christians can easily get carried away with this "Christ vs. culture" opposition, however, missing opportunities to see where gospel ideals affirm or perfect values we naturally celebrate in culture. I think this discussion of friendship may be one of those places. From my perspective, a sharp distinction between Christian love and "pagan" friendship ignores the godliness in human expressions of friendship beyond Christian circles. It cheapens the moral praiseworthiness of those kinds of relationships, and in doing so obscures the ways Christian *agape* affirms, celebrates, and builds upon the idea of friendship as a norm for relationships within Christian community as well.

Christian suspicion of friendship stems, I think, from our exaggerated preoccupation with the story of the Good Samaritan as the paradigm for Christian love. Now, I do not deny that the story of the Samaritan conveys important Christian truths about the expansive and sacrificial obligations of Christ-inspired love. In the story Jesus told, an anonymous Samaritan pauses on a dangerous road to help an assaulted and desperate stranger, a stranger whom allegedly pious individuals to that point had refused to aid. The Samaritan man helps the victim, selflessly and abundantly, putting his own life at risk and guaranteeing care with his own wealth and reputation. What makes Jesus's story so jarring, however, is that the Samaritan has not extended himself extraordinarily for a fellow countryman, but for a Jew. Jews and Samaritans were descendants of the bitter break-up between the nations of Israel and Judah, and they shared antipathy similar to Israelis and Palestinians in our day. To Jesus's Jewish audience, the Samaritans were the enemy, capitulators to the Roman plague. By telling a story of a Samaritan man sacrificing his own well-being to help this other, one considered a stranger and enemy, Jesus issued an indictment on exclusive group preference. To limit concern only for those in one's own community, tribe, religion, or nation fails to satisfy the obligations of an expansive Christ-like love of others.

Ever since Jesus first told it, the story of the Good Samaritan has been read as the quintessential tale of selfless Christian love, a sacrificial concern extended to stranger and enemy, without consideration for mutual gain or reciprocation. The importance of the story is reinforced by Jesus's teachings elsewhere. His insistence to disciples then and now, "Love your enemies, show good to those who hurt you," has become the paradigm for Christian love, especially because it is a standard for loving that is validated by Jesus's own demonstration of sacrificial and universal love on the cross. Viewed through this emphasis on universal love, friendship may be good, but it is inferior to true Christian love, because friendships are exclusive and preferential, whereas Samaritan, Christ-like love is universal and nonpreferential.

With due respect to the importance of the Good Samaritan story, however, it is far from the only way love is depicted in biblical tradition. Jesus himself talked about love and loyalty—his own, and the expressions of love he commended to his disciples—in ways that feature different expectations and employ different language than this story. One of the ways Jesus talked about his love for others and the love he encourages us to have for one another is through the concept of friendship. Recovering this Christ-like commitment to friendship as a complement to Good Samaritan love may reveal important ways of being an *agape* community that practices forbearance.

Jesus and Friends

Deep into the narrative of John's Gospel is an extended passage often referred to as Jesus's "farewell discourse," because John represents it as lessons Jesus passed on to his disciples at the table of the Last Supper, as he was preparing for his death. In these chapters, Jesus covers a lot of ground, offering his disciples hints of his divine identity, promising the coming of the Holy Spirit, and foreshadowing the persecution that would accompany a life of discipleship. In the midst of this prolonged teaching moment, Jesus offers his disciples a "new commandment":

> I give you a new commandment, that you love one another. Just as
> I have loved you, you also should love one another. By this every-

one will know that you are my disciples, if you have love for one
another. (John 13:34–35)

By identifying love as the way outsiders will recognize his followers,
Jesus suggests that it is the quintessential character trait of Christian
community. Love is the church's public persona, because love is its fundamental obligation to its founder. To say that love is a central imperative
of Christian discipleship and thus the calling card of the church is to say
nothing surprising in itself, until we focus on how John describes Jesus's
new commandment. Specifically, Jesus commands the disciples to love
one another. He does not say here that loving humanity universally, loving the stranger, or loving the enemy is the distinct commandment and
defining characteristic of Christian discipleship. These kinds of other-
regard are important reflections of Christian character as well, as we
know from themes in Jesus's teachings that the Gospel writers capture
elsewhere. But what he identifies here as his central commandment is
that the disciples love one another. This community-love does not contradict the imperative to love people in whom we are not similarly invested.
Love is not that scarce a resource that it can be extended either internally
or externally, but not both! By specifying love-in-community as the calling card of Christian discipleship, however, Jesus describes something
different than the Good Samaritan love of the enemy and stranger. In
doing so, he speaks to the importance of mutual affection among the followers of Jesus.

Jesus reminds his disciples that the love he instructs them to have for
one another is a derivation of the love he has for them: "This is my commandment, that you love one another as I have loved you" (John 15:12). In
turn, the love that Jesus has shared with them is a reflection of the love
God "the Father" has for him: "As the Father has loved me, so I have loved
you; abide in my love" (John 15:9). Inspired by John's Gospel, some would
claim that love is the essential character of the triune God. Love between
Father, Son, and Holy Spirit binds the Godhead together, so when Jesus
commands his followers to love as he and the Father love one another, we
might consider love-in-community to be one aspect of what it means to be
created in the image of God. The love Jesus expects his disciples to cultivate
in community stems from, finds its inspiration in, and testifies to the love
inherent in God the Father, Son, and Spirit. Divine love, the love Jesus
lived, and the love Jesus compels his disciples to practice are variations of
the same theme. That is what it means for Jesus to suggest love as both our

command and our character. Those who profess the triune God practice love-in-community as duty and witness.[13]

Jesus proceeds to describe this love in a way that resonates with our concern in this chapter: "This is my commandment, that you love one another as I have loved you. No one has greater love than this, to lay down one's life for one's friends" (John 15:12–13). Remarkably, Jesus captures the godly love he is describing in the language of *friendship*. This verse enjoys a prominence in Christian belief and worship that rivals the Good Samaritan story, but as much play as it gets, I wonder if we fully appreciate the significant difference between the two. Yes, here too there is an emphasis on sacrificial love, and when we invoke it in worship, this verse underscores the loving intention behind Jesus's journey to the cross. Unlike the Good Samaritan story, however, here Jesus characterizes the extension of loving self-sacrifice not as an act of "nonpreferential benevolence," or universal love of stranger and enemy, but as an expression of deep friendship. Because they have responded to his call to redirect their lives to him, Jesus names his disciples as friends, and having called them friends and shared intimately with them, Jesus asks them to do the same with one another. With the disciples, Jesus establishes the church as a community whose central obligation is to share friendship with one another as Christ has befriended them. Following that command becomes the character by which this community is known by others. Friendship, then, represents an act of collective *imitatio Christi*, an exercise in discipleship, and (to use classical theological language) a "mark" of the church.[14]

The friendship Jesus commends here is certainly compatible with the disinterested love he celebrated in the story of the Good Samaritan, but he also implies that disinterested love is not all there is to say about Christian love. This farewell discourse is clearly focused on what we might describe as a decidedly *interested* love. Jesus's new commandment to his disciples is to live, love, and serve as a community of friends. To cite the popular hymn, Jesus promises that "they will know we are Christians by our love," and the love the world shall see from the church has the character of friendship. Far from being suspicious of friendship, as Kierkegaard and others would have us believe, Jesus commandeers the concept to affirm it as the faithful expression of agape within the community of people who claim to follow him.

But what does this friendship look like? Earlier we defined authentic moral friendship as a relationship of mutuality and intimacy rooted in shared interests, loves, or goals and characterized by genuine interest in the other person as a particular other. The community of Christian disciples exhibits friendship when it lives out mutual concern the way Jesus modeled, to the point of real sacrifice. We exhibit friendship when Christians commit to being present for one another, even in hard times, as a reflection of the steadfastness of God's love disclosed in Christ. We live as a community of friends when members of the church promise to "abide in one another" as Christ abides in them. Being church, then, requires that we love one another as God in Christ loves us, and as an extension of our love for Christ. That is the force of the new commandment, not a nebulous love for humanity but the commitment to love-in-community—friendship as the character of the church, even (or especially) in hard times.

Friendship in the Early Church

Paul and the other letter writers in the New Testament understood the force of Jesus's new commandment for the newborn church. In those early attempts to discern what following Christ meant to the project of living and worshipping together, the early Christian communities energetically debated matters of theology and morality. In the midst of all of this debate and disagreement, however, the epistle writers consistently urged their readers to remain committed to Jesus's command to love one another as friends.

In one of the most famous passages in the entire Christian Bible, the apostle Paul provides a profound and poetic testament to the importance of love in Christian community:

> If I speak in the tongues of mortals and of angels, but do not have love, I am a noisy gong or a clanging cymbal. And if I have prophetic powers, and understand all mysteries and all knowledge, and if I have all faith, so as to remove mountains, but do not have love, I am nothing. If I give away all my possessions, and if I hand over my body so that I may boast, but do not have love, I gain nothing.
>
> Love is patient; love is kind; love is not envious or boastful or arrogant or rude. It does not insist on its own way; it is not irritable or resentful; it does not rejoice in wrongdoing, but rejoices in the truth. It bears all things, believes all things, hopes all things, endures all things.
>
> Love never ends. But as for prophecies, they will come to an end; as for tongues, they will cease; as for knowledge, it will come to

an end. For we know only in part, and we prophesy only in part; but
when the complete comes, the partial will come to an end. When
I was a child, I spoke like a child, I thought like a child, I reasoned
like a child; when I became an adult, I put an end to childish ways.
For now we see in a mirror, dimly, but then we will see face to face.
Now I know only in part; then I will know fully, even as I have been
fully known. And now faith, hope, and love abide, these three; and
the greatest of these is love. (1 Cor. 13)

In contemporary culture we have romanticized this celebration of love
in 1 Corinthians, which is why this passage is an all-time favorite at wed-
dings.[15] Seen in context, however, it is quite clear that Paul is not describing marital love, nor is he describing disinterested love. Coming right after Paul has finished writing about spiritual gifts in church community,
1 Corinthians 13 represents a powerful reminder that the "greatest" of their
communal gifts is the capacity to love.

Responding to apparent controversy in the Corinthian church regarding which gifts were most important, Paul insists that a gift's value depends on its contribution to the common good of the community. Proph-
ecy, healing, miracle-making, leadership, and teaching are all gifts that
serve the health of the community, and they are distributed to different
Christians in different ways. Christians are equipped and called to exercise
different gifts, but none is inherently more important than the others.
Instead, their value corresponds to their active contribution to the well-
being of the church. In fact, Paul insists that, no matter how profound or
awe-inspiring the talents individuals bring to the community, if those gifts
are not motivated by love for sisters and brothers in the community they
are for nothing. Love is the greatest of God's gifts for the church; it is the
gift that infuses value into every other gift. True love refuses to bludgeon
others with knowledge or conviction, but extends patience and kindness
toward members of the community who understand differently. True love
does not insist on its own way, celebrating when it wins an argument and
despairing when it does not, but instead bears with those who do not see
things the same way and remains hopeful that truth ultimately will prevail. Beyond all else, love-in-community remains humble, looking forward to the day when we shall see God's truth "face to face" but remaining
tempered in the meantime in its claims to know the right and the true.

As in the Gospel of John, the love commended here is *agape*, but Paul
clearly is not describing *agape* as disinterested, generic love. Here *agape* is

love-in-community, love in the context of church. This passage celebrates neither the Good Samaritan nor the perfect spouse, despite our tendency to use it these ways. First Corinthians 13 is a classic sermon about friendship, a bond of mutual care that transcends all of the other particularities and problems Christian community faces. This is a poem about being church together. All of the other virtues of forbearance are invoked in this passage—humility, patience, wisdom, and faithfulness. All of them are shaped by the overriding imperative to love one another as friends. In a letter preoccupied with congregational disagreements, Paul reminds his Corinthian friends of their obligations to Jesus's new commandment. Love one another, he insists, "that there [may] be no divisions among you, but that you be united in the same mind and the same purpose" (1 Cor. 1:10). For love is the greatest virtue for a community striving to do as Jesus commanded. Be church, writes Paul. Practice friendship.

While it is the most famous love passage in the New Testament, 1 Corinthians 13 is not the only dissertation on friendship in the epistles. The commendation of forbearance in Ephesians and Colossians that we considered in the first chapter is built in each case on the presumption of love-in-community as the prevailing norm for relationships within the church. The Letter to the Ephesians emphasizes the unifying effect of the calling to be the church of Christ. Across national, cultural, ethnic, and class identities, Christians are called together to be one community in Jesus's name. In Christ, says the writer, God "has broken down the dividing wall, that is, the hostility between us" (Eph. 2:14). Gathered together in Christ, members of the church "are no longer strangers and aliens," but instead are fellow "members of the household of God" (2:19). It is upon this familial bond that the writer calls on fellow believers to bear with each other through their disagreements. It is an appeal to the particular kinship established in the shared grace and calling of Christ. We speak truth and grace to one another because "we are members of one another." We are friends in the deepest meaning of the term, and that friendship shapes how we navigate the circumstances that threaten to divide us.

The Letter to the Colossians also stresses the reconciling, unifying love-in-community that Christ has effected in the church. The author of that letter admonishes his readers: "clothe yourselves with love, which binds everything together in perfect harmony" (Col. 3:14). That investment in one another provides the foundation for bearing with each other through disagreement. The letter even seems to contrast love-in-community with Christians' conduct "toward outsiders" (4:5), which is to be gracious and wise, but is a different kind of relationship than that enjoyed within the family of the church. In the church, Christians maintain unity as friends, bearing with one another patiently and with humility, displaying their singular connection as fellow believers called by Christ into *agape* community.

One other moment where the Bible emphasizes loving friendship as a component of discipleship is in the letters of John. It is unlikely that these letters were written by the apostle John, and they may have had multiple authors. But the letters are clearly inspired by the Gospel of John and its preoccupation with love. Here too the word used for love is *agape*, but again the love described is community affection and loyalty. The author assumes that invested love between members of the Christian community—friendship—is an essential characteristic of the community, "the message you have heard from the beginning" (1 John 3:11). In fact, friendship is something the author insists distinguishes the community from the world around it. Christians love one another because "God is love" (1 John 4:8), and God lives in the friendship Christians share in community with one another (4:12). Their kinship is deep and generous, characterized by the conviction that "we ought to lay down our lives for one another" (3:16). By contrast, the maintenance of serious discord between believers is inconsistent with allegiance to Christ:

> Those who say, "I love God," and hate their brothers or sisters [i.e., fellow Christians], are liars; for those who do not love a brother or sister whom they have seen, cannot love God whom they have not seen. (4:20)

Failure to maintain the bond of friendship betrays that we remain in the "darkness" of the world, while loving friendship serves as a sign that Christians are living in the "light" of Christ (2:9).[16]

As Frances Taylor Gench points out, the New Testament epistles make clear that the early Christian communities were wrought with internal conflict; the fact that loving one another was so prominently featured in these letters suggests that reality was much different, and the importance of Christian friendship had to be reinforced to them precisely because their discord was challenging those bonds. In the context of disagreement, the New Testament writers consistently remind their readers that the ideals of love-in-community—friendship—are both the imperative for living together in difference and the public witness the church offers as a consequence.

Forbearance and Friendship

So far we have discovered ways friendship shows up in the New Testament as an important description of both the command and the character of the community called to be the Body of Christ in the world. The Gospel of John, the letters of John, Ephesians, Colossians, and the famous dissertation on love in 1 Corinthians 13—all of these texts describe an imperative for those in the church to love one another. The love they describe, while not incompatible with love of stranger or enemy, is not adequately captured by the Good Samaritan story. Instead of disinterested love, the passages we have explored depict very interested love, invested love, the love of members of a community for one another. It is the love of friends in Christ.

Contrary to the persistent suspicion of friendship among theologians through Christian history, then, the idea of friendship captures an important dimension of discipleship. Friendship is the primary concept Jesus gives us for understanding his relationship with each of us, and therefore the relationship he expects us to have with one another. To appreciate the importance of friendship to the practice of *agape* within the church requires that we loosen the assumption that *agape* is exclusively captured by the image of the Good Samaritan—universal, disinterested, stranger or enemy love. These are vital Christian themes, too, but we should not emphasize them at the expense of Christian friendship. To denigrate the theological importance of friendship is to under-appreciate friendship as part of the ethical expectations for the Body of Christ.

At the beginning of this chapter, I suggested a general definition for friendship, to distinguish it from other kinds of relationships we might enjoy. Friendship, I argued, is a relationship of mutuality and intimacy rooted in shared interests, loves, or goals and characterized by genuine interest in the other person as a particular other. It is easy to see how this definition fits the idea of friendship in the church. The shared interest, love, or goal that brings Christians together in bonds of friendship is their allegiance to Christ, their trust in God, and their common experience of the life of the Spirit in their midst. This common identity as followers of Jesus binds Christians together in relationships of mutuality. Christians care for one another, not in an instrumental or circumstantial way, but as persons with inherent value to one another as children of God and sisters and brothers in Christ. They enjoy a bond as fellow members of a community of faith that goes beyond common activities or interests. They follow a common calling, understanding of purpose, and sense of being.

Paul Wadell's description of an Aristotelian understanding of moral friendship surely pertains to friendships in the church:

> Friendship is the community of those who seek and delight in virtue, but as a community it is not just a relationship, but a moral activity. Indeed, friendship is the activity of acquiring and growing in the virtues, a community whose purpose is its constitutive activity, namely, to be the relationship in which those who love the good actually become good.[17]

Despite the historical tension between friendship and Christian notions of love, it is easy to see how friendship actually describes an important function of love as it is experienced in faithful Christian community. Christian friendships are moral friendships, in that they represent investments in other people for who they are (not for what they give us), and they constitute relationships in which together we seek out what we consider to be the good life. For Christians, the good life is the way of Jesus, the experience and extension of the love of God. As Wadell puts it, "what distinguishes Christian friendships from other friendships is that they are means of growing together in the love of God—that is their purpose and rationale."[18] Friendship is the context in which persons who share an allegiance to Christ work out together the implications of that allegiance for a life well lived.

As we have noted, many Christian thinkers have harbored considerable hesitation about the theological value of friendship. This is because friendships are particular relationships with specific people that seem, as a matter of logical extension, to give priority to some relationships at the expense of others. I think it is right and appropriate to describe friendships as particular relationships; we cannot be friends with everyone, nor should we try. It is in the nature of a friendship to be a specific relationship with specific people based on concrete shared bonds. In this way, the bonds we share in Christian community are friendships, particular relationships of love forged in our common association with the Body of Christ. But particular relationships do not necessarily have to be exclusive, as if I cannot love X because I love Y. There can be variations in the theme of Christian *agape*. Friendship in the church and the extension of neighbor love to strangers and even antagonists are different species of the same genus, the love modeled for us by Jesus.

When Elizabeth and I were first dating and I would visit her at home, my future mother-in-law would ask me for suggestions of things I would like to have in the kitchen, as an extension of hospitality to this boy courting her daughter. She would ask me for my preference of beverages, and at the time I voiced a preference for Pepsi. She would ask me what I would like to have for dessert, and I would confess my insatiable preoccupation with pie. Sometime later, after I had been on a number of visits to her house, my mother-in-law made a comment about my hating Coke. That took me by surprise, because I had never voiced a detestation for Coke. But Elizabeth and I chuckle about it to this day, for my mother-in-law assumed that my tastes ran hot and cold, and that the things I did not request were to be avoided at all costs. If I liked Pepsi I must abhor Coke. If I requested pie, that must mean I was revolted by cake. In reality, my preferences do not run that starkly. Sometimes I drink Coke, and sometimes I drink Pepsi. If I have the choice, I normally will reach for the pie, but if there is no pie I will be more than happy to down a slice (or more) of cake. Having particular preferences does not require that they come at the expense of love for other things.

Similarly, expressions of *agape* love may give a specific character to the particular relationships we have in church, but cultivating and celebrating friendships within the Body of Christ does not mean we have nothing to extend to those outside the fellowship. Love is not that scarce a resource! It simply means that the nature of those relationships is different than the love we extend to strangers and enemies. In fact, one of the chief benefits of practicing friendship within the church is that it teaches us how to love what is *not* ourselves, including those outside our community of faith. In reality our friends are never carbon-copies of us, despite the shared interests that bring us together; we are different individuals, and even in the best of friendships those differences contrast and sometimes conflict with one another. Loving another as friend requires me to love the friend for how she is like me *as well as for how she is not like me*.[19] Christian friendship is no different. Christian friendship actually keeps us from collapsing into ourselves, because it requires us to embrace fellow believers who, despite our shared allegiance to Christ, may otherwise vary from us in background, personality, or ideology. By making us better at negotiating those differences, Christian friendship turns us out toward the world, and it trains us to encounter difference there with the same patience and grace.

For Christian friendship, like the other kinds of true friendships we experience in our lives, is not all joy and bliss. Friendships are hard, because they encourage two or more people who are not identical to invest in one another, and to stick with each other through the celebrations and the trials that visit every friendship. Wesley Hill warns us that "the calling of friendship is . . . a call to pain. Joy, yes, and consolation, but not as a substitute for pain. . . . Friendship is a call to voluntarily take up the pain of others, bearing it with and for them, by virtue of our relation to Christ."[20] Sometimes that pain is occasion for us to help our friends through hardship. Paul Wadell insists that this is an important role: "If the church is truly a community of friends committed to a shared life in Christ, then one of the obligations of discipleship is encouraging one another in living that life and helping each other with the tests and challenges of that life. Jesus predicted a cross for all of his followers, but he never said we had to bear those crosses alone."[21]

As we recall from chapter 1, Bonhoeffer reminds us that sometimes our commitment to fellow Christians requires not just that we help them through their trials, but that we suffer them as the makers of our own pain, that we show them forbearance even through what we consider their sins or errors. Fulfilling this obligation of friendship requires both fidelity and truth-telling, and both can be painful experiences for friends. Sticking with our friends even when we believe they are tragically wrong in their convictions or actions, however, is a testament to our hope for them. "To abandon our friends when they are struggling," cautions Wadell, "would suggest we had given up on them. . . . To leave when their lives are in pieces would suggest we had lost hope in them and no longer found them worthy of love. *Friends do not give up on one another*."[22] In a nutshell, this maxim of friendship is the motivating force behind the practice of forbearance.

All of this is to say that friendship is a *gift* that we exchange with one another, and the experience of it teaches us to appreciate other persons and their differences as blessings, rather than as threats. Friendship serves as the context for cultivating and sharing the virtues of forbearance that we have lifted up as important for the church. In the giving and receiving of friendship with other Christians, we not only celebrate the common faith that binds us together but we acknowledge the differences in how we understand and experience that shared allegiance to Christ. We learn to live with those differences, we learn to *learn from* those differences, and by doing so we practice the virtues of humility and patience. With friends we learn to intuit the moments to press and the moments to support, the occasions that call for challenge and the seasons that require grace and silence. Seeing church as a community of friends who are different from one another, who have seen different things and who have different needs, gives us the chance to cultivate intelligent, discerning, empathic, and imaginative wisdom in how we relate to one another. To be sure, the maintenance of those friendships requires the extension of trust and a willingness to risk. Christian friendship both relies on and makes possible the practice of forbearance in the life of the church.

When churches share the gift of friendship and look for moments to practice the virtues of forbearance as exchanges of grace, we make good on our calling to be, as Augustine evocatively put it, "schools of love." For Paul Wadell, fulfilling Augustine's charge involves teaching one another through our friendships "what it means to love God but also what it means to love *like* God."[23] Living together in church should be a transformative experience, in which we learn how to recognize and live the good life, in which we learn to be friends of God and friends in God. Wadell insists that "if the church is faithful to its identity as the friends of God, it should be a befriending community that not only welcomes all who come to it but also offers them a place where the grammar of intimacy and friendship can be learned."[24] We learn the language of friendship through moments of fellowship and activity, but also through moments of hard decision-making and disagreement. Wadell thinks that our identity as the community of friends of God should even permeate our worship: "the ongoing effect of Christian liturgy and worship should be to form us, the church, into communities of friends of God."[25]

Extending the Circle of Friends

Perhaps by now you are convinced that friendship is compatible with the broader aspirations of Jesus-like *agape*, and that friendship is in fact a wonderful way to think about the practice of godly love in the particular relationships we enjoy in church, rooted in our shared allegiance to Christ and the shared project of growing in the grace of God. Nonetheless, you still may be skeptical that we can realistically describe the broader network of Christians in and across denominations as friends. It is one thing to encourage friendships within our congregations, but can I really say that I am a friend to someone I have never met? This is an important question with regard to the project of forbearance, because I have been arguing that practicing forbearance is an antidote not just for disagreements in our congregations but also for the fractures our denominations are experiencing. So much of the destructive conflict in the church happens at the denominational or ecumenical levels, between parties who have limited (if any) face-to-face encounters. The intimate nature of friendship seems to be missing in broader applications beyond our local congregations. Does the language of friendship really help us with those conflicts? Or is it a stretch of language to call these broader church connections friendship?

Even though the application of friendship to these broader Christian connections seems to stress its meaning, I think the idea still holds. The secret to seeing our relationships within the larger church as friendships lies in another part of our basic definition, the "shared interests, loves, or goals" that bring us together in the first place. In Christian friendship, the commonality that binds us to one another is the Spirit of Christ, and that Spirit forges an intimacy that does not depend on physical proximity or even personal familiarity to create the foundation for Christian friendship. Despite lack of familiarity with another, and even in the presence of significant differences, the shared commitment to a sense of "the good"— namely, the way of Christ—draws us into relationship even with people we do not otherwise know well. The experience of divine grace, then, substitutes for personal intimacy with fellow Christians in other places.

Paul Wadell thinks that the bonds of friendship we Christians can claim with others are forged in our shared sacramental experience:

> The bond of Christian friendship is the bond of grace, the kinship we have with one another in Christ. This is why neither absence nor distance need weaken or destroy a friendship. No matter how far apart friends might be geographically, they are always one *baptismally and eucharistically.* Any person united to Christ through baptism is simultaneously joined to every other person baptized into Christ, and any person who eats the body and drinks the blood of Christ is one with every other person, no matter where they are, who partakes of that feast.[26]

If you think about it, this depiction of even Christians we do not know as friends coheres with intuition and experience. We often describe people we know at or within church as our "church friends," even if we do not hang out with them, share hobbies or pastimes with them, or engage in other activities together. Implicit in our use of that language is the recognition that sharing community in Christ creates a bond with others sufficient for the ideal of friendship. Furthermore, many of us have had the experience of meeting people from other places through the context of church and feeling an instant connection with them. A visitor from another congregation or judicatory, a pastor from a church on another continent, a new colleague on a denominational committee, a mission worker whom we have never met—we tend to embrace these kinds of encounters as being "in the family," resembling more the reunion of relatives than the introduction of strangers, because of the shared experience of being church together. The air of familiarity in these interactions among Christians betrays the reality of friendship even among Christians who do not know each other on a personal level.

The intuitive experience of friendship in the broader church may also explain why we respond to church fractures as we do. Why does denominational division bother us? Why does it seem so tragic to many of us, especially in a political environment that has otherwise numbed us to ideological disagreement and division? Why do we mourn schism within the church? We regret these breaks so deeply because they feel like arguments between friends. We experience them intimately, as divorces, even when we do not personally know much about folks on the other side of our battles. The experience of church division as tragedy betrays the reality of the bonds that are rent, even in the broader ecclesial arenas. A relationship has been severed, the blest ties that bind us together in shared allegiance to Christ have failed to endure. We have lost friends.

There is biblical precedent for this understanding of extended intimacy among Christians who otherwise do not know each other. In the Third Letter of John, the writer praises his readers for extending love to fellow Christians outside their immediate community, employing the language of friendship: "Beloved, you do faithfully whatever you do for the friends, even though they are strangers to you; they have testified to your love before the church" (3 John 5–6a). Here we see biblical extension of the concept of friendship beyond the intimate connections within a local community, as well as confirmation that the love—*agape*—that is commended throughout the New Testament is appropriately identified with friendship.

Intuitively and theologically, then, it is not a stretch to use friendship to describe the bond we have with members of the larger Christian family of faith, even if they are very different or from far-away places, even if we do not know them intimately otherwise. The connection is real, and it is morally significant, for it serves as the basis on which we love one another, in the local, denominational, and ecumenical circles in which we are church together. Our shared sacramental experience of Christ creates the space in which we cultivate humility, practice patience, exercise wisdom, and extend trust to one another. Friendship in Christ is the context in which we negotiate the differences between us. It is the theological ground on which practicing forbearance is both our command and our character.

To my knowledge, the Swiss theologian Karl Barth did not use the language of friendship to describe the church, but he did use a phrase that I find wonderfully hopeful and importantly suggestive of all that rides on this notion. Barth called the church the "provisional representation of humanity."[27] By that Barth meant that what the church experiences ideally in its own community—the love of God lived out as love for one another—foreshadows God's intentions for the world. Here lies the ultimate importance of our getting the project of forbearance in friendship right. Here we see the connection between the love of Christian friends and the Good Samaritan love with which it is so often contrasted. Christian love as friendship does not contradict the love of stranger and enemy that Jesus encouraged us to extend. Instead, practicing friendship in the church—not just in our congregations but as participants of the larger church—prepares us to represent the more universal aspects of Christian love to the world. Seeing our relationships in church as friendship imposes certain virtues on those relationships, reorients how we handle conflict, and changes our understanding of the pursuit of truth and justice together. When we are faithful to the obligations of Christian friendship, we not only make the church healthier but also strengthen its witness, by modeling a positive way of living with diversity in harmony. In this way, being the community of friends of God and friends in God implicates us, in a beautiful way, in the actualization of God's love for the world.

CHAPTER 7

Truth

Together we have imagined a new future for the church, one characterized by active forbearance of difference in a spirit of friendship. I have argued that practicing forbearance provides the church with an opportunity to embrace biblically rooted virtues in the name of its calling to be the Body of Christ in the world. To practice forbearance is to affirm the importance of that unity in the face of inevitable disagreement; to commit to a spirit of humility, patience, wisdom, faithfulness, and friendship through that disagreement; and to chart a healthier path for the church in the process.

For those of us who are tired of the incessant infighting that has come to characterize many of our denominations and congregations, this picture of forbearance and friendship may be very appealing. Practicing forbearance represents a welcome change of pace from a church life dominated by theological and moral battles. The idea of forbearance is not without its critics, however. Sexuality, climate change, abortion, economics, race—many of the issues that divide the church are not incidental to us. Instead we consider them fundamental test cases for Christian faithfulness, and the integrity of the church seems to lie in the balance of our disagreements over them. To some Christians, then, danger lurks in the theological future I have outlined so far, for emphasizing forbearance may resemble asking the church to stand down from its insistence on the truth of the gospel, to abandon its purity in the name of preserving unity. At least one Protestant formulation of the Great Ends of the Church includes "the preservation of the truth" among the church's cardinal responsibilities.[1] Some critics of forbearance argue that too zealous an effort to maintain the unity of the body risks abandoning our responsibility to represent God's truth with faithfulness, in a world of eroding moral standards. In the face of dangerous cultural counter-currents, do we not need to stand firm in our convictions? Is there no truth worthy to preserve and defend? Is not the call to forbearance simply a call for Christians to stand for nothing at all?

This charge to defend God's truth in the face of cultural opposition is often the concern of Christian conservatives, although in the next chapter we will look at the way liberals' analogous claims lead them to have their own doubts about forbearance. But for now we will consider the typical conservative's worry: does the practice of forbearance undermine the church's commitment to the preservation of God's truth? This is the heart of the conservative Christian objection to all kinds of trajectories in church and culture. The embrace of same-sex marriage and the ordination of LGBTQ individuals amounts to capitulation to cultural licentiousness around sexual standards and a denial of God's expectations for human sexuality, captured in the historical definition of "good sex" as being between a (married) man and woman. The enthusiasm for Darwinian science signals a rejection of the belief in God as the Creator of the cosmos and of the authority of Scripture as the source of truth. The use of female language and images for the divine represents a denial of the God of the Bible. Support for abortion rights denies the inherent dignity of all human beings, especially the innocent unborn. On these issues and others, many conservatives fear that the move away from traditional Christian teachings reflects a tenuous commitment to God's truth. The abandonment of traditional doctrines prevents the church from standing against the culture as a bulwark of biblical reality. Instead the church has abdicated its responsibility to preserve God's truth in an effort to mimic or absorb the dominant culture around it.

These conservative concerns are important ones. Are there moments when a church should embrace its calling to speak the truth, even if division follows? Are there convictions that are non-negotiable, so that a church that abandons them or reflects too much elasticity around them ceases to be church? Does forbearance risk sacrificing the purity of the church to an excessive commitment to unity?

A Protestant Impulse

To be sure, when conservatives insist that separation from doctrinal or moral impurity is more important than maintaining a superficial unity within the church, they are channeling an impulse that runs deep in the Protestant Christian tradition. We have been walking away from perceived impiety for hundreds of years. While he did not have schism in mind when he first posted his Ninety-Five Theses on a church door in 1517, Martin Luther eventually left the Roman Catholic fold, thus beginning the ecclesiastical fissure from which Protestantism arose. Theologically he was able to justify that break, in part by arguing that the Roman Church was not a church in the first place. In a sermon he preached in Leipzig in 1539, Luther explained that a true church "is where [Christ's] Word is preached purely and is unadulterated and kept."[2] A true church administers the sacraments according to God's institution, and encourages its fellowship to abide together in faithfulness and love.[3] By contrast, he argued that the "papists" defined the true church by their own authority and offices, by an institution that had polluted God's word and mutilated the proper form (and number) of the sacraments. "The Lord Christ and the pope each have their own church," charged Luther, but the pope's church had abandoned Christ's commands, and thus was no church at all.[4] Consequently, Luther insisted that it was not he that was responsible for tearing apart the church but the pope and his spokespersons who had ceased to be faithful.

Fellow reformer John Calvin shared Luther's understanding of the "marks" of the true church as Word and sacrament. In his *Institutes of the Christian Religion*, Calvin wrote that "wherever we see the Word of God purely preached and heard, and the sacraments administered according to Christ's institution, there, it is not to be doubted, a church of God exists."[5] On this definition he too justified his movement's break with the Roman Church. He claimed that Rome was no church, for it had departed from fundamental Christian doctrine and had distorted the sacraments beyond recognition. The papacy had so usurped Christ's authority that it was no longer possible to claim that the Roman Church and Protestant movements shared a unity "in Christ." In fact, the Roman Church's unjustified assumption of authority led it to reject Protestants first, which made Rome even more responsible for the alienation between it and the reformers.[6] Unity must be built on "mutual benevolence in Christ," argued Calvin, and, given its absence between Catholics and Protestants, he concluded that separation was inevitable and necessary. "Apart from the Lord's Word there is not an agreement of believers but a faction of wicked men."[7]

Calvin's spiritual brothers in Scotland's Presbyterian Church adopted his (and Luther's) understanding of the church, but they made even clearer the importance of doctrinal purity to the identity of the true church. In their Confession of 1560, they declared that the "notes" by which the "true Kirk" might be distinguished from the "false Kirk" are as follows: "first, the true preaching of the Word of God, . . . secondly, the right administration of the sacraments of Christ Jesus, . . . and lastly, ecclesiastical discipline uprightly ministered, as God's word prescribes, whereby vice is repressed and virtue nourished."[8] For the Scots, the maintenance of purity became an explicit mark of church identity, and the basis on which distinctions with other groups claiming to be Christian might be made. Where other bodies preached a message the Scots understood to deviate from the "plain Word of God" or encouraged practices that reflected "vice," there a true church was not to be found. With them separation was not only permissible, but necessary.

Luther, Calvin, and the Scottish Presbyterians are just a few examples of the justifying rhetoric common to sixteenth-century Protestant removals from the Roman Church. They were joined in their separatist ways by Anabaptists, who insisted on purity as a defining feature of the true church even more stridently than Luther and Calvin, so much so that they removed themselves entirely from other Protestants and from the larger society, into sectarian enclaves of like-minded believers. (The Anabaptist vein continues in contemporary Protestantism in movements like the Amish and Mennonites.) Through their history Protestants have divided not just from Catholics but from one another, and they have justified their penchant for dividing by identifying certain things as "marks" or "notes" of the faithful church, and then claiming that they had them and others did not. Certain truths are essential to the church's identity, they would say, and when those essentials are abandoned a group ceases to be church, and fellowship with such a group cannot be maintained. Since the sixteenth century, this has been an enduring Protestant principle: the church's purity must be protected, sometimes at the expense of its unity.

Dogmatic Allergies

If there is a persistent "us vs. them" mentality near the heart of historical Protestantism, modern liberal Protestants have worked hard to minimize it. Liberals reject much of the exclusivity and judgment they see in traditional Protestant invocations of the "marks" or "essential truths" of the church, preferring instead to elevate inclusivity, tolerance, and love as hallmarks of being church. They often have little appetite for dogmas, doctrines, or strict theological standards of any kind, for a focus on distinct standards of Christian identity lends itself to the construction of litmus tests for who is true church and who is not. Instead Protestant liberals have tended to concern themselves with throwing wide nets and building bridges. They have been, for instance, the driving force behind modern ecumenical movements, and in the last several decades they have cultivated allegiances with fellow Christians—and citizens outside the church— around issues like racial justice, climate concern, and LGBTQ rights.

Conservative Christians have charged these liberal efforts with the erosion of the distinct identity of the church and the abandonment of God's truth in the pursuit of cultural respectability. For their part, liberals often have contributed to this conclusion by minimizing the distinctions of Christian identity and displaying a certain allergy to explicit dogmatic conviction. To the ears of the typical conservative, the liberal desire for a tolerant and inclusive church has made liberals uncomfortable with standing for anything at all. Conservatives argue that this allergy to dogma results in a church that strains to distinguish itself from the broader culture and struggles to offer a compelling argument for what makes the church important. From a certain perspective, this conservative critique would seem to have merit; perhaps the mainline church's demographic demise in the last century (ironically dubbed the "Christian Century" by a prominent church periodical by the same name) is all the evidence we need to validate the conservative fear for what happens when the church abandons its mission to "preserve the truth."

Some years ago, in the congregation I now call home, a committee of members was commissioned to write a statement of identity for the church, in anticipation of hiring a new pastor. One line from that statement has had enduring attraction for some of my congregational sisters and brothers, but I must confess it has bothered me since I first encountered it. The line in question goes something like this: "we hold to no orthodoxy except the search for truth." A point of pride for the self-identifying liberals who helped come up with it, as well as for a number of other liberal-leaning members of the congregation, the statement strikes me as unintentionally misleading, in ways that reflect a bit of delusion that resides in some forms of Christian liberalism. At a basic level, the statement suggests that there is nothing distinctive about the community that calls itself church. A commitment to the pursuit of truth so generically defined could be the mission of any of a number of organizations. In particular, the statement fails to distinguish the community with whom

I worship from the place where I work; a broad "search for truth" is an apt description of any liberal arts college, including mine. Surely the church and a secular college are not the same species of community!

The similarity between this expression of church and the mission of a college was no accident; some of the folks who like the statement prefer to think of church not in terms of theological particularity but as a community committed to intellectual, moral, and aesthetic stimulation. In other words, for some of my friends in my congregation, church is important because of the words of wisdom that they might receive from a Sunday sermon, or the chance to talk over important issues in group studies, or the enjoyment of exquisitely beautiful music that our music director arranges each week. Church is not about believing specific theological tenets, certainly not ones that are commended primarily on the merits of historical authority. Traditional dogmas more often than not are an impediment to the pursuit of truth and a threat to the inclusivity of our community.

This rejection of dogma is fairly typical of a liberal church mindset. But to reject subscription to dogma categorically ignores the ways in which the search for truth has a particular orientation and character in church that distinguishes it from, say, a college. As Kathleen Norris points out, the word "dogma" does not necessarily deserve the connotations it has picked up over the years—irrational, thoughtless, uncritical blind adherence to authority or tradition. Instead, she notes that the term simply means "acceptance, or consensus, what people could agree on," meaning the "foundation" on which Christian faith is collectively built.[9] To understand dogma this way is to acknowledge that the church, like most communities, has traditions and histories that define it and give it identity. In this way, some matters of subscription distinguish communities that call themselves church from communities that assemble for other reasons.

Christian community is based on convictions, and those convictions are important to our sense of who we are. Presumably, despite varying understandings of who Jesus was and the significance of his life and death, Christian churches are fellowships of people who gather in the name of Jesus and assert that his legacy reveals something about God and the challenges of being human. That Jesus existed, that the Bible gives us some testament to his life and legacy, and that Jesus's life and legacy remain formative influences on Christian understandings of the world and their moral obligations in it—all of these are marks of the church that appropriately shape Christian identity. Many Christian communities might want to push this definition of church a little further, to insist that the practice of Eucharist and baptism are rituals that have served as consistent reflections of Christian identity, even if understood by Christians in drastically different ways. Commitment to the word of God in Jesus Christ, the word about Christ we receive in Scripture, and the experience of God's word in sacramental practices—these are the marks of the church identified by the early Protestant reformers, and they continue to represent orthodoxy (that is, right worship, belief, and practice) among even the most liberal of churches. But of course we interpret and practice those marks in various ways across the Christian family.

In the name of admirable virtues such as tolerance and inclusivity, I think many liberals overreact to what they consider dogmatic assertions of truth among Christians. Contrary to popular depiction, being Christian need not be an irrational or anti-rational experience, but neither has it historically been about just rational or aesthetic stimulation. As Ronald Byars writes, "The gospel is more than ideas or fodder for intellectual rumination. The gospel is the structure that supports worshipping communities, communities gathered around the risen Lord."[10] The church searches for truth with reference to the life, ministry, death, and legacy of Jesus Christ. This axis gives its search for truth a flavor that makes it different from other commitments to truth-telling and truth-seeking.

To reject categorically the idea of orthodoxy under-appreciates the distinctiveness of Christian community. To claim one's church free of orthodoxy is also normally untrue, even among proudly liberal-leaning congregations like my own. It implies that collectively we regard nothing as sacrosanct, nothing as non-negotiable as a set of convictions, but as we will explore further in the next chapter, liberal Christians subscribe to all kinds of orthodoxies, some of which they hold with all of the energy of a fundamentalist. My congregation is no different; we have shared truths that, while often unspoken and sometimes non-traditional, serve as *de facto* litmus tests for membership. Most intentionally, we recite at the beginning of each and every worship service that "no matter who you are and no matter where you are on life's journey, you are welcome here." That is an orthodoxy. That is a dogma that we consider central to who we are and what we think is "true" and "right." This commitment to radical inclusivity is rooted in further orthodoxy, namely the centrality of Jesus to our sense of the Christian Way. At the top of every Sunday's bulletin is this line: "Our mission is to live as Jesus taught, loving God and loving our neighbors as ourselves." This too is a confession of faith, a dogma to which we collectively subscribe and which shapes our understanding of what else is right and true. Now, these orthodoxies may not be Nicene trinitarianism or a belief in bodily resurrection, two theological concepts about which there is much debate in my church. But they are professions of faith that give our search for truth a different character than that of a bowling group, a social club, or a secular institution of higher education.

While we do not wield these orthodoxies like swords to wound those who would not subscribe, they do serve as measures of membership in our community of faith. They imply parameters beyond which a person likely would not feel at home in our church community. For instance, I am pretty sure that vocal homophobia would keep someone from being elected to an office of leadership in my church, and perhaps even serve as an impediment to membership. I hope that an unapologetic and public subscription to the belief in racial superiority of white people would test our inclusivity. If we are true to our mantra, we will welcome into our worship and fellowship even those who peddle in hate and intolerance—perhaps in part out of the hope that some of our inclusivity would rub off on them. But I suspect we would be uncomfortable offering membership to someone so publicly bigoted. The standard of inclusivity that demands we open the door to them serves as a conviction they would have to share to stand with us as a member, representative, and leader. We have orthodoxies in my liberal-leaning church, just not the ones liberals like to dismiss with the term "dogma."

And that is OK. It is not only appropriate but also unavoidable that we have orthodoxies, things we dogmatically consider right and true. To imply that a commitment to orthodoxy is categorically suspect confuses the idea of orthodoxy—which literally means "right belief"—with attitudes that need not accompany it. The liberal rejection of subscriptions to orthodoxy surely comes from encounters with Christians and churches for whom orthodoxy is a ruler to wield, measure, and smack down those who fail to measure up. Or it grows from a perception that those who claim orthodox convictions are necessarily ultra-traditionalists who refuse to test the tenets they claim against the things we know to be true from non-biblical sources of knowledge—reason, science, and experience, for instance. Truth be told, appeals to orthodoxy have been a consistent motive for abuse and exclusion in the church, and too often they have been an excuse for Christians to avoid critical thinking. But orthodoxy itself does not necessarily require rigidity, intolerance, thoughtlessness, or uniformity. As Byars puts it, "The label *orthodox* does not imply unanimous agreement in doctrine or ecclesiastical polity, much less unanimity on moral and ethical issues such as those so frequently debated these days. . . . The label *orthodox* points rather to the fact that . . . churches all stand in a tradition based upon and respectful of certain defining landmarks, even when the churches approach them differently."[11]

A Different Protestant Impulse

So far we have made a number of claims about the pursuit of truth that may seem incompatible. We have argued that the insistence on purity of conviction has been a part of Protestantism since its birth in the sixteenth century. We have observed how this insistence on purity has conveniently lent itself to justifying schism with others in the church. At the same time, we have asserted that there is nothing wrong with—and a lot that is appropriate to—the pursuit of deeply held conviction (what we have called orthodoxy or dogma) and the assumption that those convictions help to define a faithful church. And I have hinted that the commitment to conviction, the pursuit of truth, is possible within a church that practices forbearance, in apparent defiance of the Protestant impulse to divide. How can all of these assertions hold together?

Let me begin a response by returning to one of our examples of classical Protestant schism, John Calvin. We noted that Calvin used his definition of the "marks" of the true church—the preaching and hearing of the Word and the right administration of the sacraments—as the basis on which to conclude that the Roman Church had deviated fatally from the expectations of a true church, and thus to justify his movement's separation from Rome. In this very same section of his *Institutes*, however, Calvin offers prescient warnings about ecclesial separation and beautiful counsel on what it might take to keep the church together in the midst of disagreements. The argument is compelling—and surprising, given Calvin's role in the most notable schism in Christian history.

Calvin begins his lengthy dissertation on the church by distinguishing, as Augustine did long before him, between the invisible and the visible church. The invisible church is the fellowship of "those who are children of God by grace of adoption and true members of Christ by sanctification of the Holy Spirit."[12] In stereotypical Calvinist jargon, the invisible church is the community of God's elect, the saints of every time and place. By contrast, the visible church consists of Christian communities in the world who profess to worship God in Christ, whose institutional practices include the preaching and hearing of God's word and the regular administration of the sacraments. This visible church is made up of people with varied relationships with God, both the truly elect and the "hypocrites," as Calvin calls them, people who participate in the life of the church but do not have a saving relationship with God. The mixed nature of the visible church is the reality that comes with living in a sinful world, and rather than insisting on an impossible perfection in these fellowships, Christians must figure out how to live faithfully within communities of mixed moral and religious accomplishment.

One option that is not available, says Calvin, is to walk away from churches that disappoint us. In fact, Calvin claims that God considers "anyone who arrogantly leaves any Christian society" on account of theological, moral, or personal disagreements to be "a traitor and apostate from Christianity." To leave a church in this way is to question its identity as a church and to disrespect God by disrespecting God's church. As long as the marks of the church are present, Calvin insists that we cannot reject a fellowship, "even if it otherwise swarms with many faults." As long as a church claims fidelity to the word of God in Scripture and sacrament, we cannot question its legitimacy, even if it suffers from significant shortcomings in its doctrinal or worship life.[13]

This is an important point that bears repeating. Calvin argues that even deep disagreements about theology, morality, and worship are not grounds for division in the church. This assertion is based on Calvin's admission that "not all the articles of true doctrine are of the same sort." Some convictions of faith, he says, "are so necessary to know that they should be certain and unquestioned by all [Christians] as the proper principles of religion. Such are: God is one; Christ is God and the Son of God; our salvation rests in God's mercy; and the like."[14] Here I read Calvin to be saying that there are fundamental tenets that give Christian belief its identity. Adherence to the God recognized and worshipped in Jesus Christ is essential to Christian community, for it is the central subscription that brings us together and makes us church. Loyalty to Scripture preached and heard and participation in the sacramental life of the community make no sense beyond a loyalty to the word of God made known to us in Jesus Christ. Allegiance to God in Christ should be considered a non-negotiable principle of Christian faith.

But Calvin's list of doctrines on which the marks of the church depend does not extend much beyond the central profession of faith in Christ. In fact, he admits that there are many, many other matters of theology and morality about which Christians can expect to disagree. Yes, we might wish that all Christians could live together in theological harmony, but as we have explored in earlier chapters, that is not a reality for human communities limited by various myopia. Says Calvin, "since all [people] are somewhat beclouded with ignorance, either we must leave no church remaining, or we must condone delusion in those matters which can go unknown without harm to the sum of religion and without loss of salvation."[15] Human reality prepares us to expect disagreement, dissention, and "delusion" in the church. Differences between Christians are not going anywhere, and Calvin insists that they cannot be used as an excuse to divide the church.

So what are we to do with what we perceive to be error in the church? Should we just ignore it? Calvin anticipates that there are folks in the church who "out of ill-advised zeal for righteousness" are inclined to leave fellowships that challenge their faith convictions. "When they do not see a quality of life corresponding to the doctrine of the gospel" in the church, observes Calvin, "they immediately judge that no church exists in that place" and they leave. Calvin sympathizes with the righteous frustration among these dissatisfied Christians. He hears their concerns about theological and moral laxity in the church. "This is a very legitimate complaint," he admits, "and we give all too much occasion for it in this most miserable age." Nonetheless, he cautions those who are tempted to leave their churches. He suggests that to leave with this kind of pious indignation is to give in to "immoderate severity" in moments "where the Lord requires kindness." Departing from a church they think has given itself over to wickedness, they ironically (and tragically) respond in a way that Calvin regards as wicked, arrogant, and hateful itself.[16] Calvin is clear, then, that the concern that theological or moral truth has been compromised cannot be justification for removal from a fellowship of believers that otherwise shares allegiance to Christ and exhibits the marks of the church. "Even if the church be slack in its duty, still each and every individual has not the right at once to take upon himself the decision to separate."[17]

What then should we do when we significantly disagree with theological or moral developments within the church? We cannot leave, but neither can we ignore what we perceive to be error if we want to maintain the integrity of our faith. How can we respond to "delusion" in the church? Calvin offers some helpful hints. First, he points out that excessive insistence that the church reflect our own perceptions of truth reeks of an arrogance not befitting Christian conviction. Among the truths that

Christians profess are the majesty of God and the very real shortcomings of finite and sinful human beings, so any pursuit of truth must be colored by genuine humility.[18] He reminds us that all of us in the church are works in progress. The admission of this reality does not excuse complacency, but it does encourage us to be patient with the sometimes slow pace of faithfulness in the church. "I admit that in urging [Christians] to perfection we must not toil slowly or listlessly, much less give up. However, I say it is a devilish invention for our minds, while as yet we are in the earthly race, to be cocksure about our perfection."[19] Humility and patience, hallmarks of Christian forbearance, acknowledge the real limitations under which the church and individuals strive to be faithful.

Next Calvin reminds us to focus on our own imperfections and strivings, and to avoid exaggerating the impact that others' convictions have on the pursuit of our own. "Neither the vices of the few nor the vices of the many in any way prevent us from duly professing our faith," says Calvin.[20] Within a fellowship that hosts the true marks of the church, theological difference does not fatally inhibit our ability to be faithful ourselves, even when that difference resembles deviance from our point of view. How many times have we witnessed a fellow churchgoer exclaim that he or she cannot worship faithfully in a church that supports abortion or gay marriage or some other litmus-test issue? Perhaps we have made such declarations ourselves. Calvin claims that it is possible to be faithful within a church where others appear not to be, and in fact we might hope that those differences will give us opportunity to work on dimensions of Christian faithfulness, such as humility, patience, respect, and mutual regard.

And this brings us to the final bit of advice Calvin gives Christians concerned about apparent error in their churches. He reminds us that *forgiveness* is the backbone of Christian community. We join the church in baptism, which symbolizes our need for forgiveness and God's gracious openness to us. That sacrament signals not a one-time experience but a perpetual forgiveness that extends to the church as often as we need it. Divine forgiveness is how we become church, and divine forgiveness is the mercy that sustains the church through all of its imperfect striving toward faithfulness. Forgiveness, therefore, lies at the heart of who we are as Christian community. Furthermore, with a spirit similar to Bonhoeffer's "ministry of bearing" (see chapter 1), Calvin reminds us that God's forgiveness ought to inspire and inform our own exercise of forgiveness (and receiving forgiveness) as we struggle together in love.[21] Ultimately God's forgiveness gives us the patient hope to remain with sisters and brothers in Christ through disagreement, tension, and errors.

For reasons I do not fully understand, Calvin seemed not to appreciate how the gracious tenor of his warning against schism pushed against his own break with the Catholic Church. In fact, we might even use Calvin's words against him, suggesting that he failed to exercise the forbearance he commends here when it came to his relationship with Rome. Notwithstanding the apparent contradiction, however, Calvin's defense of unity as the context for pursuing truth is important to hear. Of course Calvin was not ambivalent to biblical truth, as anyone who has ventured into his voluminous *Institutes* knows! He was committed to the defense of God's truth, but he also believed that the Body of Christ was where Christians should pursue that right belief and right practice, and he was deeply concerned that the unity of the church not be sacrificed in the name of theological orthodoxy. For Calvin the church is the community of works in progress who proclaim loyalty to God in Christ, who gather to hear God's word and share God's sacraments, and who, in that experience, strive toward greater degrees of faithfulness without the unrealistic expectation of perfection. In contrast to the Protestant impulse to divide in the name of truth, Calvin's better angels advised a different way to navigate the differences between us.

A City on a Hill

Calvin's challenge to hold purity and unity together lived on among his theological descendants, the Puritans. In seventeenth-century England, the word "Puritan" was a pejorative, a reference to the group's preoccupation with church purity. Responding to what they perceived to be Anglican laxity, the Puritans were constantly calling English Christians to what they considered God's truth—good Calvinist theology, restrained traditional morality, and a social program that emphasized industry, piety, and cooperation. The Puritans were all about purity, which is why many of them set sail for America in the 1630s. They believed that, in order to concentrate on efforts to reform the English Church, they needed a change of scenery. Moving across the ocean also helped to put some distance between themselves and the authorities who would prefer to put them in jail.

The narrative of the Puritans in America often begins with John Winthrop's famous sermon upon the *Arbella*, adopting the biblical image of a "city on a hill" to urge his frightened band of Christians to pay due consideration to religious duty as they embarked on the formation of the Massachusetts Bay Colony:

> Consider that we shall be as a City on a Hill, the eyes of all people are upon us, so that if we shall deal falsely with our God in this work we have undertaken and so cause him to withdraw his presence from us, we shall be made a story and a by-word through the world.[22]

For Winthrop and many like-minded Puritans, God and the world would judge their faithfulness by the extent to which they protected the purity of the faith as they understood it. To live as God intended, in the midst of a world that did not, and to show that world a better way for its redemption was their mandate, their mission, and their reason for coming to the New World. Protecting the purity of God's church was their solemn duty, which led to dogged policing of religious responsibility and some intolerance for diversity in beliefs and morals.

Despite this focus on theological and moral purity, however, most Puritans looked askance at attempts to break away from the Anglican Church. To be sure, some Puritans did break away; but precisely because the Puritan majority shared Calvin's theological concern with schism, efforts to remove from the Anglican Church created considerable controversy within Puritan circles. Among the Puritans was a sub-group of dissenters known as separatists, and they taught that the established Church of England was so polluted (with Catholicism) that it failed to uphold the standards of church. In its practices and theology, it had broken away from the ancient apostolic church, so separatist Puritans gathered in enclaves of like-minded believers in England and America to reconstitute the church among their gathering of saints. This faithful remnant saw it as their responsibility to protect the purity of the faith by breaking away from a chronically ill Anglican institution—true to the Protestant impulse, we might say.

One such separatist in New England was Roger Williams, better known as the founder of Rhode Island. Williams's historical reputation is as one of the great American voices for religious freedom and tolerance, but his own theology was quite rigid and exclusive. (How he gets from a kind of religious fundamentalism to a civil doctrine of tolerance is the subject of another book![23]) As a separatist, Williams shared the belief that the Church of England had polluted the gospel and true Christians had no other choice than to leave that fellowship and form their own.[24] Williams eventually was kicked out of Massachusetts for all kinds of deviant beliefs that the authorities judged hazardous to the civil community. After his exile, Puritan leader John Cotton became Williams's chief theological antagonist, as the two men exchanged a number of treatises containing increasingly bloated justification of their own viewpoints on Williams's predicament. They debated the circumstances of Williams's exile, the balance between religious liberty and social stability, and the proper relationship between church and state. They also debated Williams's separatist theology. Williams argued that his insistence on church purity and the renunciation of the Church of England was a true reading of Christian teaching and the reason for his banishment. Cotton denied that Williams was thrown out of Massachusetts for his separatist ideas alone—but he insisted that Williams's ideas on separation were theologically suspect anyway.

Williams believed that, in order to maintain the purity of their congregations, the Puritans had to sharply and explicitly denounce the Church of England and remove themselves to their own fellowship. Cotton strongly disagreed, and among his reasons for dissent was his insistence that Williams subscribed to bad ecclesiology. Separation into pure enclaves may be a more comfortable strategy for some Christians, but Cotton argued that Jesus commended a better way. Cotton pointed to the Bible, specifically to Jesus's parable of the wheat and tares, arguing that Jesus warned Christians against the zealous pursuit of purity, lest we threaten the overall health of the church with the disturbance and violence that would ensue from searching for and casting out "weeds." Tend the garden of the church with care and gentleness instead, knowing that the garden will always be weedy until the grand Gardener returns. Of course we must defend biblical truth, said Cotton, but

> We confess the errors of men are to be contended against, not with reproaches, but the sword of the Spirit; but on the other side, the failings of the Churches (if any be found) are not forthwith to be healed by separation. It is not surgery, but butchery, to heal every sore in a member with no other medicine but abscission from the body.[25]

According to Cotton (and most Puritan divines), separation does much more harm than the struggle for truth from within the church. Separation sets the church publicly against itself, distracts it from the gospel it is supposed to preach, and frustrates the mission of which Winthrop spoke so eloquently. "The way of separation is not a way that God hath prospered," Cotton wrote. As a scholar of church and state issues, I am a big fan of Roger Williams; but as a Christian theologian interested in the good of the church, John Cotton seems the wiser counsel to keep.

Truth in Love

Few Protestants would question the Christian credentials of thinkers such as John Calvin or John Cotton, yet even these stalwart defenders of orthodoxy insisted that the pursuit of purity cannot be license to threaten the unity of the church. Believing in essential markers of Christian faith and community is one thing, but how we understand them and defend them is quite another. Dogmatic convictions are part of the Christian Way, but when our particular interpretation of fidelity to Christ becomes a basis for defining other followers of Jesus as "not church" and separating ourselves from them, we sacrifice the unity of the church for an ill-considered insistence on purity. How might we hold on to a commitment to orthodoxy, the importance of dogma to Christian believing, and the essential need for marks to define what it means to be church, without them sabotaging the project of forbearance?

The secret to maintaining a commitment to truth while practicing forbearance is to allow the latter to shape the former. Because subscribing to orthodoxy is unavoidable and appropriate, we ought not to be embarrassed to defend our sense of orthodoxy with energy. Acknowledgment of defining parameters to church community need not be exclusive, however. To quote Ronald Byars again: "All communities require boundaries, and orthodoxy may serve to define them, generously, while leaving room for diversity. Orthodoxy is less about policing than affirmation, and orthodoxy directs us to the triune God of Scripture and to the ecumenical creeds. It is neither fundamentalism nor a generic spirituality with a Christian tilt."[26] The phrase Brian McLaren has used—"generous orthodoxy"—is therefore not a contradiction in terms.[27] Orthodoxy acknowledges that the community of the church, like all human communities, has definitions and commitments that make it who it is. But *generous* orthodoxy insists that one defining commitment of the church is the character with which we pursue, preserve, protect, and promote our conception of truth. The righteousness of forbearance is one of the truths that mark the church as distinct in the world.

If the Gospels accurately capture the spirit of Jesus's teachings, he certainly acknowledged that being a Christian was going to require his followers to stand for something. Christian liberals sometimes make Jesus out to be all about inclusivity, and there is much of that in the biblical accounts of his ministry. Jesus reached out to sinners, women, the sick, and the socially marginalized, and he welcomed them to relationship with him. But it is not as though Jesus had no standards, no orthodoxy, to which he was asking would-be followers to commit. In fact, his standards were fairly severe—love the Lord your God with all your mind, heart, and soul . . . love your neighbor exactly as you love and care for yourself . . . if an enemy takes your shirt, give him your coat too . . . love your enemies . . . sell all your possessions—you get the idea.

Jesus had dogmas and standards: he believed that God was God and we are not; he believed in something called human sin from which all of us have to repent; he believed that allegiance to God should translate into a discernible life ethic. Jesus believed in truth, and he defended it in defiance of cultural accretions on his religious tradition and political threats to it. He knew that both sources of opposition would lead to threats to his band of followers, and he forecasted that they would have to choose between tranquility and integrity: "I have not come to bring peace, but a sword," he warned his followers (Matt. 10:34). He imagined a moral universe in which there were sheep and goats, and he begged his hearers to join the company of the former by loving God in neighbor-love and stranger-love (Matt. 25:31–46). Jesus was no relativist, preaching a gospel of "do what feels right to you." He had a clear sense of right and wrong, and his insistence on this theological and moral vision at times had an "either you are with us or against us" quality.

But what was the discriminating difference between those who were in Jesus's fellowship and those who were not? Where was the line between his inclusive embrace of the marginalized and his exclusive demand for righteousness? We might say that Jesus's orthodoxy was exclusive to those who failed to embrace his inclusivity, for those who refused to grant that God's love extends even to those the world considers unworthy of love. Jesus invited disciples then and now to see the truth in love. Feed the hungry, quench the thirsty, clothe the naked stranger, befriend the enemy and you can identify with me, said Jesus. If you cannot buy into God's endless love as both assurance and duty, then you are on a path that runs counter to the way of God. The non-negotiable truth Jesus preserved and defended with his life and his death on the cross was the pervasive love of God. That love was the orthodoxy that disciples, then and now, must affirm in order to identify with Jesus.

We see similar subscription to truth in the New Testament epistles. We have seen the writers of Colossians and Ephesians affirming the importance of the struggle for orthodoxy, as their churches grappled with the implications of Christ's resurrection and lordship for the direction of their communities. But each of these letters also implored those early Christians to seek the truth in love, and in fact to define what is true *through* love. Love, friendship, and forbearance help to define what is worth struggling for, as a reflection of the character of the Christ we follow.

The First Letter of John is a particularly challenging example. This letter has become one of my favorite New Testament books, because, in taking its cue from the Gospel of John, the dominant theme of the book is love. In Jesus we learn that God is love, and therefore those who identify with Jesus must also be known by love. Love is the character of the Christian community, says the writer of this letter, a character that the church exudes beyond its community. "God is love," says 1 John, "and those who abide in love abide in God, and God abides in them" (4:16).

All good, except in the middle of this letter-long celebration of love is this passage from chapter 3:

> Everyone who commits sin is guilty of lawlessness; sin is lawlessness. You know that [Christ] was revealed to take away sins, and in him there is no sin. No one who abides in him sins; no one who sins has either seen him or known him. Little children, let no one deceive you. Everyone who does what is right is righteous, just as he is righteous. Everyone who commits sin is a child of the devil; for the devil has been sinning from the beginning. The Son of God was revealed for this purpose, to destroy the works of the devil. Those who have been born of God do not sin, because God's seed abides in them; they cannot sin, because they have been born of God. The children of God and the children of the devil are revealed in this way: all who do not do what is right are not from God, nor are those who do not love their brothers and sisters. (1 John 3:4–10)

Clearly this passage is about more than just loving one another. Sandwiched between invocations of love, this set of verses contains seemingly less charitable material. People who sin are guilty of lawlessness. They are not of us. They are not of God. They are of the devil, and Jesus was sent to destroy the devil and those who follow him. Decidedly not inclusive, the middle of our text is meant to distinguish the community of God from those who do not "abide in God."

There is a backstory to this letter, of course, though nobody knows exactly what it is. The author is concerned about a division within the fellowship to which he writes. From what we can piece together, there were evidently members of the community who had rejected the idea that Jesus was a real person who had lived in the world. Seduced by Gnostic repulsion of all things bodily and material, they were teaching instead that Jesus was simply spirit and that he did not really die on the cross. On the basis of this difference, they were causing a rift in the home church community, and in fact they had taken members of that community away to form a renegade church.[28] And in response, our writer feels compelled to say two things. First and last, he insists that a central characteristic of Christian community is loving unity, not division. But second, he insists that it is important for Christians in community to understand who they are and who they are not, and he suggests that those renegade former churchgoers represent who Christians are not.

I will admit that I have a lot of trouble with this passage. Children of God versus children of the devil? This part of the letter not only seems inconsistent with the broader theme of love in 1 John but also seems to throw a wrench in the biblical basis for this project of forbearance—until we recognize the obvious, that the context for this hard passage is love itself. The exclusivity we encounter in this passage resides between bookends of love, the regard for one another as members of the Body of Christ and reflections of God's love for us. God's love is the beginning: "See what love the Father has given us, that we should be called children of God" (3:1). Our commitment to love is the end: "For this is the message you have heard from the beginning, that we should love one another" (3:11). In between, love may require us to distinguish ourselves from forces that run in the opposite direction of love. The inclusivity and patience and respect that Christian love engenders itself may from time to time become a boundary that defines us against other things. Figuring out how to balance inclusive embrace and integrity to name the wrong when we see it is a delicate endeavor. It takes wisdom and discernment, as well as humility, patience, and trust. The complexities of pursuing truth in love are why Martin Luther King Jr. insisted that it takes "strength to love." It is obviously hard to love through intense disagreement over what is right, but it does not mean that either the loving or the commitment to truth is a bad thing.

What is clear from 1 John is that commitment to truth, however important to community identity and integrity, makes theological sense only within the greater context of love, specifically fidelity to the God of love and to the divine imperative to love one another. Our commitment to what we believe to be Christian truth is not overridden by the obligations of forbearance. The pursuit of truth is *reshaped* by those fundamental virtues of being church. The defense of conviction, therefore, looks different in the church compared to how it appears outside Christian community. Pursuit and preservation of truth within a church practicing forbearance is bounded by theological humility, faith, and hope. That theology gives us permission to question ourselves and others without risk to the health of the church, for we engage in questioning with an acute awareness that we could be wrong. We question, argue, and think together with a forbearing spirit, a spirit that includes patience with those who disagree, openness to learning from one another, respect and regard for one another, trust in our fellow Christians, and a commitment to maintaining Christian friendship through the hard work of figuring out (the best we can) God's intentions for church and world in our time and place.

When we lose sight of the virtues of forbearance, our insistence on the truth dissolves into an elevation of our own perspective, knowledge, abilities, and fears to the place of God. As evangelical writer Wendy VanderWal-Gritter insists, at that moment our commitment to truth risks becoming idolatry:

> No system, no theology, no interpretive grid, no amount of scholarship guarantees absolute access to absolute truth. Our best ideas about God are incomplete and flawed. To say otherwise is simply idolatrous. To presume that our understanding of God is perfectly right makes that very understanding an idol, an image of God. It may not be carved from stone or wood, but it is indeed an idol of our own creation.[29]

Our zeal to defend God's truth must always be tempered by the equally Christian confession of our shortcomings, as well as the practice of the other virtues of forbearance: patience with generosity, empathy, intelligence, imagination, discernment, faithfulness, and trust. VanderWal-Gritter admits to having "grown weary of triumphalistic warriors for truth—who know and believe all the 'right' things but exude pride, self-centeredness, and a devaluing of anyone who disagrees with them. I would rather engage someone who might have some spotty theology," she says, "but who oozes humility, kindness, generosity, and true and deep love for their enemies." After all, this pious leakage is what it means to walk in the way of Jesus.[30]

The surety of God's love—and thus the imperative for our own—sets the context for the pursuit of truth. Christians stand for something and against other things. Sometimes what we stand for reflects the best of human culture, and sometimes it utters a prophetic word against culture. Much of the theology that Christians have articulated—past and present—has been at some level an attempt to flesh out the precise meaning of that something for particular times and places. Investing in these theological undertakings is a useful exercise in the continual effort to shape faith identity.

But at its heart, the truth for which we stand mimics the One for whom we stand, the Christ who showed us the persistent inclusivity of God's love, and who commanded us to develop inclusive embraces of our own. Loyalty to Christ is the orthodoxy that defines us; the love of God in Christ Jesus our Lord is the truth we are called to preserve, not particular explanations of the inner workings of the Godhead or a precise recipe for resurrection. Christians are called to defend the truth that God so loved the world that God sent the Son, who calls us to love God with our whole being, to love each other as we love ourselves, and to preach the gospel of love to the world in Jesus's name. Forbearance does not ask us to grow soft in our convictions in the name of unity; the message of forbearance is not "don't sweat the details." Biblical forbearance endorses the pursuit of truth, but it insists that this exercise always happen in the service of love. If it happens that way, then arguments over biblical truth are not at cross-purposes with the call to forbearance and friendship. Forbearance and friendship are in fact the character of the truth we pursue together.

Marks of a Forbearing Church

So what does this commitment to truth in a spirit of forbearance look like in practice? What does a church that holds to these marks do? Allow me to end this chapter with a few quick "rules of thumb" for Christians committed to the preservation of God's truth through the practice of forbearance.

First, Christians who pursue truth through forbearance embrace rather than run from exposure to other points of view. An embrace of different views flies in the face of the dominant impulse in many of our congregations and denominations, where Christians often respond to disagreements by leaving those confrontations and gathering with folks who parrot what they believe. But the pursuit of truth in forbearance sees truth-seeking differently. Truth-seeking in forbearance causes us to recognize that Christians who believe differently than we do are not the enemy, and they are not threats to our piety. They are fellow travelers on the pilgrimage of faith who deserve our Christ-centered love, even if they are in a different place on the journey. Seeking truth with forbearance also allows us to recognize that you seldom learn anything by surrounding yourself with people who think exactly like you do. So if the point of pursuing truth is to grow in godly wisdom and knowledge, then we are better served by the critical encounter with Christians who understand truth in a different way.

Second, forbearance as the character of a truth-seeking church leads to an investment in critical study. Study is important to a forbearing church for the reason I just stated: you do not grow in truth by reinforcing your own myopic views. Truth emerges in deep reflection on the Bible and Christian theological tradition, in which Christians are encouraged to challenge, inform, test, and add nuance to their beliefs, and to one another's. A forbearing church should want to learn, which means having a robust Christian education program that deepens theological literacy, while bringing together members with diverse faith and life perspectives, to learn from one another.

Third, Christians who seek truth with forbearance never close the door on changing their minds. The virtues of wisdom, humility, and faith keep alive the possibility that God is trying to tell us something new through our differences with others. This means that, in seeking out opportunities to live, think, and talk with Christians with different views, we remain open to the possibility that we could be influenced by that encounter in some way. This does not mean that forbearance always *requires* us to change our mind. But being aware of our limitations, attentive to others, and faithful to the God who ultimately governs compels us to be open to the possibility. Forbearance reminds us that changing our minds need not be capitulation to doubt or a crisis of faith. It can be an opportunity for piety.

Fourth, the pursuit of truth through forbearance changes how Christians win and lose their theological battles. Patiently and persistently pursuing the truth through theological debate and struggle, even a forbearing church eventually will need to make decisions on matters before it. Congregations and denominations will vote, leaders will take a stand, and in those moments there will be winners and losers. In a season of forbearance, winning becomes a moment not for triumph but for healing and reconciliation. Losing becomes a moment to exercise grace and faith. In fact, with trust in God's sovereignty and concern for our fellow Christians at the fore, ceding the struggle may represent a gift we give to the unity of the church.[31] When the moment seems wise, we yield the struggle, even if we are dissatisfied with the result, for we care about the health of the Body of Christ, and we trust that the decisions of fallible human beings will not discourage the enduring grace of God.

Finally, a church that seeks God's truth with forbearance reinforces the virtues of forbearance by regularly sharing Word and sacrament, the practices that mark us as church. We commit to the regular reading, hearing, preaching, and study of the Word for the collective wisdom of the body, but more broadly to inform its health and harmony. In the encounter with the Word, we dwell on the shared allegiance to Jesus Christ that makes us community, the Lord who stands at the center of even our most biting crises and controversies. Baptism and Eucharist become intense holy reminders of the reconciling bond we share in Christ. Weekly worship, then, becomes a regular affirmation of the love of God that draws us and keeps us together, and a chance to practice the virtues of community with people who are otherwise very different from us. A forbearing church is one where sacramental worship lies at the heart of its life.

A church that worships, prays, studies, and loves together creates a foundation on which truth may be pursued and preserved, in a way shaped and not threatened by forbearance. For much of this chapter, we have treated this concern for truth as the preoccupation of conservatives in the church. As I mentioned near the beginning, however, the typical liberal also worries that a preoccupation with forbearance may encourage a questionable abandonment of godly principle. Liberals tend to express this concern not so much in the language of preserving truth as in the rhetoric of pursuing justice. To the relationship between forbearance and justice we turn next.

CHAPTER 8

Justice

"Snap! Snap! Snap!" The room seemed to explode with snapping fingers, like a kettle of popcorn reaching its zenith. I sat at a table in the front of the lecture hall with two others, having been invited by a student to contribute to a panel discussion on religious opposition to the contraceptive provisions in the Obamacare health insurance mandates. The objections of several evangelical and Catholic organizations to having to cover employee access to birth control was in the news and heading through the courts. Students at my school were talking about it.

To my far right was a spokesperson from a local Planned Parenthood office, who gave an impassioned, if not terribly deep, presentation on the importance of contraceptive access to women's health and autonomy. The room responded with a murmur of approval. Next up was a student of mine, Andy, who was invited to offer a perspective as a traditional Catholic for whom the religious objection to birth control is important. Andy was a serious but gracious student, and he responded with integrity, clearly laying out his position but signaling a desire to engage others' viewpoints with respect. The audience did not think highly of Andy's position, however, for the murmur that followed his presentation was clearly more negative. Then it was my turn to talk about the First Amendment implications of this debate. I spoke about the historical importance of protecting conscientious conviction and about the concept of a "compelling state interest" that sometimes defines the social limits of freedom of conscience. I suggested that, in my view, a priority on women's health served as a public interest compelling enough to justify the birth control provisions in Obamacare, especially since they provided religious organizations some distance from the financing of it. Finally, I ended with a call for civility in the debate, given that there were hard and respectable moral concerns at stake on each side.

My remarks were largely met with silence, until the first member of the audience rose to speak. The young man was well known on campus, for he fancied himself a social radical and had instigated protests over college policies on diversity and investment in fossil fuels. (I will admit to a bit of cynicism over the ease with which economic privilege sometimes purchases the luxury of smug radicalism for certain students at my school.) The student stood up and offered not so much a question as a charge: "I can't help noticing," he said, "that the only people on the panel who are insisting on civil and respectful debate on this matter are both men, whose reproductive freedom is not at risk here." And then he sat down. "Snap! Snap! Snap!"

The room exploded with audience members snapping their fingers, an odd shared code that I quickly took as support for his remark and as a sign of rebuke for Andy and me.[1] I do not remember exactly how I responded, but I was stung by the charge. I consider myself a social liberal who shares the views on Obamacare dominating the room that day. My own ethics is deeply influenced by feminist and other liberationist perspectives, and I had made clear my judgment that access to birth control was an issue important enough to women's freedom and well-being that it justified the provisions, despite religious objection. Yet my call for civility was heard as capitulation, a retreat from women's reproductive choice. Apparently others too in the room heard my desire for civility as a threat to the struggle for justice.

In the time I have been working on this book, I have received a number of similar responses to the notion of forbearance. Insisting on forbearance, I have been told, is akin to asking women, persons of color, LGBTQ persons, and other oppressed groups to slow down the pace of justice, to have patience and wait for church or society to come around, to retreat from the struggle for what is right. Or at least the word "forbearance" *sounds like* that is what I am asking. Defined this way, an ethics of forbearance cannot be compatible with prophetic Christianity and its commitment to social justice.

That is a misunderstanding of forbearance, at least as I understand it. To be sure, the word has had the connotation of what Martin Luther King Jr. called "gradualism." It has been used to ask perceived social agitators to calm down. But I am unwilling to abandon this important theological idea just because it has been used unhelpfully in the past. Think of the wake of jettisoned religious concepts that would follow that precedent! Should we not use words like "sin," "truth," "authority," "justice," "church," or "God" because they have been misused as well? In this chapter, I want to explore how a proper understanding of forbearance is absolutely compatible with a persistent struggle for social justice. Liberals are not the only Christians to care about social justice (see the likes of Tony Campolo and Ron Sider, for instance), but the objection to forbearance in the name of social justice is most likely to come from liberals, so this chapter is primarily offered as a conversation with them. But first I want to consider how similar this objection to forbearance is to the one we considered in the previous chapter. Here, too, we need to move past the idea that practicing forbearance is somehow incompatible with maintaining strong conviction in disagreement.

Justice and Truth Are Not Opposites

First things first, we must push back against the notion that a commitment to "God's truth" and a commitment to "social justice" are somehow distinct. This assumption too often serves as the structure for what divides conservatives and liberals in the church, and strangely enough we see this binary reinforced from both sides. Conservatives characterize themselves as the defenders of biblical truth in debates over sexuality and other matters, while deriding Christian progressives' preoccupation with social justice as the infiltration of secular liberalism into authentic Christianity. Conservatives often argue that Christianity is properly focused on individuals' saving experience of Christ and adherence to a largely personal morality taught by the Bible. Christianity does not offer a social program per se, and progressives' concerns about power and their predictable commitment to a welfare state are a confusion of Christianity with Democratic politics. Christianity is about a commitment to God's truth; "social justice" often serves as theological code for the abandonment of traditional Christian teachings in favor of socialism.

In their own way, Christian progressives often play into this stereotypical opposition between "truth" and "justice." Too often progressives characterize all that truth-talk by conservatives as anti-intellectual dogmatism. Conservatives are ideological, liberals tell us, statically and intolerantly committed to outdated convictions they insist are right and true. Making grand assumptions about what Christianity really stands for, they use "truth" as a weapon against individual conviction and betray their discomfort with diverse perspectives. By contrast, progressives embrace diversity and consider themselves the defenders of tolerance and inclusion—except sometimes when it comes to being open to and listening to conservative viewpoints. Blind to the ways in which liberal principles work as their own form of dogmatism, many liberals in the church turn their noses up in judgment at conservatives who treat theological concepts such as the divinity of Christ and the historical heterosexual definition of marriage as essentials of Christian orthodoxy, while failing to see that their commitment to their own ideals, including gender and racial equality and the embrace of diverse sexual identities, is equally unflinching. In other words, liberals do what conservatives do—they draw lines between what are essential and nonessential matters of Christian belief. They simply draw the lines in different places.

By pointing this out, I am not suggesting that a liberal commitment to principle is theologically suspect. As a progressive Christian myself, I strongly identify with most if not all of the values that the stereotypical liberal raises up as important. My point is that, in our dogmatic commitment to progressive convictions, we liberal Christians distinguish ourselves from conservatives in substance but not in form. We make interpretive choices about what Christianity really means in our time and place. We read the Bible selectively, treating some parts as essential and softening the impingement of other parts on our circumstances. We claim that our understanding of the ideals of the faith is right, and that those who oppose our views, particularly on matters of social justice, subscribe to an inauthentic version of Christianity. And often we make these claims as dogmatically as our conservative counterparts, wondering out loud how anyone could disagree with us and call herself a Christian.

Progressive commitments to social systems of inclusion, fairness, and mutual assistance—that is, principles of social justice—are themselves claims about what is right or true. As such, progressives' commitment to the truth can be just as confident, just as dogmatic, and at times just as intolerant as the defense of traditional notions of "biblical truth" that one finds among conservative Christians. So the reality that divides the two groups is not that Christian conservatives believe in the truth of their religion and progressives do not; nor is it that Christian conservatives are intractably dogmatic and progressives are not. The reality is that conservatives and progressives are frequently just as dogmatically committed to very different notions of what truth requires on matters of interpersonal and social responsibility. They are doing the same thing from opposite directions.

Allow me to illustrate this point with a couple of examples, one of them from the early part of the twentieth century and one a bit more recent. The Social Gospel was a liberal Protestant movement that emerged as a response to social problems caused by rapid industrialism in the United States. In the early decades of the twentieth century, the proliferation of factories resulted in deplorable conditions for millions of American workers. Industrialists offered their laborers wages that were insufficient to sustain a decent existence, demanded long work days and weeks without days off, exploited the need for families to send their children to work, and took advantage of the labor class's complete lack of power to negotiate better conditions. The promise of work in those factories, however, caused many people to flock to the cities, especially waves of immigrant populations. Urban housing was insufficient for the numbers, and landlords took advantage of their tenants by charging excessive rents and providing virtually no upkeep of their properties. The American worker was abused and powerless to insist on change.

Into this void stepped Christian leaders who argued that the nation had a moral obligation to improve the condition of the poor and working classes. Drawing in some cases from socially progressive evangelicalism and in others from theological liberalism, these largely Protestant spokespersons argued for social justice as a matter of religious conviction.[2] They argued that the heart of Jesus's ministry was the encouragement of solidarity with our fellow human beings, the insistence on fairness, and a special priority on the poor and oppressed. In other words, the message Jesus preached was a "social gospel," and a country that claimed to be a "Christian nation" must respond to the divine imperative to improve its care of the most vulnerable in society.

The best-known spokesperson for the Social Gospel was a Baptist pastor named Walter Rauschenbusch. Serving for years in the infamous Hell's Kitchen section of New York City, Rauschenbusch saw firsthand the effects of industrialization and unbridled capitalism on American workers. He wrote a book entitled *Christianity and the Social Crisis*, in which he claimed that "the essential purpose of Christianity was to transform human society into the kingdom of God by regenerating all human relations and reconstituting them in accordance with the will of God."[3] According to Rauschenbusch, Jesus lived and taught in the lineage of the prophets, who insisted that good religion is not focused on ceremonial observance, nor is it excessively concerned with rewards and punishments and the afterlife, but instead it should be preoccupied with the transformation of present life according to divine ideals. For the prophets of the Hebrew Bible, he argued, "religion and ethics are inseparable" and the "morality which the prophets had in mind in their strenuous insistence on righteousness was not merely the private morality of the home, but the public morality on which national life is founded."[4] In other words, faithfulness was relevant not just to individual heart and conscience but also to social structures and institutions.

Jesus himself perpetuated this religious call to social conversion. Rauschenbusch claimed that subsequent generations of Christians had domesticated Jesus's message by interpreting the social ethic out of it, reading it instead as an individualistic call to a private moral code, motivated by a desire to get into heaven. But the kingdom of God as Jesus understood it, as he inherited it from Amos, Micah, and John the Baptist, was inherently a "social hope":

> The kingdom of God is still a collective conception, involving the whole social life of man. It is not a matter of saving human atoms, but of saving the social organism. It is not a matter of getting individuals to heaven, but of transforming the life on earth into the harmony of heaven. If he put his trust in spiritual forces for the founding of a righteous society, it only proved his sagacity as a society-builder. If he began his work with the smallest social nuclei, it proved his patience and skill. But Jesus never fell into the fundamental heresy of later theology; he never viewed the human individual apart from human society; he never forgot the gregarious nature of man. His first appeal was to his nation.[5]

In the spirit of this understanding of Jesus's ministry, Rauschenbusch called for a "revolutionary Christianity" that would combine Christ's religious ethic with modern sociological understanding of systems and institutions to lead the efforts for national reform in the spirit of the "social gospel."[6]

Note that Rauschenbusch did not offer this interpretation of Jesus's message as one among many possible readings. Nor did he develop his social ethic as an alternative to biblical truth. He argued that the social gospel *is* truth; it is the *only* right way to understand Jesus's gospel, and competing interpretations that squelch the social imperative to Christianity are *heresy*. That is not the language of tolerance! It is a reflection of the righteous dogmatism of the Social Gospel, evidence that Rauschenbusch was convinced that his reading of the tradition was right. To be sure, said Rauschenbusch, there are understandable historical explanations for the church's turn away from a social ethic, but Christianity's continued rejection of its social obligation represents a pollution of the gospel. In *Christianity and the Social Crisis*, Rauschenbusch argued that the Social Gospel is biblical truth, and a church that is not social in its outlook and its understanding of faithfulness misunderstands its commitment to Jesus.

The Social Gospel is a vivid demonstration that a progressive appeal to social justice can be accompanied by a tenacious commitment to biblical truth. Rauschenbusch's rhetoric reminds us that liberals can be just as dogmatic, just as committed to their understanding of truth and faithfulness, as conservatives. Our second example illustrates this even more clearly. James Cone is one of the most important voices in modern Christian thought. He is also one of the most controversial. His 1970 book, *A Black Theology of Liberation*, fundamentally changed how we think about the relationship between religious conviction, racial justice, and the American church's complicity in bigotry. In his book, Cone asserts that "God is black"—not that God cares about black Americans or that God disapproves of racism, but that God *is* black. His theological claim about the nature of God is meant to insist that God radically identifies with people of color, and more broadly "has made the oppressed condition God's own condition."[7] Drawing from prophetic literature and Jesus's affinity for the marginalized, Cone argues that Christianity is theology of liberation at its core. As a result, any understanding of Christianity that does not centralize the condition of the oppressed misses the whole point of the religion. Cone argues that the incarnation assures us of God's intention to live with human beings as a liberating presence. In Jesus, God is revealed to live with and in the oppressed. For Cone, then, there is no place where God may be more genuinely discovered than in the black community. God is black.

Cone anticipates that white Christians will object to his depiction of God as having color. God exists above and beyond human particularities, his critics will say; God is neither black nor white. But Cone insists that white theology does not depict a colorless God but a *white* God. Whites implicitly globalize white experience as objective or universal experiences of the divine, propagating images of God in ways that reinforce their own power. So the objections to a God who has color are the discomfort of an oppressive majority unwilling to define God as anything besides a mirror reflection of themselves. White Christians reject the assertion that God is black because they are unwilling to give up all of the religious and social power that comes from the implicit assumption that God is white.

One way white Christians maintain the whiteness of God is to neutralize the social message of the faith, preferring to characterize Christian faith as an individual experience and private spirituality rather than a radical social ethic. Cone argues that, by "making the gospel into private moments of religious ecstasy or into the religious sanctification of the structures of society," the white church has polluted Christianity.[8] "God-talk is not Christian-talk unless it is *directly* related to the liberation of the oppressed," he writes. "Any other talk is at best an intellectual hobby, and at worst blasphemy."[9] Cone offers a reading of Christian faith that "proclaims the reality of the biblical God who is actively destroying everything that is against the manifestation of black human dignity."[10] Social revolution and racial emancipation are religious imperatives. Christian theology is a call to arms, so to speak, for black liberation.

James Cone does not argue for racial justice at the expense of biblical truth. Instead he claims that racial justice *is* biblical truth—God is black. And the flip side of this assertion is equally true for Cone—God is most certainly not white. God does not identify with white people and their oppressive power. God is not present in the experience of white privilege. God is not represented faithfully in the white church. White readings of the Bible that are too distracted by esoteric concerns like the Trinity to commit to social justice fundamentally misunderstand the gospel of Christ. They read into the gospel preoccupations that serve to de-center the theme of liberation, thereby silencing Christianity as a liberating voice and rendering it a reinforcement of white domination. White Americans misunderstand Christianity, and the predominantly white class of theologians in the United States perpetuates "basically a theology of the white oppressor."[11] Cone goes so far as to say that white Christians must become black in order to truly understand the gospel. "There will be no peace in America until whites begin to hate their whiteness, asking from the depths of their being: 'How can we become black?'"[12]

As Cone's rhetoric suggests, Christian traditionalists have no corner on the market of truth claims that are dogmatic and exclusive in consequence. Like the contemporary Christian conservative who insists that belief in the bodily resurrection of Jesus or the inerrancy of the Bible is a litmus test for inclusion in the Christian family, so radical liberals such as James Cone argue that a commitment to justice—"blackness," as he calls it—is essential to call oneself a faithful Christian. Cone is not just offering an alternative reading of the Christian gospel. He is asserting his interpretation of what is fundamentally true and important to Christianity as the right reading, the only reading. His understanding of the faith is dogmatic, binary, and intolerant of contrary views. All other readings are disingenuous and inauthentic.

Why is it important to point this out? First, if we are to have any hope for progress in our entrenched debates within the church, it is helpful to realize that the opponents in those debates are not actually peddling in apples and oranges. They are doing the same thing, making interpretive claims about what God's truth requires for human behavior. There is nothing inherently irreligious about progressives' theological claims about justice, nor are those claims somehow less dogmatic than conservatives' defense of their convictions. It may not be much, but I think it is important for both conservatives and progressives to recognize that they are playing the same theological game.

Second, to acknowledge that progressive commitments to social justice are another form of ardent commitment to conviction clarifies how we might respond to the expected objection to forbearance on the part of progressives. As I argued in the previous chapter with respect to conservative depictions of truth, here too with progressives I want to be quick to affirm the legitimacy of strongly held conviction. There is nothing categorically wrong with dogmatism, if by that we mean firmly held beliefs about what is right and true. By offering up Rauschenbusch and Cone as examples of dogmatic, radical, liberal Christian thinkers, I am not suggesting that there is something illegitimate about the stridency of their truth claims. Personally I find both thinkers compelling, and my own theological convictions are deeply shaped by them. They are doing what we should expect from people "thinking theologically"—they are articulating clear and confident claims about who God is and what it means to be a follower of Jesus in our world. But these strongly held beliefs might seem, at first glance, to be incompatible with forbearance. And for their part, liberals deeply committed to social justice might initially find a call for forbearance of difference in the church as unsatisfying as it is for some Christians defending traditional expectations of marriage. How is forbearance not what Martin Luther King Jr. dismissed as "gradualism," a tepid commitment to justice that is unwilling to risk social disruption for the cause of what is right?[13] How is a call to forbearance not a request for progressive Christians to yield the urgency of their struggles for justice?

Are Forbearance and Justice at Odds?

In April 1963, while King languished in a Birmingham jail cell in the aftermath of protests over racial segregation and police brutality, eight white religious leaders published a letter in a local newspaper, calling on white and black citizens of the city to distance themselves from the protests and find more peaceful ways to work for justice. The writers of the letters considered themselves friends of the black community in Birmingham, and in fact they had written an earlier letter supporting the address of racial injustice in their city. But now they were reflecting their collective discomfort with the upheaval caused by the recent march through Birmingham. Heavily insinuating that the marches were instigated by outsiders, the clergymen appealed to local citizens to abide by the "principles of law and order and common sense." They acknowledged the legitimacy of "the natural impatience of people who feel that their hopes are slow in being realized." But they insisted that the public demonstrations were "unwise and untimely." Things were happening too fast and too stridently. While "technically" nonviolent, the protests actually elevated the chance of violence in their unapologetic disturbance of the peace. The "responsible" and "proper" recourse, they argued, was to slow down, to take black Americans' grievances through the courts, and to seek out "honest and open negotiation" rather than the shock value of public protest. The white clergymen were asking their fellow citizens to temper their push for justice, and early in the letter they explicitly used the word "forbearance" to summarize what they were asking for.[14]

King had no time for this kind of forbearance. Writing a now famous letter of his own in response, he charged those religious leaders with preferring "a negative peace which is the absence of tension to a positive peace which is the presence of justice."[15] He rejected their assumption that "law and order" were uncontestable goods, insisting that the public tension caused by the marches would serve to wake society to greater justice and understanding.[16] The cause of justice necessitated that they provoke the status quo, and the need was urgent. The book in which his "Letter from a Birmingham Jail" was reprinted was titled *Why We Can't Wait*, a clear rejection of the suggestion that King and his movement show patience and "bide their time." For his part, King suggested that his clergy antagonists were not the friends of justice that they represented themselves to be, and that their tepid response to segregation in Birmingham amounted to capitulation to injustice. He rejected their insinuation that what he and his movement were doing was somehow contrary to the principles of Christianity. For King, the church was not responsible for maintaining the level temperature of law and order but for serving as a prophetic voice for justice. If forbearance means what those clergymen suggested it meant—dialing down the pursuit of what we think is right—then King wanted no part of it.

African Americans in Birmingham are not the only oppressed group in the United States to hear a message—normally in a white, male voice—to slow down and wait. Women routinely have been advised to temper their insistence on social, economic, and political equality as well. Historically women have been told by a patriarchal culture that humility is a virtue, a reflection of the self-sacrificial character of Christ, especially suited to the "weakness" of women. At its most dangerous, the prescription of deference to women as the demeanor of Christ has given theological legitimacy to violence against women and has sabotaged resistance to that violence.[17] Even when it does not take a physically abusive form, however, an exaggeration of the virtue of humility into a gendered ethic of docility has served to "keep women in their place." The push for women's equality has often been regarded as too aggressive—"not fitting for [their] sex," as Puritan John Winthrop charged the early feminist Anne Hutchinson when she had the gall to teach theology to men.[18] Women have been told that what passes admirably as leadership in men is bossiness in women. They have been cautioned not to come off as "bitchy" in relationships, in the workplace, or in the political arena—by which is usually meant a caution against asserting themselves. In other words, in the name of humility, women have been asked to stand down in the struggle for equal respect. In a church in which women still struggle for access to leadership opportunities—denied by theological principle in some denominations, and by glass ceilings and pay differentials in others—it is more than fair to ask whether we can risk softening our pursuit of justice by commending something like forbearance. Is forbearance just another way of telling women to stop asserting themselves?

Members of the LGBTQ community have been hearing the instruction to stand down for years. At first glance, the recommendation to temper the call for inclusion in the church might actually sound gracious. After all, shriller voices routinely request that gay sisters and brothers simply go away—or die. Compared to that clear rejection, those calling for patience and subtlety in the name of peace might feel like allies. But when those voices ask fellow Christians to wait for the church to catch up to their inclusive ideals, when they insist that we bide our time until a consensus on sexuality issues emerges, that commendation of passivity rightly looks like another impediment to the righteous cause. Should not prophetic Christianity work to shape the new consensus, rather than standing back and hoping it appears? Should not a just faith do more than just wait for a more compatible cultural climate for LGBTQ persons wanting to marry or wanting to serve? How is bearing with exclusion a faithful sign of the liberating gospel of Christ?

Something like forbearance—call it gradualism or patience, "knowing your place" or "waiting your time"—has often been code to encourage marginalized communities within church and society to put the brakes on their efforts for change. If that is all forbearance is, then perhaps it does not surprise that a straight, white, male writer like myself should find it easy and attractive to call for patience, humility, and trust in the church. The most poignant injustices in church and society do not affect me as an individual. I am not marginalized by capitulation to dominant expectations of race, gender, or sexual orientation. Could it be that forbearance only looks good if you have nothing to lose in the retreat from social justice?

Bearing with the Struggle for Justice

If forbearance were primarily a call to pull back in the struggles against injustice, to slow down and wait for church or society to catch up, then the charge of gradualism or capitulation would have merit, and forbearance would not be much of an ethic. But forbearance does not require a retreat from social justice, at least not as I understand it. It does not require us to give up the good fight for what we know in our hearts and minds is right and true. It does not ask us to temper our energy, reduce the urgency of our cause, or avoid tension and conflict at all costs. What forbearance does ask is that we engage the other in church and society in a certain way, in a way consistent with Christian virtue and the art of Christian friendship. It invites us to be dogged in our conviction while remaining open to the possibility that we might learn something from people with very different beliefs. It invites us to be persistent in our commitment to what is right and true while perfecting the art of listening to others. It affirms our dedication to principle while encouraging us to empathize with others, imagine how the world looks from their points of view, and discern the best strategies for persuading them of our perspective. Perhaps above all, forbearance encourages us to fight for what is right, good, and true with a commitment to friendship with others in the church, and in a spirit of mutual trust and faith in God's future.

What I have in mind here is similar to what King called the "transformed nonconformist." Never did King argue that nonconformity—that is, nonviolent resistance to civil or social norms—was an inappropriate strategy for Christian social witness. Christians should be concerned for justice, and we should be concerned enough to serve as "creatively maladjusted" instigators for change when we see injustice in church or society. He explicitly rejected the "passive sort of patience which is an excuse to do nothing."[19] But what sets Christian social witness apart from other protest endeavors, argued King, is the spirit in which the pursuit of justice is engaged. King taught a nonconformity "controlled and directed by a transformed life" rooted in Christ.[20] The transformed nonconformist combines a "toughminded" commitment to conviction with a "tenderheartedness" that refuses to give up on his antagonists as people and fellow Christians.[21] The transformed nonconformist "pleads patiently" and persistently with those who have lost the true meaning of Christianity. "With understanding and goodwill" he takes up the obligation to change their minds.[22] King commended an ethic of social change that never loses sight of its ultimate ends: reconciliation, love, and friendship.[23] As a result, the transformed nonconformist is saved "from speaking irresponsible words which estrange without reconciling and from making hasty judgments which are blind to the necessity of social progress. He recognizes that social change will not come overnight, yet he works as though it is an imminent possibility."[24] Committed to the imperative of justice, the transformed nonconformist resists oppression and works for the good and the right aggressively, but does so with a spirit of grace, hope in the power of friendship, and an enduring commitment to the unity of the Body of Christ.[25]

King was a leader in this transformed nonconformity, combining his persistent commitment to racial justice in the United States with motivation rooted in reconciling love and the desire for Christian friendship. Similarly prophetic voices in the Dutch Reformed Mission Church in South Africa gave voice to the combination of justice and a spirit of reconciliation in the face of apartheid, witnessed in the Confession of Belhar, adopted by the church in 1986. In that confession, the church rejected the segregation of people on account of race, color, identity, or heritage. Such separation was a profound injustice, and any attempt to baptize segregation with Christian theology was anathema to the statement of faith. But this insistence on the full respect and inclusion of all people was explicitly articulated as part of a larger witness to Christ's work of reconciliation: "Unity is . . . both a gift and an obligation for the church of Jesus Christ," says the Belhar Confession. The reality of our unity in God is the context for the church's insistence on justice, and thus it provides the flavor for a particularly Christian commitment to justice. Reconciliation—including reconciliation with the oppressor—is the ethos in which Christians insist on justice. In this way, justice and the virtues of forbearance are more than compatible; the virtues of forbearance transform the Christian understanding of justice and its ends.

Christians struggling for the inclusion of LGBTQ persons in the church have embodied the compatibility between justice and forbearance in their work as well. In my denomination, an organization called the Covenant Network has worked tirelessly for years to make the ordination and marriage of LGBTQ persons constitutionally permitted. They have persistently stoked the debates in the PC(USA), organizing national, regional, and local efforts to educate and persuade their fellow Presbyterians and to keep the concerns of the gay community on the front burner. The Covenant Network refused to hear the warning that "now is not the time," insisting that justice was overdue, but pushing the conversation in such a way that it always pointed to the unity of the church in Christ. Their mission statement commits them explicitly to the maintenance of unity, all the while laboring for a moment when the church would open its marital blessings and ordination opportunities to those who had been long excluded.[26] They do not use the term, but in insisting on both inclusion and reconciliation for the church, their work testifies to the truth that the practice of forbearance is compatible with the work of justice.[27]

Writing for *Christian Century*, Nicole Chilivis tells the story of her difficult relationship with the church of her youth, a church that stands for starkly different values from hers. An ordained clergywoman herself, Chilivis grew up in a congregation that does not approve of women in ministerial leadership positions. When she returns to her church on family visits, the disconnect between her values and theirs provokes strong feelings. She says those differences were never more acute than on the day when "15 men—and only men—stood up to serve communion. I couldn't deny my hurt and frustration—or my inclination to become an apologist for my own beliefs. I wanted to build a wall so I wouldn't have to see or hear those men." And yet she loves the congregation. She neither apologizes nor retreats from her commitment to women's ordination, but as she insists on the rightness of that conviction she also hopes for reconciliation with those who disagree:

> So I will continue to sit in those pews when I make my yearly journeys to the place of my youth. I will sing, pray, worship, delight in, and grapple with the culture that played a part in forming me. I will do so because of a deep and abiding hope that if we are faithful and committed to staying in relationship, living in the tension, Christ will show up with a healing love for us that may even reach the ends of the earth.[28]

If Chilivis's hope is not misplaced, then the equal embrace of justice and forbearance is not only possible; it is a recipe for grace.

Does Forbearance Have Its Limits?

One of the great challenges to a commitment to forbearance and friendship in the church comes in the form of those who strike us as less committed to these same ideals. In other words, how does a Christian extend forbearance and friendship to people in the church who themselves exercise neither? This is an especially poignant concern for those committed to social justice. Sometimes our opponents articulate their opposition in ways that seem to undermine justice itself. Sometimes their opposition strikes us not only as incorrect but as lacking in mutual respect and humility. For instance, the theological debates over homosexuality in the church often are mired in insinuations of moral depravity and promiscuity of gay, lesbian, and transgendered persons. As a result, advocates for marriage or ordination for gay and lesbian persons contend not only with fellow Christians who have principled theological commitments to the normativity of heterosexual relationships but also with persons who combine with (or substitute for) those principles what can only be called homophobia—a fear or hatred of gay people. The former convictions may represent a theological disagreement over the proper reading of Christian

moral obligation, but the latter dynamic denies the morality and humanity of individuals with different sexual identities. As a result, some of us
may object to the imperative to extend forbearance to Christians peddling
in homophobia as part of their defense of traditional marriage or ordination litmus tests.

But of course Christians holding conservative beliefs are not the only
ones capable of participating in theological debate in ways that transgress
the ideals of forbearance. In rejecting traditional interpretations of theology or morality, or the understanding of biblical authority that may root
them, progressives often dismiss the intelligence, motives, or worth of
those who hold traditional convictions. Christians who subscribe to traditional beliefs in the Trinity, or the authority of the Bible, or the physical
reality of the resurrection are lumped in the category of "fundamentalists"
and dismissed as backward, anti-modern, and unintelligent. Christians
who voice support for law and order, for strict immigration laws, or for a
reduced social welfare system are labeled as racist, regardless of the precise
principled roots of their convictions. Christians who believe that nature
and biblical theology affirm heterosexual relationships as a social and
moral norm that the church should defend are declared homophobic, even
as they try to distinguish between a defense of civil rights for all persons
and a restriction of the definition of marriage. As a self-identifying liberal,
I have been in the company of many fellow progressives who regularly
bathe in self-congratulation for their alleged intellectual or moral superiority over people who believe such supposedly stupid things. As a result,
we liberals often come off as the parabolic Pharisee obliviously praying
next to the sinner at the altar, thanking God that we are not like those
brainless, Darwin-denying, bigoted conservatives (see Luke 18:9–14). Elitism has been part of liberal Christianity as long as there has been a liberal
Christian movement, and its result is that progressive Christians often
treat conservative Christians as if they are not their intellectual or moral
equals.

From both directions, then, what we often encounter is not just a
theological or moral disagreement, but an attack on the character and
value of those on the other side of the debate. When these kinds of ungracious arguments and attitudes show themselves in ecclesial debates,
are we obligated to extend forbearance to them? I think we can make two
distinctions that might help us navigate these moments that challenge an
ethics of forbearance.

First, even in moments when those on the other side of the ideological divide promote disrespect for others' humanity, perhaps we can distinguish between the message and the messenger. Here again, the wisdom of Martin Luther King is helpful. Committed to seeing the *imago Dei* in all people, King was able to embrace the humanity of his opponent even while rejecting his message of racial hatred. "We must recognize," he wrote, "that the evil deed of the enemy-neighbor, the thing that hurts, never quite expresses all that he is. An element of goodness may be found even in our worst enemy."[29] By virtue of their being children of God and reflections of God's image, even the most hateful antagonists possess human dignity, which obligates us to persist in loving them, even as we reject the values for which they stand.

Especially in church community, where the bond of Christian friendship sets the context for exercising forbearance, we are called to confront injustice and disrespect in a way that always has an eye on conversion and reconciliation. To embrace the humanity of our opponent does not mean that we always will be able to put our arms around him. As King admitted, to love another as a child of God does not guarantee that I will necessarily like him: "'Like' is a sentimental and affectionate word. How can we be affectionate toward a person whose avowed aim is to crush our very being and place innumerable stumbling blocks in our path?"[30] But love transcends mere liking, for it is animated by "redemptive goodwill" and aims for reconciliation. Love encourages me to see past the hurtfulness of another's beliefs and rhetoric to hope for a time when we can share in greater mutual respect. That hope energizes the persistence it takes to maintain community with people whose views seem reprehensible to us, whose opposition to us cuts to the heart of who we are, who our friends are, and the principles we hold dear.

Another distinction we might make is between categories of ideas themselves. Many of our disagreements in church are the result of honest differences in interpretation of the faith tradition, the Bible, or the needs of our time. Such differences invite persistent navigation through the virtues of forbearance. But not every opinion is worthy of patient hearing. Some ideas fly in the face of the very ethos of Christian community. Some arguments do not simply exhibit differences in understanding but are hateful or dismissive. Should we bar those who hold such opinions from our ecclesial debates, or remove ourselves from them?

Thinking about public discourse in his book *Religion in Public Life: A Dilemma for Democracy*, Ronald Thiemann cautioned against "threshold requirements" for the kinds of arguments permitted to be shared. Responding to claims that religiously based reasoning is categorically inappropriate in public debate, Thiemann recommended against litmus tests in a pluralistic democracy in which the freedom of speech is held in such high esteem. Instead, he claimed that any arguments that are compatible with the ideals of democracy ought to be given credible hearing. But how do we distinguish between arguments that support those ideals and those that do not? Thiemann suggested that we need to cultivate the "virtues of citizenship" among participants in public debate, so that we collectively learn to recognize perspectives that further the ideals of mutual respect, moral integrity, and public accessibility and those that compromise them. In a democracy, we ought not to outlaw certain kinds of arguments because they are inaccessible or even offensive. But as citizens we ought to learn to tell the difference between arguments that are compatible with the ideals of democracy and those that are not, giving hearing to the former viewpoints and respectfully ignoring those that do not.[31]

Similarly, I hesitate to put hard-and-fast parameters on the things Christians are allowed to say to one another in the context of ecclesial debate. What I would prefer is to see Christians so internalize the virtues of Christian love, respect, and friendship that we become good at recognizing viewpoints that clearly run so contrary to those principles that they are not worth serious consideration. In other words, arguments that run counter to the Christian spirit *disqualify themselves* from serious consideration in the context of faith community. Viewpoints that are clearly racist, misogynist, homophobic, elitist, or otherwise hateful in their intent or rhetoric can and should be ignored by Christians. These kinds of attitudes fail to reflect the spirit of Christian love, kinship, and respect from which the imperatives of forbearance and friendship derive. I do not think that Christians need to entertain such expressions of profound disrespect in the name of pious patience. There are bounds to the inclusivity that the Body of Christ is obligated to exhibit, and ideas that are obviously dehumanizing ought to be disqualified as such in Christian discourse. In other words, from time to time Christians are justified in being exclusionist in the name of the inclusive love of God. While our hope for reconciliation with the holder of such viewpoints remains, our rejection of disrespectful ideas and opinions themselves is entirely consistent with the virtues we are exploring here. It is, in fact, an act of integrity to reject them.

But how do we know when a more exclusivist position is warranted? Circumstances in which fellow Christians make arguments based in *explicit* assumptions about the inferiority of women or persons of color, or in a demeaning set of assumptions about the sexual lives of gay and lesbian persons, may be easy to recognize, but happily they also are relatively rare these days. More often in ecclesial debate we are confronted with arguments that are *implicitly* based in homophobia or stereotypes of women or persons of color. Sometimes the persons who offer these arguments are unaware of the prejudices lurking in their views, and in fact they may adamantly deny that they harbor biases against sexual differences, women, or persons of color. Nonetheless their arguments strike us as wrong, but not just wrong. They strike us as *hurtful*. Are we to judge these arguments out of bounds too, and dismiss them categorically, or should we exercise forbearance in these cases?

As difficult as these moments are, my own inclination is to commend forbearance in the confrontation of even arguments that strike us as hurtful but fall short of unapologetic assertions of race, gender, or sexual hatred. For to engage in these cases with forbearance and friendship represents the most likely avenue toward change and progress without injury to the church's aspirations to reconciliation. In other words, even in these difficult circumstances, of which many Protestant churches have recently had plenty, I would counsel against the inclination to split and run. The exercise of forbearance with integrity is a better reflection of faithfulness, and a more practical way to increase justice in the church. Doing the hard work of staying involved, meeting ignorance, callousness, and prejudice with the antidotes of love and persistent presence, offers more hope for the emergence of a just truth than refusing to engage at all.

Just Forbearance, but Not *Just* Forbearance

Forbearance does not ask us to lessen our commitment to conviction. Instead, it reshapes our zeal so that, armed with the grace of Christ, we pursue what we believe to be right with equal dedication to the maintenance of community, even with those with whom we painfully disagree. And even in those moments when fellow Christians and their values promote disrespect and dishonor the charity of God, forbearance prepares us to meet that injustice defiantly, with persistent love and patient hope that, through our presence and benevolent agitation, we will witness a day when reconciling grace makes us friends in Christ again.

To be sure, much of what I have argued in defense of forbearance finds root in an understanding of difference as not only inevitable but also a

reflection of a theological reality that it makes sense for Christians to celebrate from time to time. We navigate differences with forbearance because
we know that God is good, that we are not God, that human beings are
wonderfully diverse and frustratingly myopic, and that the church is invited in all this mess to be community in the name of Christ. We would not
have disagreements if we were not convinced that certain things are right
and other things are wrong. Often our investment in our differences with
others runs deep; what we think is at stake are basic tenets of righteousness and faithfulness, indeed, imperatives from God. Even in these times,
however, the maintenance of church as a community of forbearance and
friendship is a faithful way to doggedly follow the truth and unflappably
pursue the demands of justice. Even in those moments when we mourn
that many in the church apparently have misunderstood God's intentions,
the virtues of forbearance and friendship reinforce our commitment to
learn, grow, repent, and change together. And if we can manage to protect
Christian fellowship while we live in the tensions of difference, we just
might have a compelling ministry to offer the world. Forbearance as social
witness is where this commitment to virtue ultimately takes us.

CHAPTER 9

Forbearance as Social Witness

On a Monday morning, as I first sat down to work on this chapter, details were still emerging from a shooting at an Orlando nightclub two nights before, an act of hatred that left forty-nine people dead and more than fifty injured. It was the worst mass shooting in American history, and an act of loathing intolerance. The shooter targeted the nightclub because it was a social hot spot for members of the LGBTQ community; and by the trail of homophobia he left in the days before the crime, we know that the perpetrator harbored an intense hatred of gay people, stoked by an air of religious extremism. This was a hate crime, an act of terror inflicted on a community out of a pathological rejection of not only their sexual identity but also their humanity.

In the 911 call he placed during the shooting, the perpetrator proclaimed allegiance to ISIS, the global terrorist group that boasts of representing the righteous path of Islam. Anyone who knows anything about Islam knows that neither ISIS nor the Orlando shooting represents the heart of Islam as billions of Muslims worldwide practice it, any more than the crusades represent the heart of Christianity. Like Christianity, Islam is a complicated religious tradition, with texts and histories that admittedly lend themselves to justifications of violence against persons and groups deemed to be outside the teachings of the faith. But this rich tradition also features many communities, adherents, thinkers, and leaders who understand peace and respect to be the true pillars of Islam. Nonetheless, the shooter's attack on the LGBTQ community in the name of Islam gave license to an uptick in intolerance of Muslims in the aftermath of the shooting—ironic, since many who hold to Islamophobia are not exactly warm to gay people either. His self-identification as a Muslim gave many Americans (and a few politicians) permission to call for more restrictions on Muslims—those in the United States and those trying to emigrate to the United States—based solely on their religious difference.

Soon after Orlando, we experienced a week of public violence in the United States like few others. In successive evenings, two African-American men, one in Baton Rouge and the other in St. Paul, were shot and killed in confrontations with police. With a dynamic that is too familiar by now, the circumstances surrounding the shootings were unclear (were the men actually a threat to police or bystanders?), but the incidents aggravated the resentment and frustration that communities of color harbor for a law enforcement culture that many believe targets them with excessive force. Then, during a peaceful protest by Black Lives Matter in Dallas, a sniper unaffiliated with this movement opened fire on police providing crowd control, killing five officers and wounding several others. Several days later, a gunman assassinated three more police officers in Baton Rouge, making it the deadliest span of days for law enforcement since 9/11, and the string of events left many Americans wondering if our national fabric is coming apart at the seams.

The events I have recounted here are tragic examples of the violent end to which intolerance of others can lead, especially in a society that stokes suspicion and hatred of those who are different. If we are honest with ourselves, we will admit that American political culture in the last twenty-five years or more has been the fuel for just this kind of fire. To be clear, no politician, political party, or social movement directly caused these tragedies. American leaders do not make a habit of explicitly inciting violence. But some of them have perpetuated the us-versus-them culture of mutual suspicion in which understanding, cooperation, and a sense of the common good give way to division, ideological distrust, and a profound disrespect for those who are different from us. It should come as no surprise, then, that in this unhealthy national climate, occasionally someone will mix that intolerance with pathology and take their hate to the extreme.

I am writing in the days immediately following President Donald Trump's inauguration, and nothing confirms the depths of intolerance and disrespect to which American politics has descended like the presidential election cycle that put him in the White House. It would be naïve to assert that politics before this most recent campaign was devoid of name-calling, baiting, character attacks, and intentional hyperbole. In the last couple of decades, Clinton-bashing, ridicule of George W. Bush's intelligence, and suspicion of Barack Obama's citizenship have been rooted in a deeper hyper-partisan paralysis that elevates the goal of beating the other guy over serving the country. The 2016 election season hit some new lows, however, and the poster child for political spite was Mr. Trump himself. During the campaign, Trump directed crude and gendered insults at a female news anchor, resurrected his "birther" rhetoric to call into question a Republican rival's eligibility for the presidency, mocked a reporter's physical disabilities, and publicly questioned the professional credibility of a sitting judge based on his ethnicity. He ridiculed a rival's spouse for her looks, disparaged another politician's claimed Native American heritage, and regularly referred to journalists as "disgusting" people peddling in "fake news." He began his campaign by insinuating that most undocumented Mexican immigrants are murderers and rapists, and he finished it by referring to his Democratic rival as a "nasty woman" and threatening to jail her when he won. Left and right, Trump violated norms of political decorum and public civility; yet, not only did his insults not cost him votes, but they clearly contributed to his victory, as voters underestimated by professional pollsters flocked to Trump's war on "political correctness" and found voice in his penchant for "telling it like it is."

As bad as Trump was during the campaign, though, he was not alone in the abandonment of decency. Some of Trump's critics tried to rise above it all, but that seldom led to political reward (see John Kasich). Others met Trump in the rhetorical gutter, with one Republican contestant making euphemistic public references to parts of Trump's anatomy, and a Democratic critic calling him a "loser," a "small insecure money grubber," and a "disgrace."[1] More broadly, Trump's attacks on various communities, and apparent disdain for anyone who disagrees with him, led to violent flare-ups on the campaign trail. Trump supporters attacked protestors at his rallies, and protestors occasionally got violent outside venues where Trump was speaking.

Now reducing this kind of political venom will not completely eliminate acts of violence like those we saw in 2016. But to deny that living in a culture of political barbarism intensifies publicly orchestrated violence is to ignore the fundamental connection between cultural context and the cultivation of character. The great theologian and public intellectual Reinhold Niebuhr once wrote, "Whenever the followers of one political party persuade themselves that the future of the nation is not safe with the opposition in power, it becomes fairly certain that the nation's future is not safe, no matter which party rules. For such public acrimony endangers the nation's health more than any specific policies."[2] The rhetoric and character of our politics shape who we are as citizens, how we speak to one another, and how we view one another. Violence is a predictable outcome when our political culture teaches us to despise one another. To a certain extent, the adage is true: we reap what we sow.

In his State of the Union speech in January 2015, well before the verbal carnage of the recent presidential campaign, President Barack Obama named the problem in our political culture and yearned for a different kind of politics:

> Imagine if we broke out of these tired old patterns. Imagine if we did something different. Understand—a better politics isn't one where Democrats abandon their agenda or Republicans simply embrace mine. A better politics is one where we appeal to each other's basic decency instead of our basest fears. A better politics is one where we debate without demonizing each other; where we talk issues, and values, and principles, and facts, rather than "gotcha" moments, or trivial gaffes, or fake controversies that have nothing to do with people's daily lives. . . . If we're going to have arguments, let's have arguments—but let's make them debates worthy of this body and worthy of this country.[3]

In calling for a better politics built on genuine and open discourse, President Obama gave voice to a hope many of us have, that American political culture could cultivate virtues of honest and informed debate, a public exchange rooted in mutual respect and a shared commitment to the national good. It is not a hope for unrealistic ideological uniformity, but a desire for us to find healthier ways to navigate the real differences that reside among Americans.

It is here that the church is poised to minister to the world around it, by providing leadership in this important project of healthier civic community. By practicing forbearance in their religious communities, Christians model a better way for navigating difference. By doing so, we might contribute to the recovery of American public life, from a contest of division and disdain to an exercise in conversation, cooperation, and the common good.

Deliberative Democracy

Over the last two decades or so, while the sinews of American politics have been coming apart, a number of political theorists have been calling for us to return to the heart of democracy, which they believe is respectful and constructive discourse. Calling their perspective *deliberative democracy*, they contend that "public deliberation of free and equal citizens is the core of legitimate political decision-making and self-government."[4] Deliberative political theorists acknowledge that legitimate disagreement can result from all kinds of things: the scarcity of resources and competing claims for those resources, disparate values and the priorities that stem from them, power inequities, or inadequate understanding of facts and circumstances. Whatever the source of our disagreement, however, they believe that our divisions can be reduced by a social commitment to open and accessible discussion.[5] Best represented in the work of Amy Gutmann and Dennis Thompson, "the core idea [of deliberative democracy] is simple: When citizens or their representatives disagree morally, they should continue to reason together to reach mutually acceptable decisions."[6] A commitment to public deliberation—and the practices and venues that support regular conversation—encourages political participation, promotes a collective investment in the legitimacy of civic decision-making, and inspires a broader public spirit about socially divisive issues.[7] Voting and protests still play roles in deliberative politics, but they are secondary to public discourse. The heart of healthy democracy is time for conversation, which itself is based in a respect for all citizens and their participation in collective self-governance.

A commitment to discuss and debate respectfully together does not promise to resolve all disagreement, but it does contribute to achieving what Gutmann and Thompson call an "economy of disagreement," by which they mean minimizing differences through mutually accommodating one another's moral convictions, to the degree that it is possible without totally abandoning our own considered values.[8] An economy of disagreement may be achieved in a number of ways. When we explore our differences through deliberative practices, we often discover that a certain amount of our disagreement results from misunderstanding. Deliberation, then, presents us with the opportunity to identify and correct our factual misunderstandings or our misperception of others' convictions, thus reducing the divisions that result from them. Deliberation educates us in the views of others, positioning us to better respond to their views and to translate our own convictions into language that may make more sense to them. Similarly, others will be in a better position to communicate with us, and all of this translation into one another's languages will make our exchanges more productive. Finally, deliberation may allow us to discover and affirm the points on which we share substantial agreement, thus strengthening a sense of the common good. None of this real talking together guarantees the total elimination of differences, but it sets the stage for reducing the fronts on which we have entrenched and dangerous disagreement. This in turn fosters a greater sense of the common good among citizens, and that leads to a healthier public life together.

In describing what deliberative democracy looks like in real-time politics, Gutmann and Thompson provide three principles that they think should govern. The first of these principles is what they call *reciprocity*, by which they mean the collective pursuit of "fair terms of social cooperation for their own sake."[9] Reciprocity is a commitment to fairness, rooted in our mutual respect for fellow citizens as legitimate social participants and equally valuable to ourselves.[10] A simple idea, respect for other citizens, shapes how we think about public participation. When we share respect for others and a commitment to reciprocity, then we look for ways to maximize inclusion in the political process as a public priority. We will want to ensure that those who wish to participate can be involved in political discussion and decision-making, and we will reject any policies or social attitudes that try to restrict citizens' access to the political process, including voting restrictions, massive campaign financing inequities, and lack of access to public officials or forums. Rather than overpowering our opponents with political force, we will instead, out of respect for them, persuade them with arguments that can be broadly recognized as legitimate, because they "appeal to reasons that are shared or could come to be shared by our fellow citizens" (whether they ultimately are judged persuasive or not).[11] Out of respect for others in the conversation, we express our convictions in ways that are intentionally comprehensible, rather than talking past them in the "jargon" of our ideology.[12] As a corollary, reciprocity also insists that we ground our claims as much as possible in verifiable facts.[13] The basic idea behind reciprocity is that, for a well-ordered democracy, more participation is better in a society whose citizens legitimately respect one another.

In addition to reciprocity, a principle of *publicity* requires that "the reasons that officials and citizens give to justify political actions, and the information necessary to assess those reasons, should be public."[14] While only the most naïve observer would deny that there are moments that require public officials to employ secrecy, Gutmann and Thompson maintain that public access to information should be the norm in political decision-making, for it is a "fundamental requirement of deliberative democracy."[15] Again, this would seem painfully obvious if the principle of publicity were not ignored so routinely in contemporary politics. Publicity insists that we know what is really going on and why. It demands that leaders be truthful, responsible, and open with their reasons for the acts and decisions they discharge in their offices. Access to accurate information and the chance to question or debate allows the average citizen to participate in democracy with integrity, by making it possible for us to understand decisions made in our name, to consent or object to them, and to reward or change our leadership as a consequence of the decisions they make. "Through the give-and-take of argument" that enjoys open publicity, say Gutmann and Thompson, "citizens and their accountable representatives can learn from one another, come to recognize their individual and collective mistakes, and develop new views and policies that are more widely justifiable."[16]

Of course, honoring the principle of publicity requires cooperation not only from public officials but also from an independent news media committed to honest and comprehensive coverage of the issues. News outlets must live up to their responsibility to report all the important news, rather than focusing on issues or personalities that boost their entertainment ratings or appeal to a partisan audience. The selective attention of many news sources has been a problem at least since the advent of 24-hour cable news channels and the competition for ratings that ensued with the challenge of presenting news around the clock. Mr. Trump capitalized on Americans' suspicion of major outlets by categorically dismissing them as producers of "fake news" when they criticized him. This past election also featured the proliferation of web sources that disseminated verifiably false claims as "alternative facts" (to use a phrase employed by one Trump official), infesting public debate and decision-making with disinformation. In an age of informational chaos, when it is easy to get lost in the volume of data available on the internet, and when the lines between information and agenda are blurred beyond recognition, we need reliable news sources to help us sort through the noise.

We also need citizens who are responsible information-gatherers, checking their facts against sources with which they disagree ideologically, instead of assuming everything they read or hear from their favorite sources is true. In other words, the principle of publicity commits leaders and media sources to responsible and honest presentation of information, but it also implies an obligation on our part to demand accurate and adequate information, to exercise healthy suspicion of the sources, and to do the necessary homework to ensure that we know what is true and what is false. When citizens, leaders, and the media are accountable to the principle of publicity, the political process gains legitimacy. The openness that publicity demands allows us citizens to evaluate and, when necessary, to correct past decisions. Adherence to the principle of publicity also serves an educational function, by providing wide exposure to arguments on public issues that over time will broaden our moral and political perspectives. In all of these ways, the principle of publicity conveys the respect for citizens on which a deliberative democracy depends.

Finally, a principle of *accountability* requires that public officials provide good reasons for their decisions to those to whom they are responsible. Accountability cautions officials against pandering to special interests, and warns them against paternalistic decision-making rooted in an assumption that they always know better than we do. By insisting on a wide scope of accountability, we resist concentrations of power, an acute problem in American politics that gets worse when officials hold themselves primarily accountable to those with money or influence.[17] Like the principle of publicity, accountability serves an educational role; our views are more likely to be challenged and broadened by exposure to the range of explanations public officials would normally have to give for their decisions, in order to speak persuasively to a diverse constituency. Officials will learn by being accountable too, because it forces them to remain engaged with constituents. Ultimately, accountability encourages political leaders to be responsible to us: "A deliberative principle of accountability asks representatives to do more than try to win reelection. . . . In a deliberative democracy, representatives are expected to justify their actions in moral terms."[18]

The principles of reciprocity, publicity, and accountability, then, define truly deliberative political life. Gutmann and Thompson make clear that these principles do not promise easy resolution of conflict, which is an unrealistic—and arguably unhealthy—aspiration for a genuinely pluralistic society. Instead, the aim of deliberative democracy is to provide a more productive means by which we navigate our differences: eliminating some occasions of disagreement when we discover new levels of understanding, forging partial consensus when improved understanding makes it possible, and deepening our respect for fellow citizens and their convictions where differences remain. The principles of deliberative democracy set the conditions for affirming the legitimacy of even those public policies with which we do not agree, because they were the product of respectful and inclusive deliberation. When that happens, less animosity, fear, suspicion, and mutual loathing are likely to follow.

Virtues of Civility

The principles of deliberative democracy give us guidelines for building and maintaining a public culture that is less antagonistic and more cooperative. For these principles to work, however, they need a commitment from us, the people, a citizenry with the moral character to desire healthy democracy. To talk of character is, as we have been doing throughout this book, to invoke virtues. In this case, political virtues are the traits that make us the kind of society we want to be, the kind of people who more often than not demand, recognize, and follow principled standards for healthy democracy. As I have written elsewhere, I think there is a constellation of virtues that define the ideal political character for American democracy, for citizens and leaders alike. The virtues of *civility* promote healthy democracy by encouraging "the exercise of patience, humility, integrity, and mutual respect in civil conversation, even (or especially) with those with whom we disagree."[19] Civility creates the public ethos in which the practices of deliberative politics may be widely affirmed as good.

Allow me to unpack this notion of civility for a moment. As you will see, there is a lot of common ground between public civility and the virtues that shape a forbearing church. The first virtue of civility, *patience*, prompts us to engage others in our public life together with the intent of understanding them and the values and interests that animate them, rather than seeing them only as obstacles to getting what we want. Patience asks us to take the long view on public discourse and decision-making, honoring the hard process of minimizing disagreement and creating consensus, resisting ideological entrenchment and instead embracing active engagement with difference. Patient civility describes citizens who wish to persuade and are open to persuasion, and who recognize that the effectiveness of arguments requires open exchange, persistent communication, and mutual understanding.

That openness promotes the development of *humility* as a public virtue. Humility reminds us that the limits of human knowledge and understanding are real, that individual perspectives on moral and political issues are necessarily partial, and that we may possess incomplete or incorrect information on any issue. Humility reminds us that there may be limits to our vantage point, and that our perception of debates is likely skewed by biases and prejudices we bring to the table. Political humility prepares us to acknowledge and confront these limitations to our perspectives, and to be open to having our minds changed by the deliberative process. As a result, encounters with different perspectives may correct our understanding of an issue, may fill out our perception of convictions different from ours, and sometimes may persuade us that the view to which we are accustomed does not encompass all there is to consider on a particular issue. Humility does not require us to retreat from our convictions, but it does train us to be open to new information and perspectives, instilling in us the expectation that conversation will affect our views in some way, even if that effect is as subtle but important as a deeper understanding of perspectives different from our own.

Closely related to the virtues of patience and humility is the cultivation of *integrity*. Integrity involves a commitment to openness and honesty in how we represent our public positions and the convictions that give rise to them. It requires consistency between what we believe and what we say, between what we say and what we do, and between what we say should be true for others and the norms we apply to our own lives and circumstances. Integrity also requires consistency between our positions on different issues.[20] Finally, integrity demands that we represent the views of others as accurately as possible in public debate. Obviously the mischaracterization and trivialization of ideological opponents—the "gotcha moments" that President Obama rejected in his State of the Union address—run afoul of the virtue of integrity, even if they remain exceedingly popular political strategies.

The commitment to engaged, honest, and open conversation captured in the first three virtues exhibits the commitment to the fourth, *mutual respect*. By commending mutual respect, civility requires us to acknowledge the legitimacy of other participants in a true democracy. The cultivation of respect as moral habit trains us to see others, even our ideological opposites, as moral agents with serious convictions worthy of due consideration. It shapes our practices in public life with the reminder that those we encounter in that shared life together are citizens just like us, with equal right to be at the proverbial table of debate. A character of mutual respect invites us to take one another seriously as participants in the deliberative process, and makes us less likely to dismiss each other as illegitimate, ignorant, or somehow unqualified to participate in the conversations of civic society.

In shaping the character of healthy public life, civility encourages us to commit to, among other things, the ideal of a deliberative democracy. Widespread exercise of patience and humility encourages deliberative practices, for deliberation looks more attractive when we recognize the limits on our own understanding and the good that comes from listening to and learning from others. Similarly, integrity and mutual respect undergird the principles of reciprocity, publicity, and accountability.[21] The commitment to reciprocal fair play requires an appreciation for honestly representing oneself and others, as well as an acknowledgment of other people's worthiness to participate in the political process. Citizens who take integrity and respect seriously affirm and reward efforts toward publicity and accountability from fellow citizens and leaders. Mutual respect encourages habits of self-reflection, discernment, serious consideration, moral dexterity, openness, and accommodation of differences. Deliberation does not happen without first being disposed to the benefit of learning from others, to the good of conversation and openness to discovery, born of the recognition that we have something to gain from listening to each other.

So civility's virtues make it possible to imagine a society in which the principles of deliberative democracy govern, because these virtues shape us into citizens who accept those principles as binding and recognize them as good. The virtues of civility also provide us with the character necessary to keep ourselves and each other, as well as our institutions and leaders, accountable to the aspirations of healthy democracy. Furthermore, the virtues of civility prepare us to live with the reality of moral and political disagreement in the long term, knowing that deliberation may achieve an "economy of disagreement," but it will never eliminate difference entirely in a truly pluralistic society.

For, like forbearance, civility does not imply artificial nicety or passive acquiescence in public disagreements. It does not insist on the avoidance of real conflict that regularly characterizes pluralistic society. Instead, as a set of virtues, civility equips citizens of a pluralistic society to negotiate differences constructively, not to avoid conflict but to make our exchanges more productive and our coexistence more peaceful. Public priority on the virtues of civility promises deeper moral debate, more respectful collective participation, and more frequent moments of agreement. It would set a political climate in which persistent disagreement is navigated in ways that maintain a sense of community and mutual accountability and lead less often to apathy or hostility.

Communities of Character

If the virtues of civility sound familiar to you, it might be because they correspond closely to how we have described the practice of forbearance. I think there is deep affinity between the ideals of a virtuous life lived in ecclesial community (forbearance) and the definition of a virtuous public life (civility). Both are rooted explicitly in the virtues of humility and patience. Both exhibit the virtues of respect and integrity, forbearance capturing these two norms within the ideals of faithfulness and friendship. Both are constellations of virtues on which depends the maintenance of community in the face of deep division. Because of these connections, I think the modeling of forbearance is perhaps the best gift the church can give to a political culture that is desperate to learn how to navigate its own differences in heathier ways. A church that excels at forbearance is admirably equipped to extend those gifts to the project of civility.

Given the importance of civility to healthy democracy, and the distance between healthy democracy and the one in which we now live, we need to nurture this public character intentionally among citizens and political leaders. As Gutmann and Thompson say, "to flourish—sometimes even to survive—in the face of fundamental moral disagreement, institutions need to cultivate these virtues."[22] The cultivation of virtue, however, depends on institutions and organizations to promote and habituate desirable traits in persons. As we noted early in this book, communities support and educate citizens in the development of good character.[23] They supply the moral worldview in which some traits are seen as commendable and others as detrimental. Communities also provide institutions that reinforce moral values with intentional formation and relationships of accountability. Communities shape us into the persons we ought to be.

The cultivation of public virtue is no different, and toward this end Gutmann and Thompson argue for the importance of what they call "intermediary institutions" to develop the habits of healthy democracy. Intermediary institutions are organizations, associations, venues, and sub-communities within a democratic society that encourage their members to develop the moral character necessary to honor and contribute to democratic life. They foster relationships, microcosms of our public roles in which we learn to live, work, learn, or play with one another admirably and productively. Families, schools, colleges, and clubs all serve this purpose of providing practice in living well together. Involvement in intermediary institutions provides us with the chance to practice living in a pluralistic society respectfully:

> Unless citizens have the experience of reasoning together in other institutions in which they spend more of their time they are not likely to develop either the interest or the skill that would enable them to deliberate effectively in politics. That is why it is so important that the processes of decision making that citizens encounter at work and at leisure should seek to cultivate the virtues of deliberation. The discussion that takes place in these settings not only is a rehearsal for political action, but also is itself a part of citizenship in deliberative democracy.[24]

Curiously, in their discussion of intermediary institutions, Gutmann and Thompson do not mention religious communities as an example, but it seems to me that they are describing precisely the exposure to respectfully living with difference that we have been discussing in this book. The practice of forbearance within Christian community is good for the health of the church, but it also serves as a primer for the practice of civility within democratic society. In this way, the virtues of forbearance serve as skills that can be transferred to the political realm. Without a doubt, Ronald Thiemann correctly asserts that "communities of faith can be among the most important associations within which the virtues of citizenship are fostered."[25]

Luke Bretherton, who has a different take on the heart of healthy democracy than the deliberative democracy theorists we have been considering, nonetheless ends up in a similar place with regard to the importance of institutions like churches in contributing to the improvement of our public life. To Bretherton, healthy democracy is not primarily about talking with one another, but about *doing* things together, namely contributing to the common good in community action. In other words, democratic politics is about "practices rather than theory."[26] In a perspective deeply informed by broad-based community organizing, Bretherton argues that pluralistic democracy on the ground "is a constellation of practices that mediate between a wide variety of traditions."[27] Community action, such as social service projects and advocacy efforts, provides a focus on discrete political goods and a sense of solidarity around those goods that brings a wide diversity of people together, but then requires the navigation of difference in order for anything to get done. The challenge for our democratic life is to develop through practices enough of a "shared story" or sense of common good that it serves as "a context for real relationship where all participants—however distasteful their views to others—can begin to touch on difficult issues in a place of trust."[28] Dialogue, while not the starting point, is an important by-product of shared political activity on behalf of common concerns.[29] It is "the formation of a shared political life through particular kinds of democratic practices . . . that is able to foster self-restraint and the conciliation of different interests and visions of the good within a particular place."[30] Democracy seen through the lens of community organizing becomes the project of "enabling the formation of shared speech and action that forms a public arena of communication between diverse traditions."[31]

Bretherton thinks it is obvious that churches are well positioned to host, organize, and support community action efforts that serve the broader public culture in this way—because many churches are doing this kind of work already! As a result, they also are in a good position to bring together people from a variety of ideological traditions to work and live together in the name of healthier public life. "The only places in which to listen to others and learn judgment and responsibility for goods in common and from which to contradict, demand, or contribute to the judgments of political and economic power holders is within the kinds of non-pecuniary, tradition-situated institutions of which congregations are paradigmatic examples."[32] Churches are communities of people "who do not come together for solely commercial or state-directed transactions, but who instead come together primarily to worship and care for each other."[33] When they instill in their members the virtues necessary for a life of faith together, they imbue them as well with the mutual respect and character necessary to engage in the projects of citizenship.[34] As a result, Bretherton thinks churches can be "the building blocks of a more complex space that inhibits the totalizing, monopolistic thrust of the modern market and state that seek not only to instrumentalize persons and the relationships between them, but also to subordinate all other interests to a single, dominant interest."[35] To use the language we have been developing in this book, congregations that practice forbearance equip their members with the dispositions necessary to contribute to pluralistic democracy in productive, healthy ways, and, in doing so, they provide a model for healthier coexistence for the greater society. They bring persons together to live productively and respectfully, while honoring (and not obliterating) their differences.

A Ministry of Reconciliation

But why bother? Why should Christians care to model respectful disagreement? It is one thing to claim that forbearance satisfies our obligation to maintain our unity as the Body of Christ. It is quite another to suggest that we have an obligation to extend those virtues beyond the church, to contribute to some project of civility. Why should we feel responsible for that?

That responsibility comes from recognizing that being church is not an end in itself, but a means to an end, for in being church we are the "provisional representation" of God's intentions for all people (Barth again). What we know, experience, and live out imperfectly in the church is the gospel God wishes for the world. For this reason, says Douglas Ottati, the church necessarily lives *in* and *for* the world. While there always has been a segment of Christianity that has viewed the best path to faithfulness as withdrawal from the messy seduction of the world, Ottati reminds us that the true responsibility we derive from the gospel is to live actively in the world. God has charged the church with a *public* ministry, a ministry of reconciliation.[36]

As we have discussed already in this book, the story of the Christian gospel *is* one of reconciliation. It is the story of humanity's alienation overcome by God's reconciling love. From Scripture we hear the story of a God who created human beings for righteous companionship, only to see us wander away out of pride and selfishness. As many of us recite in the prayers of confession that we feature in our Sunday worship, we are prone to transgress God's intentions for us "in wandering from [God's] ways, in wasting [God's] gifts, in forgetting [God's] love."[37] Through generations, God sent prophets to call us to return to God's ways, but we rebuffed God's overtures and abused those who spoke for God. "Then in the fullness of time," rehearse the Eucharistic prayers, God sent Jesus Christ "to redeem us and heal our brokenness."[38] For God so loved the world, we are told, that God sent the Son to show us the way back to God (John 3:16). Him too we rejected, of course, and Christ was crucified in a brutal exhibition of the sin that plagues humanity and alienates us from God and one another. But God raised Jesus from the dead, as a testament to the ultimate triumph of reconciling love over hate and division. The light shines in the darkness, and the darkness did not overcome it (John 1:5)! This is the good news of the gospel, that "neither death, nor life, . . . nor anything else in all creation, will be able to separate us from the love of God in Christ Jesus our Lord" (Rom. 8:37–38).

Caught up in this theological narrative, we Christians are called to affirm and proclaim the reality of God's reconciling love for the world. Having experienced reconciliation ourselves, we share that grace with one another and embrace the opportunity to be part of the community of God's friends. Then we are called to export that experience of reconciliation, sharing the good news of God's redeeming grace with the world. We proclaim that "there is no longer Jew or Greek, there is no longer slave or free, there is no longer male or female," for all have been made one in Christ Jesus (Gal. 3:28). We make known that, in Christ, God is working the ways of peace in our broken world, demolishing the walls of hostility between us, reconciling us to God and to one another (Eph. 2:14; 2 Cor. 5:19). As the Presbyterian Confession of 1967 aptly put it, "to be reconciled to God is to be sent into the world as God's reconciling community." What we have experienced as community is who we are, and who we are is our charge. Reconciliation is the ministry to which we the church have been called. The church "is entrusted with God's message of reconciliation and shares God's labor of healing the enmities which separate people from God and from each other."[39]

To be clear, this ministry of reconciliation with which we are charged is not ours because we have somehow mastered living in the light of God's reconciling love.[40] As we have discussed throughout this book, the opposite is often true. At times church conflict rivals the intensity of division and pain in the world around us. In fact, had we perfected reconciling love, this book would be unnecessary! Reconciliation is still a work in progress within the church, but while we struggle with it ourselves, we who have heard the message of God's reconciling grace in Christ are still commissioned to share that message, however imperfectly, with the world. We share it by proclamation, declaring words of peace, justice, and friendship to a world marred by the opposite. We share it in our living, modeling a spirit of reconciliation in our struggles to maintain Christian unity within church—that is, living out forbearance and friendship. We share it through service, cooperating with others to help those afflicted by injustice and estrangement, to contribute to efforts to bridge differences in the world around us.

One way we satisfy our calling to reconciling ministry is by extending the practice of forbearance beyond the church. Cultivating the virtues of forbearance as the righteous character necessary to live with difference in the church, we preach these same virtues as the moral character necessary for healthy public life together. For example, the limits on human understanding pertain not just in church but also in the world, so we implore our fellow citizens to be open to the possibilities in learning from one another, as we practice that openness publicly as well. The pace of history, like the future of the church, is in God's hands, and so we proclaim a message of patient hope that God will reveal what is right and true in God's time, as we listen and learn and discern together what makes for the common good. We celebrate the virtue of wisdom as a pillar of a good society, and we encourage the use of imagination, intelligence, discernment, and empathy in the pursuit of our common life together. The virtue of mutual faithfulness is not only the backbone of a healthy church but also the foundation of a civil society in which all citizens flourish, so we commend the courage it takes to trust one another, and we speak out against a politics of mutual suspicion. Finally, we remind our civic neighbors that moral friendships built on mutual respect are ultimately a much surer basis for a free and secure society than enmity and rancor. For friendship accentuates the mutual dependence that links us together, and it reminds us of the inherent value all human beings possess as creatures made in the image of God.

The virtues of forbearance define not just what we preach in this ministry of reconciliation but how we in the church engage the world. In other words, forbearance governs our relationships both within and beyond the church. Recognizing the limitations of human knowledge under which the church operates, we remain open to the likelihood that we will learn something about what it means to be good moral citizens from those outside our faith. Inspired by the virtue of hopeful patience, we take the time to truly listen to those who might speak a complementary or corrective word to our understanding of truth. Schooled in the many faces of wisdom, we seek to learn from the imagination, discernment, empathy, and intelligence of others in our world. Committed to the virtue of faithfulness, we show the courage to trust our civic neighbors and to assume the best intentions in them as we cooperate in the activities that build a healthy society. Trained in the art of friendship, we do our best to give and

191

receive friendship with our neighbors, even those beyond the community of church. Committing to a ministry of reconciliation requires that we practice what we preach, so we embrace the world with forbearance even as we commend forbearance for the world.

The virtues of forbearance represent faithfulness in a church community striving to be the Body of Christ in the world, but those same virtues bring out the best in a good society, a healthy democracy, a civil community bound together in pursuit of the common good. In that way, the public preaching and practice of forbearance fulfill the obligations of our God-given ministry of reconciliation to the world. When we shape our church communities around the practice of forbearance, we provide a template for how citizens of diverse ideological backgrounds might coexist in healthy and productive ways. Forbearance is the church's gift to the world, so by preaching and practicing forbearance we discharge one of the Great Ends of the Church, to "exhibit the kingdom of heaven" to a world desperate for a glimpse of good news.

As theological vision goes, this may all sound quite nice, but what does forbearance actually look like as a practice of ministry in the world? Here is an example: a couple of years ago, my friend J. Herbert Nelson, then in charge of the Office of Public Witness of the Presbyterian Church (USA), came up with what I thought was a brilliant idea. He proposed that we invite Presbyterians from across the denomination to gather together for intensive training as moderators of civil conversations. Then we would send those folks back home, not just to serve as facilitators but to pass the training on to other cohorts of potential moderators in their congregations and presbyteries. The result would be exponential multiplication of the art of healthy discourse. Dubbed the Respectful Dialogue Initiative, the project aimed at improving the quality of conversation and protecting the integrity of communities around the United States, not just churches but also other associations in the civic realm, by teaching people how to discuss hard issues respectfully. The initiative was a way for the church to provide public leadership in dealing with disagreement and difference. Due to logistical obstacles (not the least being the denomination's wisdom in tapping J. Herbert to be its next Stated Clerk), the project has yet to live up to its righteous ambitions, but the template is a sound one—Christians witnessing to a different way of dealing with disagreement by exploiting the virtues of Christian community.

Or take the story of Oak Mountain Presbyterian Church and Urban Hope Community Church in Birmingham, Alabama, a city that continues its struggles with a deep history of racism. Oak Mountain, a predominantly white and affluent congregation, and Urban Hope, a predominantly black church with a substantial number of its congregants living in poverty, have taken it upon themselves to create counter-cultural bridges across racial and socio-economic lines. The congregations came together to watch the 2014 film *Selma* and to talk about the struggle for civil rights. They have worked together on community-action programs related to job procurement, small business development, spiritual wholeness, and youth education. Through it all, they have pushed back against the assumption that white Americans and black Americans cannot create true communities of justice and friendship together. According to Alton Hardy, Urban Hope's pastor, the question that animates their efforts is this: "What would it look like for African-American Christians and white Christians to build with the common denominator of Christ?"[41] What it looks like is the honest and authentic partnership between these two congregations, modeling a better way of navigating racial differences in the city they call home.

Or consider the just peacemaking initiative, a Christian movement spurred on by the late Glen Stassen and other theological leaders desperate to chart a new way for us to deal with global conflict. Dissatisfied with moral reflections on war that seem unable to go beyond providing justifications or categorically condemning military action, just peacemaking advocates focused their efforts on the economic, political, and environmental conditions that *lead to* armed conflict. Their work resulted in the identification of ten practices that could facilitate a reduction of war around the world—efforts like fostering non-predatory economic development, encouraging grassroots peacemaking initiatives, and concentrating attention on the reduction of the global weapons trade. Born of Christian concern with the proliferation of state violence, the just peacemaking movement is now an interfaith endeavor aimed at helping the world navigate conflict in healthier ways.[42]

Or consider the Charter House Coalition, a cooperative effort between Christian congregations and other community partners in Middlebury, Vermont, who ignored their ideological differences and disparate priorities to establish a set of programs to help the underserved in the community. Now a flourishing independent organization, Charter House Coalition provides food for people who could use a hot meal, a warming shelter so homeless citizens can escape the harsh New England winter, and transitional housing to assist individuals and families struggling to be independent. The calling card of Charter House, though, is its community lunch and supper program, intentionally organized not as "free meals for the poor" but as a table set for anyone in the community who wants to participate. It is a regular occurrence to see people of very different levels of economic privilege sitting together and enjoying food and conversation, in a testament to how the bonds of human community cut across socio-economic divides. In Charter House, the gospel of forbearance and friendship is on powerful display.

What does forbearance as social witness look like? It resembles these efforts, and many more like them. A congregation that reaches out to its local mosque to facilitate greater understanding between Christians and Muslims practices forbearance as social witness. A cohort of churches hosting an organizing forum to welcome Syrian refugees into the local community practices forbearance as social witness. An evangelical network of environmentally concerned Christians that forms an alliance with the Sierra Club (an organization not exactly known for embracing traditional religion), so that they might combine strengths and combat climate change together, practices forbearance as social witness. Congregations who host local non-partisan discussions of public issues, to intentionally bring together ideologically different groups as an educational alternative to dysfunctional media coverage, practice forbearance as social witness. Christians who light up Facebook with messages of sympathy and solidarity for an LGBTQ community rocked by terrorism offer forbearance as social witness. Anytime the church extends the virtues of Christian community beyond itself into a world desperate for reconciling love, we practice forbearance as public ministry. In extending forbearance and friendship from the church to the world, we testify to the emergence of the kingdom of God.

Conclusion

In doing the work of forbearance, churches have opportunity to be what James Gustafson called "communities of moral discourse" in a society starving for this kind of servant leadership. Gustafson defined a true community of moral discourse as "a gathering of people with the explicit intention to survey and critically discuss their personal and social responsibilities in the light of moral convictions about which there is some consensus and to which there is some loyalty."[43] As I have tried to make clear in this book, I think that the "consensus" that binds us together need not (and will not) be shared convictions on a broad spectrum of theological and moral issues. Instead, our commonality comes from our shared loyalty to the good of the Body of Christ itself, and the oneness in Christ that serves simultaneously as the church's *raison d'être* and its obligation. Armed with this common calling, a theologically profound respect for our differences, and a rich and varied intellectual tradition from which to draw wisdom and insight, the church is supremely equipped to host the kinds of critical conversations Gustafson imagined, and to model serious but respectful exchange to the world beyond it. And as Gustafson emphasized, it is the *process* of dialogue and conversation that is important, not the achievement of consensus. Participation in theological discourse deepens and enriches Christian community and our investment in it.[44] Correspondingly, participation in public discourse deepens and enriches our civic health and our collective investment in it.

Practicing forbearance gives the church an opportunity to get its own house in order, to live more faithfully with one another in the spirit of the unity of Christ. If we are faithful to the practice of forbearance, however, we may not only improve the health of our common life together as church; we may also seize a chance to witness to the world an alternative way to navigate difference, by demonstrating the powerful potential in forbearance as a set of "transferrable skills" that our political culture desperately needs. Forbearance as social witness may be our response to Danielle Allen's call for "political friendship," the recognition of the public life we hold in common and the development of habits that contribute to a spirit of trust among the strangers who encounter one another in that life together.[45] To take up this mantle, to serve as communities that nurture virtues of faithful living and healthy public life, we must commit to what James Davison Hunter has called a ministry of "faithful presence" in the world.[46] Rather than retreating from the world or seeking cultural supremacy, we lead by living and serving in the world, modeling a better way of negotiating the differences between us.

If we practice forbearance successfully in our Christian lives together, the export of these virtues beyond the church is easier and has more integrity. For the old hymn is right: they will know we are Christians by our love. They will know through our words and actions, in moments of difficult conflict and concern, what impact, if any, Christian virtue has on the navigation of difference. They will know by our behavior, by our choice between schism and fidelity, whether the church's proclamation of Christ as our peace is truth or a lie. They will know by our willingness to be reconciled ourselves whether we preach a genuine message of reconciliation for the world. Forbearance is a practice of faithfulness within church and a powerful witness beyond it, perhaps our most compelling ministry and mission in this moment. In a time when churches seem to be tearing themselves apart from the inside, and when American democracy appears unhealthier than ever, the future of both church and world just might depend on our commitment to forbearance as a theological ethic for a disagreeable church.

Appendix

The following statement of congregational identity was developed by a task force led by my two good friends, Nancy Jakiela and Albert Zaccor, and approved in my home church in 2016. I think it offers a fine example of a church explicitly committed to both the pursuit of conviction and the practice of forbearance as the character of its calling to be the Body of Christ.

The Congregational Church of Middlebury, United Church of Christ, is an open and affirming church. We welcome you, no matter who you are or where you are on life's journey.

We are a self-governing community of faith in covenant with the United Church of Christ, active in the local and global mission of the church. It is our aim to offer welcoming hospitality to all. Our belief in the one God of love compels us to embrace one another, people from other Christian denominations, followers of other faiths, and individuals who do not identify as religious at all. Our goal is to see Christ in every human being and to value each person as an individual. We endeavor to love each other as God loves us.

We are a church that is constantly growing in faith, with great diversity in conviction. There is no creed you must profess to be a member. Instead, we encourage one another to learn and grow in faith, to own and speak our convictions freely, and to respect those who believe differently from us. Indeed, as Paul wrote to the Ephesians, we long to live a life worthy of the calling we have received, to be humble, gentle, and patient with each other, bearing with one another in love and making every effort to keep the unity of the Spirit through the bond of peace (Eph. 4:1–3).

*   *   *

Our unity comes from gathering and living in the name of Jesus, the one whom Christians have called Jesus of Nazareth, Jesus Christ, the Messiah of God. For some of us, we follow Jesus because we believe he taught and modeled the quintessential life of goodness. Jesus showed us the way, the truth, and the life lived with grace. He taught us to love God with our whole being, to love others as we love ourselves, and to labor for the reign of God through the pursuit of justice and peace. For others of us, we also follow Jesus because we believe he was the incarnation of the triune God. In his life, death and resurrection, Jesus testified to the reality of God-with-us. Jesus is the Son of God who came into the world so that we might be reconciled with God through grace, and experience new life in the Spirit of divine love.

Within our faith community, we embrace very different understandings of Jesus and the meaning of his life and death. Nonetheless, we are united in our allegiance to Jesus as the heart of our fellowship. His enduring presence lives in our regard for one another, as well as in our outreach to those beyond our congregation.

*   *   *

As followers of Jesus, we recognize that we are on a journey of personal and spiritual growth. We grapple with questions of life and death and the mysteries of faith. No matter where we are on our journey, we are committed to supporting one another in nurturing our spiritual lives, throughout every stage of life. We embrace a multi-faceted ministry to children and young adults, while also offering educational opportunities for adults and pastoral care for all. We give individual care to the homebound, the sick, the elderly, and the dying with a love grounded in faith.

As a Christian congregation, we honor Scripture and tradition as pillars of our faith. In these texts and histories, we are heirs to a rich and varied treasure of stories, myth, poetry, and music. For some of us, the Bible represents the word of God, while for others it is one source of wisdom and knowledge among many. Nonetheless we are intentional in our commitment to study Christian Scripture and tradition for wisdom, moral guidance, and an understanding of God and the world in which we live. No matter our approach to Scripture and tradition, we are united in our conviction that "God is still speaking."

As a community of faith, we assemble weekly for public worship. We pray privately and together, share music, and celebrate the sacraments. We deepen our connection to God and each other through Scripture and sermon. We come together as the Body of Christ to be present for one another and in the presence of God. For it is written that, ". . . where two or three are gathered in my name, I am there among them" (Matt. 18:20).

Our congregation embraces two sacraments: baptism and communion. The sacrament of baptism symbolizes God's gracious claim on each of us and welcomes us into the church, the Body of Christ. We baptize during worship when the community is present because baptism includes the community's promise of love and care for the baptized.

We believe that all are welcome at Christ's table for the sacrament of communion. As long as there has been church, Christians have come together to break bread and share a cup in remembrance of the life and death of Jesus Christ. For some of us this provides a deeply spiritual and personal connection to God, while for others of us it is a symbolic meal representing the love that binds us together as a community. However we experience the meal, we celebrate Christ's presence in our midst.

United as a community by our allegiance to Jesus, we are called to work together to help realize the reign of God on Earth. We do this by promoting peace and justice in our communities, our nation, and the world. We promote peace by building strong communities and seeking nonviolent solutions in situations of conflict. We promote justice by caring for the sick, feeding the hungry, and helping the disadvantaged among us, both at home and abroad. As stewards of God's creation, we strive to protect Earth and all the gifts it brings us. As Christians, we confidently look for opportunities to partner across denominational and interfaith lines to foster cooperation and good will in the world.

This is who we are: A church united in its diversity, with a faith centered on Jesus, committed to living out the Christian vision captured in the words of the prophet Micah: "What does the Lord require of you but to do justice, and to love kindness, and to walk humbly with your God?" (Mic. 6:8).

Notes

Notes to the Preface

1. James Calvin Davis, *In Defense of Civility: How Religion Can Unite America on Seven Moral Issues That Divide Us* (Louisville: Westminster John Knox Press, 2010).

Notes to Chapter 1

1. Amy Frykholm, "A Time to Split? Covenant and Schism in the UMC," *The Christian Century* 131, no. 8 (April 3, 2014).

2. See Sarah Pulliam, "Richard Cizik Resigns from the National Association of Evangelicals," *Christianity Today*, December 11, 2008; David P. Gushee, *The Future of Faith in American Politics: The Public Witness of the Evangelical Center* (Waco: Baylor University Press, 2008), chapter 7. As Pulliam's article makes clear, the last straw for Cizik's tenure at the National Association of Evangelicals was a supportive response he gave to a question on civil unions on an NPR broadcast. But the hostility toward his leadership had been growing for over a year before his resignation, largely over his outspokenness on climate change. For his part, Gushee has represented an intellectual support for environmentalism within evangelicals for years, and more recently has shifted his support for gay rights in progressive directions as well.

3. I intentionally have obscured the specific identity of this congregation, but I am grateful to Andrew Kort for his contributions to the case study.

4. James Luther Adams was largely responsible for giving us the term "voluntary association" to describe the sociological existence of sub-communities within western democracies. See D. B. Robertson, ed., *Voluntary Associations: A Study of Groups in Free Societies* (Richmond, VA: John Knox Press, 1966), for a glimpse of the impact Adams's concept of voluntary association had on the study of American Christianity in the twentieth century.

5. The outward vector that properly characterizes theology is nicely captured in the

work of James M. Gustafson, who commended a "theocentric piety" that pushes against more truncated conceptions of God and the morally relevant world, in part by intentional conversation with a range of sources of knowledge. See his *Ethics from a Theocentric Perspective*, 2 vols. (Chicago: University of Chicago Press, 1981, 1984).

6. Douglas F. Ottati, *Theology for Liberal Protestants: God the Creator* (Grand Rapids: Eerdmans, 2013), 91.

7. On this point, therefore, I agree with Ottati that, when properly done, "Christian theology seems bound to include dialogical and apologetic dimensions, and . . . it stands against false dogmatisms that assume that nothing more is necessary for Christian faithfulness than is supplied by received doctrines and creeds." *Theology for Liberal Protestants: God the Creator*, 91–92.

8. Readers familiar with political philosophy will recognize a similarity between my bidirectional understanding of good theology and how John Rawls talks about "reflective equilibrium" in political philosophy. Like philosophy, theology begins with our considered convictions. We then subject those convictions to rigorous logical elaboration and analysis. But the product of our theological reflection always must cohere with what we know outside the theological exercise (that is, from other sources of knowledge) to be true or appropriate. See Rawls, *Political Liberalism* (New York: Columbia University Press, 1993), 8–11.

9. See, for instance, 1 Samuel 23:13; 1 Kings 22:15; 2 Chronicles 25:16; Nehemiah 9:30.

10. For an appreciation of this point, and in my interpretation of this passage more generally, I am indebted to Ralph P. Martin, *Ephesians, Colossians, and Philemon*, in *Interpretation: A Bible Commentary for Teaching and Preaching* (Louisville: Westminster John Knox Press, 1991), 45–62.

11. Martin, *Ephesians, Colossians, and Philemon*, 81–94.

12. I am indebted to Frances Taylor Gench's treatment of this section of Romans in *Faithful Disagreement: Wrestling with Scripture in the Midst of Church Conflict* (Louisville: Westminster John Knox Press, 2009), 33–53. Of special note is her insistence that the NRSV's translation of the verb in Romans 15:1 is terribly misleading; instead of "putting up" with the weak, Gench argues that Paul's word choice commends the more positive "bearing with," returning to that theme of imitating the forbearance that God extends to us.

13. See David W. Torrance and Thomas F. Torrance, eds., *Calvin's New Testament Commentaries*, vol. 11., trans. T. H. L. Parker (Grand Rapids: Eerdmans, 1965), 171–72, 350–51.

14. For instance, as helpful as his commentary is for an understanding of the conflict preoccupying both of these letters, Ralph Martin's study of Ephesians and Colossians makes nothing of the specific imperative to forbearance.

15. Columbia Seminary's statement can be found here: http://www.ctsnet.edu/files/documents/pr%20Faculty%20Statement%20PCUSA%200501114.pdf. The Austin Seminary version of the statement can be found at https://www.austinseminary.edu/cf_news/view.cfm?newsid=1587.

16. See, for instance, "Seminary Call for Mutual Forbearance Rejected by Both Sides as Gay Bashing and Adultery," *The Layman*, May 19, 2014; David Oliver-Holder, "An Open Letter to the Faculties of Columbia and Austin Seminaries," *The Presbyterian Outlook*, May 28, 2014.

17. Stanley Hauerwas, *Approaching the End: Eschatological Reflections on Church, Politics, and Life* (Grand Rapids: Eerdmans, 2013), 157.

18. Beverly Wildung Harrison, "The Power of Anger in the Work of Love: Christian Ethics for Women and Other Strangers," in *Making the Connections: Essays in Feminist Social Ethics*, ed. Carol S. Robb (Boston: Beacon Press, 1985), 14–15.

19. Hauerwas, *Approaching the End*, 109.

20. I am grateful to my colleague and friend Glen Ernstrom for the evocative image of "productive discomfort" that I employ here.

21. Dietrich Bonhoeffer, *Life Together*, trans. John W. Doberstein (New York: Harper, 1954).

22. Bonhoeffer, *Life Together*, 100.

23. Bonhoeffer, *Life Together*, 101.

24. Bonhoeffer, *Life Together*, 101.

25. Bonhoeffer, *Life Together*, 101.

26. Bonhoeffer, *Life Together*, 102–3.

27. Bonhoeffer, *Life Together*, 102.

28. Bonhoeffer, *Life Together*, 30.

29. See Aristotle's *Nicomachean Ethics*, trans. J. A. K. Thomson (New York: Penguin, 1955).

30. See Thomas Aquinas, *Summa Theologica*, trans. Fathers of the English Dominican Province (Westminster, MD: Christian Classics, 1981).

31. See, for instance, Stanley Hauerwas, *Character and the Christian Life: A Study in Theological Ethics* (San Antonio: Trinity University Press, 1975); idem, *A Community of Character: Toward a Constructive Christian Social Ethic* (Notre Dame: University of Notre Dame Press, 1981).

32. The emphasis on "communities of character" in the work of Hauerwas and other contemporary virtue theorists is indebted to the groundbreaking work of Alasdair C. MacIntyre in *After Virtue: A Study in Moral Theory*, 2nd ed. (Notre Dame: University of Notre Dame Press, 1984). MacIntyre powerfully pointed out the disconnect in modern ethics between moral norms and the communities and traditions that once gave them context. In other words, moral values make sense only within the communities and their stories that give them meaning and significance.

33. Hauerwas, *Character and the Christian Life*, 33.

34. See chapter six of this book for more on friendship as an occasion for exercising virtue.

Notes to Chapter 2

1. For exploration of the Christian convergences in Schulz's cartoon strip, see Robert L. Short, *The Gospel According to Peanuts* (Richmond, VA: John Knox Press, 1965).

2. See, for instance, Matthew 25:31–46.

3. See 2 Corinthians 1:1–14 and Philippians chapters 1 and 3.

4. John H. Leith, ed., *Creeds of the Churches*, 3rd ed. (Louisville: John Knox Press, 1982), 31.

5. The story of the Nicene Creed is, of course, much more complicated than I have

summarized here, and was driven by political divisions in the church and empire as well as theological concerns.

6. The Nicene Creed, as appears in *The Nicene and Post-Nicene Fathers*, series 2, vol. 14, ed. Philip Schaff and Henry Wace (New York: Charles Scribner and Sons, 1900), 3.

7. Leith, *Creeds*, 441.

8. From Martin Luther, "The Pagan Servitude of the Church," in *Martin Luther: Selections from His Writings*, ed. John Dillenberger (New York: Anchor Books, 1961), 250–54.

9. For an introduction to the fundamentalist movement of the early twentieth century, see George Marsden, *Fundamentalism and American Culture*, 2nd ed. (New York: Oxford University Press, 2006).

10. *Book of Order, The Constitution of the Presbyterian Church (USA), Part II* (Louisville: Office of the General Assembly, 2015), F–1.0304. While I affirm the priority of the pursuit of truth, the specific formulation in the Great Ends is too restrictive for me. "Preservation" implies that we had truth in the past and we need to protect it from erosion in the present and future. I prefer to think of the pursuit of truth as being a mixture of protecting the wisdom of the past and the discovery of new manifestations of truth in the present, and an openness to additional ways of understanding in the future.

11. John Calvin, *Institutes of the Christian Religion*, ed. John T. McNeill (Philadelphia: Westminster Press, 1960), 4.17.32, pp. 1403–4.

12. "Immortal, Invisible, God Only Wise," lyrics by Walter Chalmers Smith (1867) as included in *Chalice Hymnal* (St. Louis, MO: Chalice Press, 1995), 66.

13. The late evangelical ethicist Allen Verhey wrote a provocative essay on the notion of "playing God," in which he argued that the idea is not incontrovertibly bad, as the normal invocations of the phrase assume. If by "playing God" we mimic the biblical God's priority on healing and concern for justice, for instance, then standing in for God might be an entirely appropriate discharge of Christian responsibility. See "'Playing God' and Invoking a Perspective," in *On Moral Medicine: Theological Perspectives in Medical Ethics*, 2nd ed., ed. Stephen E. Lammers and Allen Verhey (Grand Rapids: Eerdmans, 1998), 287–96.

14. Reinhold Niebuhr, *The Nature and Destiny of Man* (Englewood Cliffs, NJ: Prentice Hall, 1964), 1:181.

15. Niebuhr, *Nature and Destiny of Man*, 1:190–94.

16. Niebuhr, *Nature and Destiny of Man*, 1:194–203.

17. For the philosophical tension between our subjective and apparently objective human perspectives, see Thomas Nagel, *The View from Nowhere* (Oxford: Oxford University Press, 1989).

18. Niebuhr, *Nature and Destiny of Man*, 1:194.

19. Calvin, *Institutes*, 1.6.1, p. 70.

20. Calvin, *Institutes*, 1.6.2, p. 72.

21. Brian D. McLaren, *A Generous Orthodoxy* (Grand Rapids: Zondervan, 2004), n. 129.

22. I am familiar with the passages many Christians claim are direct references to abortion and same-sex relationships in the Bible. Space does not permit arguing adequately for why I do not read them as directly relevant as other Christians do, but I can state my position quickly on several of them. Exodus 21:22 is often raised as a biblical acknowledgment of the immorality of abortion, but I think it is pretty clear from the passage that the injury being punished was not seen as the taking of "innocent life" but as an assault on a woman and the "property" of her husband. Psalm 139 describes a di-

vine value for the individual person that precedes even birth, but the text itself does not actually draw any implications for abortion. The story of David and Jonathan is taken by some as biblical celebration of same-sex amorous relationships, but it is speculative at best to suggest that the story has anything like contemporary same-sex relationship in mind. Finally, Romans 1 is often at the center of the biblical battle over homosexuality, and I deal with it quickly above. Christian interpreters may persuasively employ some of these passages (and others) to construct a theological permission or rejection of abortion or homosexuality. But my point is that such arguments would be just that—*constructive*. They do not follow automatically from the texts themselves.

Notes to Chapter 3

1. Given the negative consequences impulsivity has yielded in American political and corporate life in the last couple of decades, you would think we would have learned to value the deliberate soul more. But "act first, think later" still tends to define what most Americans identify as a "strong leader," as the bravado on display in the 2016 presidential campaign disturbingly illustrated.

2. As reported by CNN at http://www.cnn.com/2016/11/11/politics/popular-vote -turnout-2016/. According to the Bipartisan Policy Center, the turnout for the 2012 presidential election was only around 60 percent; see their report at http://bipartisanpolicy .org/library/2012-voter-turnout.

3. My interest here is the impatience with American "politics as usual" that motivates many Americans' failure to vote. But while many of the Americans who failed to vote simply chose to stay home, many others *could not* vote because of circumstances that kept them away from the polls. The disenfranchisement of millions of Americans, including the intentional efforts to keep citizens from the polls by racially motivated and targeted voter registration policies, continues to be a crisis in American politics.

4. "PCUSA Continues Membership Decline," *The Layman*, May 13, 2015.

5. The latest attempt to establish these non-geographical presbyteries was rejected soundly at the denomination's biennial General Assembly in 2012.

6. See the Pew Research Center's 2014 Religious Landscape Study at http://www.pew forum.org/religious-landscape-study/.

7. Augustine, *On Patience*, in *The New Advent Fathers of the Church* at www.newadvent .org/fathers/1315.htm.

8. Charles R. Pinches, "Time for Patience," in *Attentive Patience*, ed. Robert B. Kruschwitz (Waco: Institute for Faith and Learning at Baylor University, 2016), 20.

9. Thomas Aquinas, *Summa Theologica*, trans. Fathers of the English Dominican Province (Westminster, MD: Christian Classics, 1981), II-II q. 136.

10. See Ephesians 4:1–2 and Colossians 3:12–13.

11. Thomas Aquinas, *Summa Theologica*, II-II q. 123.

12. Thomas Aquinas, *Summa Theologica*, II-II q. 136.

13. See, for instance, Paul's vindication of his ministry in 2 Corinthians 6:3–12, in part by calling attention to the virtues with which he and his colleagues have discharged that ministry. Chief among those virtues was their exercise of patience toward friends and persecutors alike. See also 1 Timothy 1:16 and James 5:7–10. The writer of the Second

Letter to Timothy makes reference to the patience of Paul's endurance of suffering as a model for Christian leadership in a traumatized early church.

14. Karl Barth, *Church Dogmatics*, II/1, ed. G. W. Bromiley and T. F. Torrance (Edinburgh: T&T Clark, 1978), 417.

15. "Great Thanksgiving Prayer A," in *Book of Common Worship* (Louisville: Westminster John Knox Press, 1993), 69–70.

16. "A Brief Statement of Faith," in *The Constitution of the Presbyterian Church (USA), Part I: The Book of Confessions* (Louisville: The Office of the General Assembly, 2014), 303.

17. Luke Bretherton, *Christianity and Contemporary Politics* (Chichester, UK: Wiley-Blackwell, 2010), 96–104.

18. Theologian Mark Achtemeier began the process as a reliable conservative critic of homosexuality, but through the experience of participating in this group and intensively studying the issue on his own, he discovered what he believes is biblical warrant for blessing same-sex relationships. See his courageous book, *The Bible's Yes to Same-Sex Marriage: An Evangelical's Change of Heart* (Louisville: Westminster John Knox Press, 2014).

19. As an indication of that respect, Anna invited Andy to participate in a panel discussion on contraception access in a subsequent semester. Anna's invitation was not designed as a way to sucker-punch Andy, by inviting him to share the podium with a representative of Planned Parenthood, in a room of students disproportionately committed to that organization's mission. She invited him because she thought he could speak on the issue with intelligence, integrity, and strength of conviction. Despite a somewhat hostile room, Andy did not disappoint. I relate this story in chapter 8 in pursuit of another point.

20. Susan Cain, *Quiet: The Power of Introverts in a World That Can't Stop Talking* (New York: Crown Publishing, 2012).

21. Barbara Brown Taylor, *When God Is Silent* (Boston: Cowley Publications, 1998), 38–39.

22. See Galatians 2.

Notes to Chapter 4

1. See Aristotle's *Nicomachean Ethics*, trans. J. A. K. Thomson (New York: Penguin, 1955), Book 6.

2. See Plato's *Apology* in *The Dialogues of Plato*, ed. Erich Segal (Toronto: Bantam, 1986), 6–8.

3. See, for instance, Ecclesiastes 2:26.

4. For example, Proverbs 4:6–7.

5. John Calvin, *Institutes of the Christian Religion*, ed. John T. McNeill (Philadelphia: Westminster Press, 1960), 1.1.1, p. 35.

6. Matthew B. Crawford, *Shop Class as Soulcraft: An Inquiry into the Value of Work* (New York: Penguin Books, 2009).

7. Richard Dawkins, *The God Delusion* (Boston: Houghton Mifflin, 2006), 5.

8. Former President George W. Bush's regular appeals to religious conservatives by playing the anti-intellectual card were particularly pernicious, to my mind, because he managed to denigrate the importance of intelligent wisdom to both religious faith and responsible political citizenship in one fell swoop.

9. For instance, in his 1995 encyclical, *Evangelium Vitae*, Pope John Paul II attempted to hold on to his tradition's theoretical support of capital punishment while essentially condemning the practice, by lumping it with other cultural trends he found illustrative of the "culture of death, abortion and euthanasia."

10. The literature around just peacemaking continues to grow. For an introduction, see Glen Stassen, *Just Peacemaking: The New Paradigm for the Ethics of Peace and War* (Cleveland: Pilgrim Press, 2008).

11. David Tracy, *The Analogical Imagination* (New York: Crossroad, 1981), 13.

12. Tom L. Beauchamp and James F. Childress, *Principles of Biomedical Ethics*, 7th ed. (New York: Oxford University Press, 2012), 39.

13. Elizabeth Liebert, *The Way of Discernment: Spiritual Practices for Decision Making* (Louisville: Westminster John Knox Press, 2008), ix.

14. Liebert, *Way of Discernment*, 23.

15. Liebert offers this interpretation of the biblical stories in this paragraph in *Way of Discernment*, 12. The story of Samuel's calling appears in 1 Samuel 3.

16. Jesus's commendation of the wisdom of serpents can be found in Matthew 10:16; the story of the wise bridesmaids is in Matthew 25:1–13; and the parable of the dishonest manager is in Luke 16:1–9. The famous "thief in the night" passage in 1 Thessalonians 5:1–11 is just one example of the epistles cautioning Christians to discern the signs of the times and respond to God's movements with faithfulness.

17. Thomas Aquinas, *Summa Theologica*, trans. Fathers of the English Dominican Province (Westminster, MD: Christian Classics, 1981), I-II, q. 57 a.4.

18. Aquinas, *Summa Theologica*, I-II, q. 57 a.5.

19. Aquinas, *Summa Theologica*, II-II, q. 47 a.3.

20. Aquinas, *Summa Theologica*, I-II, q. 57 a.6.

21. Aquinas, *Summa Theologica*, II-II, q. 47, a.1.

22. Aquinas considered prudence in the context of a medieval moral psychology that would seem antiquated to us—the belief that there are distinguishable moral faculties we might call the "intellect," the "will," and the "appetite," the operation of which practical wisdom helped to regulate. Even if we have moved beyond a scholastic understanding of moral psychology, however, there is something to be said for its evocative representation of integrity in a holistic depiction of moral character.

23. Aquinas, *Summa Theologica*, I-II, q. 57, a.6, reply 4. For a brief discussion of "accumulated learning," see Liebert, *Way of Discernment*, 13.

24. H. Richard Niebuhr, *The Responsible Self: An Essay in Christian Moral Philosophy* (New York: Harper & Row, 1963).

25. Niebuhr, *The Responsible Self*, 65.

26. Leslie Jamison, *The Empathy Exams* (Minneapolis: Graywolf Press, 2014), 23.

27. Paul Bloom, "The Case Against Empathy," *The New Yorker*, May 20, 2013.

28. The history of western philosophical demands for the exercise of "reason alone" is itself a case in point. As contemporary feminists have pointed out, those appeals to reason betray a stereotypically male understanding of the rational—emotionless and preoccupied with the theoretical and hypothetical. The expansion of perspective to include feminist critiques challenges the validity of any understanding of reason that excludes the importance of affection, the importance of relationships, and the legitimacy of subjective experience.

29. Wendy VanderWal-Gritter, *Generous Spaciousness: Responding to Gay Christians in the Church* (Grand Rapids: Brazos Press, 2014), 52.

30. Martin Luther King Jr., "I Have a Dream," in *A Testament of Hope: The Essential Writings and Speeches of Martin Luther King, Jr.* (New York: HarperCollins, 1986), 217–20.

31. Presbyterian Church (USA), *Book of Occasional Services: A Liturgical Resource Supplementing the Book of Common Worship, 1993* (Louisville: Geneva Press, 1999), 58. Emphasis mine.

32. Kathleen Norris, *Amazing Grace: A Vocabulary of Faith* (New York: Riverhead Books, 1998), 305–6. If there is any truth to this characterization of classical Protestant thought as unimaginative, surely African-American Protestantism is an exception to the rule. From its beginning, African-American Protestantism has featured stories and imagination to convey meaning. The priority on narrative was necessary during slavery, when literacy among African Americans was not encouraged and oral storytelling served as an effectively subversive way of passing on both the religion and the hope it conveyed. Thus it should be no surprise that one of the best examples of imaginative wisdom in modern Protestantism, Martin Luther King Jr., emerged from that tradition.

33. The idea that theology's native language is poetry is fruitfully explored in Douglas F. Ottati, *Hopeful Realism: Reclaiming the Poetry of Theology* (Cleveland: Pilgrim Press, 1999). The phrase "play in the joints" is a metaphor the US Supreme Court has invoked from time to time to describe the imprecise negotiation of government's obligations under the Free Exercise and Establishment clauses of the First Amendment. See, for instance, *Locke v. Davey* (2004).

Notes to Chapter 5

1. This is made clear in both of the explanations for the Sabbath's origin. In Exodus the Sabbath is tied to God's activity in creation. In Deuteronomy it is tied to Israel's emancipation from Egypt. In both cases, the people of God are encouraged to celebrate and demonstrate the trustworthiness of God by trusting that God will uphold the community even through a day of relative inactivity. For a subsistence culture like ancient Israel's, this was a radical act of trust. Similarly, in our workaholic culture today, the honoring of the Sabbath by refraining from work is a counter-cultural testament to God's reliability to care for us.

2. See, for instance, Jeremiah 15:6.

3. The story of the woman with the hemorrhage can be found in Luke 8:40–48; Peter walking with Jesus on the water is in Matthew 14:22–32; and the story of Thomas's disbelief is told in John 20:19–29.

4. Martin Luther, "A Mighty Fortress Is Our God" (1529), trans. Frederick Henry Hedge, 1852), in *The Presbyterian Hymnal* (Louisville: Westminster John Knox Press, 1990), 260.

5. Friedrich Schleiermacher, *The Christian Faith* (Edinburgh: T & T Clark, 1989), 13. See also Schleiermacher, *On Religion: Speeches to Its Cultured Despisers* (Louisville: Westminster John Knox Press, 1994), especially the Second Speech.

6. Paul Tillich, *Systematic Theology* (Chicago: University of Chicago Press, 1951), 1:211–18. See also Douglas F. Ottati, *Theology for Liberal Protestants: God the Creator* (Grand Rapids: Eerdmans, 2013), 40–43.

7. Karl Barth, *Church Dogmatics*, IV/1, ed. G. W. Bromiley and T. F. Torrance (Edinburgh: T&T Clark, 1978), 760.

8. Barth, *Church Dogmatics*, IV/1, 761.

9. Richard Gillard, "Sister, Let Me Be Your Servant," in *Chalice Hymnal* (St. Louis: Chalice Press, 1995), no. 490.

10. Frances Taylor Gench, *Faithful Disagreement: Wrestling with Scripture in the Midst of Church Conflict* (Louisville: Westminster John Knox Press, 2009), 26.

11. *The United Methodist Hymnal* (Nashville: The United Methodist Publishing House, 1989), 48–49.

12. Incidentally, I think this would be a healthy way to understand ordination services too. Highlighting the mutual covenant that church and the candidate for ordination make with one another, our liturgies reinforce that ordination is a commitment of faith in one another. The church entrusts the candidate with responsibility for leadership and service, while the church promises to trust, support, and serve those whom it calls to particular office.

13. By the way, this model of a conversation based on honesty, integrity, and listening is a pretty good recipe for approaching civil discourse as well, as I suggested in my previous work, *In Defense of Civility: How Religion Can Unite America on Seven Moral Issues That Divide Us* (Louisville: Westminster John Knox Press, 2010). The parallels between my definition of civility there and the kind of Christian faithfulness I am describing here are not accidental. In the final chapter of this book, I will have more to say about the church's potential for leadership in public efforts at civility.

14. Karl Barth, *Dogmatics in Outline* (New York: Harper & Row, 1959), 72–81.

15. John Calvin, *Commentaries on the Book of Joshua* (1564), trans. Henry Beveridge. Reprinted in *Calvin's Commentaries* (Grand Rapids: Baker Books, 2003), 29–31.

16. Martin Luther King Jr., *Strength to Love* (Minneapolis: Fortress, 1980), 123.

17. H. Richard Niebuhr, "The Grace of Doing Nothing," *The Christian Century*, March 23, 1932.

18. John Calvin, *Institutes of the Christian Religion*, ed. John T. McNeill (Philadelphia: Westminster Press, 1960), 3.7.1, p. 690.

Notes to Chapter 6

1. How I have imagined friendship might resemble how we would describe a *spouse* or *domestic partner*, and that should not surprise us. Ideally a spouse or domestic partner is a more specific kind of moral friend, a friend with whom the level of commitment, intimacy, and mutual investment runs especially deep (uniquely, in fact, for those of us who remain fans of monogamy), often (though not always) including a sexual dimension we normally do not share with our other friends. Spouses and domestic partners normally are "friends with benefits," to use a popular phrase.

2. See Aristotle's *Nicomachean Ethics*, trans. J. A. K. Thomson (New York: Penguin, 1955), 261–64. See also Paul J. Wadell, *Friendship and the Moral Life* (Notre Dame: University of Notre Dame Press, 1989), 51–55.

3. Gilbert Meilaender, *Friendship: A Study in Theological Ethics* (Notre Dame: University of Notre Dame Press, 1981), 3.

4. Meilaender, *Friendship*, 53.

5. Meilaender, *Friendship*, 3. Here Meilaender is citing Matthew 5:45.

6. Meilaender, *Friendship*, 54.

7. Meilaender, *Friendship*, 65.

8. Søren Kierkegaard, *Works of Love*, trans. Howard Hong and Edna Hong (New York: Harper & Row, 1962), 59.

9. Kierkegaard, *Works of Love*, 58–72.

10. Kierkegaard, *Works of Love*, 62.

11. Kierkegaard, *Works of Love*, 68.

12. Kierkegaard, *Works of Love*, 70.

13. For a helpful discussion of the interpretation of Trinity as divine community, see Shirley C. Guthrie, *Christian Doctrine*, revised ed. (Louisville: Westminster John Knox Press, 1994), 88–95.

14. I have more to say about forbearance and friendship as marks of the church in chapter 7.

15. I would agree that the application of passages like this to the covenant of marriage is a natural and helpful extension of the meaning of the text, insofar as marital love should be understood to consist of a deep bond of friendship lived in (domestic) community. Where we err is not in applying it to marital friendship but in limiting its relevance to such. Marital friendship is but one subset of the kind of Christian friendship Paul and other early Christian leaders are describing in the New Testament.

16. The theme of loving one another as a satisfaction of Christ's commandment and a reflection of love for God continues in the Second and Third Letters of John as well. That being said, there exists in 2 John a passage that strains against the friendship imperative and is difficult to resolve. In verses 10–11, the author recommends that members of his audience deny basic hospitality to his theological opponents. He justifies this advice by warning them that tolerance of these opponents will make others complicit in their errors and the harm they bring the church. There is no easy way to reconcile this suggestion that there are limits to Christian love and kinship with the more prevalent suggestion in the Johannine letters that those who love God love one another (2 John 5). If the writer of this letter experienced a moment of self-contradiction in the navigation between conviction and forbearance, however, it does not distinguish him from a great cloud of Christians and Christian communities from biblical time onward. See also Frances Taylor Gench, *Faithful Disagreement: Wrestling with Scripture in the Midst of Church Conflict* (Louisville: Westminster John Knox Press, 2009), chapter 1.

17. Wadell, *Friendship and the Moral Life*, 63.

18. Wadell, *Friendship and the Moral Life*, 99–100.

19. If it is right to describe our relationship with God as friendship (as Thomas Aquinas and others would endorse), then that relationship makes clear that friendships do not depend on the annihilation of differences. In our friendship with God, we are brought closer to the divine, but we do not (or need not) become God. In fact the value for us of that friendship is in the juxtaposition of the differences between God and ourselves.

20. Wesley Hill, *Spiritual Friendship: Finding Love in the Church as a Celibate Gay Christian* (Grand Rapids: Brazos Press, 2015), 99.

21. Paul J. Wadell, *Becoming Friends: Worship, Justice, and the Practice of Christian Friendship* (Grand Rapids: Brazos Press, 2002), 72.

22. Wadell, *Becoming Friends*, 116.

23. Wadell, *Becoming Friends*, 84.

24. Wadell, *Becoming Friends*, 53.

25. Wadell, *Becoming Friends*, 16.

26. Wadell, *Becoming Friends*, 91.

27. Karl Barth, *Church Dogmatics*, IV/2, ed. G. W. Bromiley and T. F. Torrance (Edinburgh: T&T Clark, 1978), 614.

Notes to Chapter 7

1. *Book of Order*, *The Constitution of the Presbyterian Church (USA)*, *Part II* (Louisville: Office of the General Assembly, 2015), F-1.0304.

2. Martin Luther, "Sermon in Castle Pleissenburg," in *Martin Luther: Selections from His Writings*, ed. John Dillenberger (New York: Anchor Books, 1961), 247.

3. Luther, "Sermon," 243.

4. Luther, "Sermon," p. 246.

5. John Calvin, *Institutes of the Christian Religion*, ed. John T. McNeill (Philadelphia: Westminster Press, 1960), 4.1.9, p. 1023.

6. Calvin, *Institutes*, 4.2.10, p. 1051.

7. Calvin, *Institutes*, 4.2.5, p. 1047.

8. Arthur C. Cochrane, ed. *Reformed Confessions of the Sixteenth Century* (Louisville: Westminster John Knox Press, 2003), 176–77.

9. Kathleen Norris, *Amazing Grace: A Vocabulary of Faith* (New York: Riverhead Books, 1998), 324–25. Norris points out that the Greek root for dogma means "what seems good, fitting, becoming." In this light, she suggests that "'beauty' might be a more fitting synonym for dogma" than its current connotation as prescription, and that "it appeals to my poetic sensibility, rather than to my more linear intelligence."

10. Ronald P. Byars, *Finding Our Balance: Repositioning Mainstream Protestantism* (Eugene, OR: Cascade Books, 2015), 9.

11. Byars, *Finding our Balance*, 45.

12. Calvin, *Institutes*, 4.1.7, p. 1021.

13. Calvin, *Institutes*, 4.1.10, pp. 1024–25.

14. Calvin, *Institutes*, 4.1.12, pp. 1025–26.

15. Calvin, *Institutes*, 4.1.12, p. 1026.

16. Calvin, *Institutes*, 4.1.13, p. 1027.

17. Calvin, *Institutes*, 4.1.15, p. 1029.

18. Calvin, *Institutes*, 4.1.16, pp. 1030–31.

19. Calvin, *Institutes*, 4.1.20, p. 1034.

20. Calvin, *Institutes*, 4.1.19, p. 1033.

21. Calvin, *Institutes*, 4.1.20–21, pp. 1034–35.

22. John Winthrop, "A Modell of Christian Charity," in *American Sermons* (New York: Library Classics of the United States, 1999), 42 (modernization mine).

23. See James Calvin Davis, *The Moral Theology of Roger Williams: Christian Conviction and Public Ethics* (Louisville: Westminster John Knox Press, 2004).

24. This separatism, in fact, contributed to Williams's exile from the Massachusetts Bay Colony, for both political and theological reasons. Politically, rejection of the Church

of England was an affront to the head of that church, the king of England, and the authorities in Massachusetts were not enthusiastic about such treasonous positions being known from their colony. Theologically, most Puritans believed that their mission was to protect and reform the church, not separate from it. Geographically, they had removed to America to model what they believed was Christianity with integrity: biblically based preaching, conservative morality, congregational polity, and the eradication of anything that resembled Catholic ostentation. However, the Puritan experiment was meant as a pattern of reform for the mother church, not an alternative to it.

25. Sargent Bush, ed., *The Correspondence of John Cotton* (Chapel Hill: University of North Carolina Press, 2001), 220.

26. Byars, *Finding Our Balance*, 11–12.

27. Brian D. McLaren, *A Generous Orthodoxy* (Grand Rapids: Zondervan, 2004).

28. Frances Taylor Gench, *Faithful Disagreement: Wrestling with Scripture in the Midst of Church Conflict* (Louisville: Westminster John Knox Press, 2009), chapter 1.

29. Wendy VanderWal-Gritter, *Generous Spaciousness: Responding to Gay Christians in the Church* (Grand Rapids: Brazos Press, 2014), 125–26.

30. VanderWal-Gritter, *Generous Spaciousness*, 14.

31. This notion of "loss as gift" in the church is indebted to Danielle Allen's similar description of sacrifice as a display of trust within democratic politics. See Danielle S. Allen, *Talking to Strangers: Anxieties of Citizenship since* Brown v. Board of Education (Chicago: University of Chicago Press, 2004), especially chapter 4.

Notes to Chapter 8

1. I since have come to understand that this relatively new phenomenon of snapping as a substitute for clapping is not always a sign of derision, and in fact is meant as a signal of support that is less disruptive of public events (or more subtly respectful of the serious nature of some public presentations) than applause. For an interesting discussion, including its connection to the generation of social media, see Katherine Rosman, "Snapping Is the New Clapping," *New York Times*, November 22, 2015, ST10.

2. What is commonly understood as the Social Gospel in the United States was predominantly a Protestant movement, but it had a counterpart among American Catholics, appealing to their own social justice tradition to critique the injustices of modern industrialism. For more on Protestant and Catholic social movements in the early-twentieth-century United States, see Gary Dorrien, *Social Ethics in the Making: Interpreting an American Tradition* (Malden, MA: Wiley-Blackwell, 2011), especially chapters 2–3.

3. Walter Rauschenbusch, *Christianity and the Social Crisis* (1907; reprint, Louisville: Westminster John Knox Press, 1991), xxxvii.

4. Rauschenbusch, *Christianity and the Social Crisis*, 7–8.

5. Rauschenbusch, *Christianity and the Social Crisis*, 65–66.

6. Rauschenbusch, *Christianity and the Social Crisis*, 91.

7. James H. Cone, *A Theology of Liberation*, Fortieth Anniversary Edition (Maryknoll, NY: Orbis Books, 2010), 67.

8. Cone, *Theology of Liberation*, 32.

9. Cone, *Theology of Liberation*, 63.

10. Cone, *Theology of Liberation*, 58.

11. Cone, *Theology of Liberation*, 4.

12. Cone, *Theology of Liberation*, ix.

13. Martin Luther King Jr., "I Have a Dream," in *A Testament of Hope: The Essential Writings and Speeches of Martin Luther King, Jr.* (New York: HarperCollins, 1986), 218.

14. The "Statement by Alabama Clergymen" (April 12, 1963) can be found at http://kingencyclopedia.stanford.edu/kingweb/popular_requests/frequentdocs/clergy.pdf.

15. Martin Luther King Jr., *Why We Can't Wait* (New York: Harper and Row, 1963), 84.

16. King, *Why We Can't Wait*, 82–86.

17. The late Grace M. Jantzen powerfully explored the ways that Christianity has served to underwrite violence against women in its historical elevation of certain metaphors—including military might, courtroom ferocity, and the self-sacrificial model of the crucified Christ—to portray attributes of God. See "The Courtroom and the Garden: Gender and Violence in Christendom," in *Violence against Women in Contemporary World Religion*, ed. Daniel C. Maguire and Sa'diyya Shaikh (Cleveland: Pilgrim Press, 2007), 29–48. The theological antidote to these destructive metaphors, she wrote, is to be found in more affirming symbols in the tradition, including the "organic" images of garden and creation.

18. See "The Examination of Mrs. Anne Hutchinson," in *The Puritans in America: A Narrative Anthology*, ed. Alan Heimert and Andrew Delbanco (Cambridge: Harvard University Press, 1985), 156.

19. Martin Luther King Jr., *Strength to Love* (Philadelphia: Fortress, 1963), 27.

20. King, *Strength to Love*, 26.

21. King, *Strength to Love*, 19.

22. King, *Strength to Love*, 141.

23. King, *Strength to Love*, 50–51.

24. King, *Strength to Love*, 27.

25. King, *Strength to Love*, 140.

26. That day came at the General Assembly in the summer of 2014, when the denomination's highest body approved provisions that liberalized the liturgical definition of marriage and opened up the approval of ordination to local standards. A necessary majority of presbyteries in the PC(USA) endorsed the latter move later in the year.

27. For another example of an effort to work for full inclusion with an explicit commitment to some of the reconciling virtues we have identified with forbearance, see the Reconciling Ministries Network of the United Methodist Church.

28. Nicole Chilivis, "Humble Connections: Staying in Challenging Relationships," *The Christian Century*, December 14, 2015.

29. King, *Strength to Love*, 51.

30. King, *Strength to Love*, 52.

31. Ronald F. Thiemann, *Religion in Public Life: A Dilemma for Democracy* (Washington, DC: Georgetown University Press, 1996), chapter 6.

Notes to Chapter 9

1. Jennifer Steinhauer, "Fighting with Gusto, Senator Goes Taunt-for-Taunt with Trump," *New York Times*, June 10, 2016, A20.

2. Reinhold Niebuhr, "Democracy and the Party Spirit," in *Love and Justice: Selections from the Shorter Writings of Reinhold Niebuhr* (Louisville: Westminster John Knox Press, 1957), 66.

3. President Barack Obama, State of the Union (January 2015), accessed at http://www.cnn.com/2015/01/20/politics/state-of-the-union-2015-transcript-full-text/.

4. James Bohman, "The Coming of Age of Deliberative Democracy," *The Journal of Political Philosophy* 6, no. 4 (1998): 401. Bohman's essay provides a quick survey and analysis of the maturation of this movement within political philosophy, through the isolation of two theoretical questions that preoccupy the literature and distinguish members of the "family" of deliberative democracy theorists: the relationship between epistemic and moral justifications and the complex issues associated with the institutionalization of deliberative ideals. For deeper introduction to deliberative democracy and its critics, see Amy Gutmann and Dennis Thompson, *Democracy and Disagreement* (Cambridge: Belknap Press of Harvard University Press, 1996); James Bohman and William Rehg, eds., *Deliberative Democracy: Essays on Reason and Politics* (Cambridge: The MIT Press, 1997); Jon Elster, ed., *Deliberative Democracy* (Cambridge: Cambridge University Press, 1998); Stephen Macedo, ed., *Deliberative Politics: Essays on Democracy and Disagreement* (New York: Oxford University Press, 1999).

5. Of course, this picture of democratic decision making contrasts with the view of political encounter as fundamentally a contest of power. For a critique of deliberation from this perspective, see Ian Shapiro, "Enough of Deliberation: Politics Is about Interests and Power," in Macedo, ed., *Deliberative Politics*, 28–38.

6. Gutmann and Thompson, *Democracy and Disagreement*, 1.

7. Amy Gutmann and Dennis Thompson, *Why Deliberative Democracy?* (Princeton: Princeton University Press, 2004), 10–12.

8. Gutmann and Thompson, *Democracy and Disagreement*, 3.

9. Gutmann and Thompson, *Democracy and Disagreement*, 2.

10. Gutmann and Thompson, *Democracy and Disagreement*, 52. Of course, regard for others corresponds to an expectation that they will extend similar treatment to us.

11. Gutmann and Thompson, *Democracy and Disagreement*, 14.

12. What constitutes an "accessible" or "comprehensible" public reason has been a matter of robust debate in political philosophy, especially around the issue of religious reasoning in public discourse. Famously, both Richard Rorty and John Rawls claimed that religion is inappropriate as public reasoning because it is not an accessible source of argumentation and justification for citizens who do not subscribe to its truth claims. For their equally important but significantly different arguments for this general position, see Richard Rorty, "Religion as Conversation-stopper," in *Philosophy and Social Hope* (London: Penguin Books, 1999), 168–74; John Rawls, *Political Liberalism* (New York: Columbia University Press, 1995). Both men rethought their positions somewhat late in their careers, and they inspired a library of scholarly affirmations and rebuttals. For a sample, see Ronald F. Thiemann, *Religion in Public Life: A Dilemma for Democracy* (Washington, DC: Georgetown University Press, 1996); Robert Audi and Nicholas Wolterstorff, *Religion in the Public Square: The Place of Religious Convictions in Political Debate* (Lanham, MD: Rowman & Littlefield, 1997); and Jeffrey Stout, *Democracy and Tradition* (Princeton: Princeton University Press, 2004).

13. Gutmann and Thompson, *Democracy and Disagreement*, 15.

14. Gutmann and Thompson, *Democracy and Disagreement*, 95.

15. Gutmann and Thompson, *Democracy and Disagreement*, 95.

16. Gutmann and Thompson, *Democracy and Disagreement*, 43.

17. Gutmann and Thompson, *Democracy and Disagreement*, 133. See also Gutmann and Thompson, *Why Deliberative Democracy?*, 16.

18. Gutmann and Thompson, *Democracy and Disagreement*, 129. In theory, the accountability this principle prescribes is "universal"—that is, officials are accountable beyond the restricted scope of their immediate constituents.

19. James Calvin Davis, *In Defense of Civility: How Religion Can Unite America on Seven Moral Issues That Divide Us* (Louisville: Westminster John Knox Press, 2010), 159. The following discussion of civility is a quick summary of the argument I make in the last chapter of that book. Of course, the ingredients of political civility are best not limited to these four virtues. Other character traits might prove useful contributors to civility, such as discernment, imagination, and a sense of humor. But I argue that these four virtues are essential and foundational, and perhaps many of the other character traits we might associate with civility may be seen to derive from these first four.

20. One of the best examples of public integrity remains Joseph Cardinal Bernardin's insistence on a "consistent ethic of life" among Catholics in the 1980s. His was a call for consistency between the reverence for life that animated traditional Catholic opposition to abortion and the church's stance on capital punishment. See Joseph Cardinal Bernardin, "A Consistent Ethic of Life and the Death Penalty in Our Time," in *Capital Punishment: A Reader*, ed. Glen H. Stassen (Cleveland: Pilgrim Press, 1988).

21. Despite the relative lack of virtue language in their approach, Gutmann and Thompson themselves identify integrity and mutual respect (what they sometimes call "civic magnanimity") as dispositional "extensions" of the principle of reciprocity. As I argue here, we might easily describe them as correspondent to the other principles as well. See Gutmann and Thompson, *Democracy and Disagreement*, 79–81.

22. Gutmann and Thompson, *Democracy and Disagreement*, 360.

23. See Stanley Hauerwas, *A Community of Character: Toward a Constructive Christian Social Ethic* (Notre Dame: University of Notre Dame Press, 1981).

24. Gutmann and Thompson, *Democracy and Disagreement*, 359.

25. Thiemann, *Religion in Public Life*, 153.

26. Luke Bretherton, *Resurrecting Democracy: Faith, Citizenship, and the Politics of a Common Life* (New York: Cambridge University Press, 2015), 217.

27. Bretherton, *Resurrecting Democracy*, 92.

28. Bretherton, *Resurrecting Democracy*, 92.

29. Bretherton, *Resurrecting Democracy*, 95.

30. Bretherton, *Resurrecting Democracy*, 192.

31. Bretherton, *Resurrecting Democracy*, 192.

32. Bretherton, *Resurrecting Democracy*, 195.

33. Bretherton, *Resurrecting Democracy*, 195.

34. Bretherton, *Resurrecting Democracy*, 198–99.

35. Bretherton, *Resurrecting Democracy*, 195.

36. See Douglas F. Ottati, "The Ministry of Reconciliation," in *Hopeful Realism: Reclaiming the Poetry of Theology* (Cleveland: Pilgrim Press, 1999), 103–12.

37. Prayer of Confession 2, *Book of Common Worship* (Louisville: Westminster John Knox Press, 1993), 53.

38. Great Thanksgiving Prayer A, *Book of Common Worship*, 69.

39. Presbyterian Church (USA), *The Confession of 1967* (Inclusive Language Text, 2000), 9.31.

40. See Ottati, *Hopeful Realism*, 107–8.

41. Carmen K. Sisson, "Building Relationships across Racial Lines," *The Christian Century*, August 3, 2015.

42. For more on the just peacemaking movement, see Glen H. Stassen, ed., *Just Peacemaking: The New Paradigm for the Ethics of Peace and War* (Cleveland: Pilgrim Press, 2008); and Susan Brooks Thistlethwaite, ed., *Interfaith Just Peacemaking: Jewish, Christian, and Muslim Perspectives on the New Paradigm of Peace and War* (New York: Palgrave Macmillan, 2011).

43. James M. Gustafson, *The Church as Moral Decision-Maker* (Philadelphia: Pilgrim Press, 1970), 84.

44. Gustafson, *Church as Moral Decision-Maker*, 93.

45. Danielle S. Allen, *Talking to Strangers: Anxieties of Citizenship since* Brown v. Board of Education (Chicago: University of Chicago Press, 2004).

46. James Davison Hunter, *To Change the World: The Irony, Tragedy, and Possibility of Christianity in the Late Modern World* (New York: Oxford University Press, 2010).

Selected Bibliography

Achtemeier, Mark. *The Bible's Yes to Same-Sex Marriage: An Evangelical's Change of Heart*. Louisville: Westminster John Knox Press, 2014.

Allen, Danielle S. *Talking to Strangers: Anxieties of Citizenship since Brown v. Board of Education*. Chicago: University of Chicago Press, 2004.

Aristotle. *Nicomachean Ethics*. Translated by J. A. K. Thomson. New York: Penguin, 1955.

Barth, Karl. *Church Dogmatics*. Edited by G. W. Bromiley and T. F. Torrance. Edinburgh: T&T Clark, 1978.

———. *Dogmatics in Outline*. New York: Harper & Row, 1959.

Beauchamp, Tom L., and James F. Childress. *Principles of Biomedical Ethics*. 7th ed. New York: Oxford University Press, 2012.

Bernardin, Joseph Cardinal. "A Consistent Ethic of Life and the Death Penalty in Our Time." In *Capital Punishment: A Reader*. Edited by Glen H. Stassen. Cleveland: Pilgrim Press, 1988.

Bloom, Paul. "The Case against Empathy." *The New Yorker*, May 20, 2013.

Bohman, James. "The Coming of Age of Deliberative Democracy." *The Journal of Political Philosophy* 6, no. 4 (1998): 400–25.

Bohman, James, and William Rehg, eds. *Deliberative Democracy: Essays on Reason and Politics*. Cambridge: The MIT Press, 1997.

Bonhoeffer, Dietrich. *Life Together*. Translated by John W. Doberstein. New York: Harper, 1954.

Bretherton, Luke. *Christianity and Contemporary Politics*. Chichester, UK: Wiley-Blackwell, 2010.

———. *Resurrecting Democracy: Faith, Citizenship, and the Politics of a Common Life*. New York: Cambridge University Press, 2015.

Bush, Sargent, ed. *The Correspondence of John Cotton*. Chapel Hill: University of North Carolina Press, 2001.

Byars, Ronald P. *Finding Our Balance: Repositioning Mainstream Protestantism*. Eugene, OR: Cascade Books, 2015.

Cain, Susan. *Quiet: The Power of Introverts in a World That Can't Stop Talking*. New York: Crown Publishing, 2012.

Calvin, John. *Calvin's Commentaries*. Grand Rapids: Baker Books, 2003.

————. *Institutes of the Christian Religion*. Edited by John T. McNeill. Philadelphia: Westminster Press, 1960.

Cochrane, Arthur C., ed. *Reformed Confessions of the Sixteenth Century*. Louisville: Westminster Press, 2003.

Cone, James H. *A Theology of Liberation*, Fortieth Anniversary Edition. Maryknoll, NY: Orbis Books, 2010.

Crawford, Matthew B. *Shop Class as Soulcraft: An Inquiry into the Value of Work*. New York: Penguin Books, 2009.

Davis, James Calvin. *In Defense of Civility: How Religion Can Unite America on Seven Moral Issues That Divide Us*. Louisville: Westminster John Knox Press, 2010.

————. *The Moral Theology of Roger Williams: Christian Conviction and Public Ethics*. Louisville: Westminster John Knox Press, 2004.

Dawkins, Richard. *The God Delusion*. Boston: Houghton Mifflin, 2006.

Dillenberger, John, ed. *Martin Luther: Selections from His Writings*. New York: Anchor Books, 1961.

Dorrien, Gary. *Social Ethics in the Making: Interpreting an American Tradition*. Malden, MA: Wiley-Blackwell, 2011.

Elster, Jon. ed. *Deliberative Democracy*. Cambridge: Cambridge University Press, 1998.

Gench, Frances Taylor. *Faithful Disagreement: Wrestling with Scripture in the Midst of Church Conflict*. Louisville: Westminster John Knox Press, 2009.

Gushee, David P. *The Future of Faith in American Politics: The Public Witness of the Evangelical Center*. Waco: Baylor University Press, 2008.

Gustafson, James M. *Ethics from a Theocentric Perspective*. 2 vols. Chicago: University of Chicago Press, 1981, 1984.

————. *The Church as Moral Decision-Maker*. Philadelphia: Pilgrim Press, 1970.

Guthrie, Shirley C. *Christian Doctrine*. Revised edition. Louisville: Westminster John Knox Press, 1994.

Gutmann, Amy, and Dennis Thompson. *Democracy and Disagreement*. Cambridge: Belknap Press of Harvard University Press, 1996.

————. *Why Deliberative Democracy?* Princeton: Princeton University Press, 2004.

Harrison, Beverly Wildung. "The Power of Anger in the Work of Love: Christian

Ethics for Women and Other Strangers." In *Making the Connections: Essays in Feminist Social Ethics*, edited by Carol S. Robb. Boston: Beacon Press, 1985.

Hauerwas, Stanley. *A Community of Character: Toward a Constructive Christian Social Ethic*. Notre Dame: University of Note Dame Press, 1981.

———. *Approaching the End: Eschatological Reflections on Church, Politics, and Life*. Grand Rapids: Eerdmans, 2013.

———. *Character and the Christian Life: A Study in Theological Ethics*. San Antonio: Trinity University Press, 1975.

Heimert, Alan, and Andrew Delbanco, eds. *The Puritans in America: A Narrative Anthology*. Cambridge: Harvard University Press, 1985.

Hill, Wesley. *Spiritual Friendship: Finding Love in the Church as a Celibate Gay Christian*. Grand Rapids: Brazos Press, 2015.

Hunter, James Davison. *To Change the World: The Irony, Tragedy, and Possibility of Christianity in the Late Modern World*. New York: Oxford University Press, 2010.

Jamison, Leslie. *The Empathy Exams*. Minneapolis: Graywolf Press, 2014.

Jantzen, Grace M. "The Courtroom and the Garden: Gender and Violence in Christendom." In *Violence against Women in Contemporary World Religion*, edited by Daniel C. Maguire and Sa'diyya Shaikh. Cleveland: Pilgrim Press, 2007.

Kierkegaard, Søren. *Works of Love*. Translated by Howard Hong and Edna Hong. New York: Harper & Row, 1962.

King, Martin Luther, Jr. *A Testament of Hope: The Essential Writings and Speeches of Martin Luther King, Jr.* New York: HarperCollins, 1986.

———. *Strength to Love*. Minneapolis: Fortress, 1980.

———. *Why We Can't Wait*. New York: Harper and Row, 1963.

Leith, John H., ed. *Creeds of the Churches*. 3rd ed. Louisville: John Knox Press, 1982.

Liebert, Elizabeth. *The Way of Discernment: Spiritual Practices for Decision Making*. Louisville: Westminster John Knox Press, 2008.

Macedo, Stephen, ed. *Deliberative Politics: Essays on Democracy and Disagreement*. New York: Oxford University Press, 1999.

MacIntyre, Alasdair C. *After Virtue: A Study in Moral Theory*. 2nd ed. Notre Dame: University of Notre Dame Press, 1984.

Marsden, George. *Fundamentalism and American Culture*. 2nd ed. New York: Oxford University Press, 2006.

Martin, Ralph P. *Ephesians, Colossians, and Philemon*. In *Interpretation: A Bible Commentary for Teaching and Preaching*. Louisville: Westminster John Knox Press, 1991.

McLaren, Brian D. *A Generous Orthodoxy*. Grand Rapids: Zondervan, 2004.

Meilaender, Gilbert. *Friendship: A Study in Theological Ethics*. Notre Dame: University of Notre Dame Press, 1981.

Nagel, Thomas. *The View from Nowhere*. Oxford: Oxford University Press, 1989.

Niebuhr, H. Richard. *The Responsible Self: An Essay in Christian Moral Philosophy*. New York: Harper & Row, 1963.

Niebuhr, Reinhold. *Love and Justice: Selections from the Shorter Writings of Reinhold Niebuhr*. Louisville: Westminster John Knox Press, 1957.

———. *The Nature and Destiny of Man*. Englewood Cliffs, NJ: Prentice Hall, 1964.

Norris, Kathleen. *Amazing Grace: A Vocabulary of Faith*. New York: Riverhead Books, 1998.

Ottati, Douglas F. *Hopeful Realism: Reclaiming the Poetry of Theology*. Cleveland: Pilgrim Press, 1999.

———. *Theology for Liberal Protestants: God the Creator*. Grand Rapids: Eerdmans, 2013.

Pinches, Charles R. "Time for Patience." In *Attentive Patience*, edited by Robert B. Kruschwitz. Waco: Institute for Faith and Learning at Baylor University, 2016.

Rauschenbusch, Walter. *Christianity and the Social Crisis*. 1907; reprint, Louisville: Westminster John Knox Press, 1991.

Rawls, John. *Political Liberalism*. New York: Columbia University Press, 1993.

Robertson, D. B., ed. *Voluntary Associations: A Study of Groups in Free Societies*. Richmond, VA: John Knox Press, 1966.

Schaff, Philip, and Henry Wace, ed. *The Nicene and Post-Nicene Fathers*. Series 2. New York: Charles Scribner and Sons, 1900.

Schleiermacher, Friedrich. *The Christian Faith*. Edinburgh: T & T Clark, 1989.

Segal, Erich, ed. *The Dialogues of Plato*. Toronto: Bantam, 1986.

Stassen, Glen. *Just Peacemaking: The New Paradigm for the Ethics of Peace and War*. Cleveland: Pilgrim Press, 2008.

Taylor, Barbara Brown. *When God Is Silent*. Boston: Cowley Publications, 1998.

Thiemann, Ronald F. *Religion in Public Life: A Dilemma for Democracy*. Washington, DC: Georgetown University Press, 1996.

Thistlethwaite, Susan Brooks, ed. *Interfaith Just Peacemaking: Jewish, Christian, and Muslim Perspectives on the New Paradigm of Peace and War*. New York: Palgrave Macmillan, 2011.

Thomas Aquinas. *Summa Theologica*. Translated by Fathers of the English Dominican Province. Westminster, MD: Christian Classics, 1981.

Tillich, Paul. *Systematic Theology*. Chicago: University of Chicago Press, 1951.

Tracy, David. *The Analogical Imagination*. New York: Crossroad, 1981.

VanderWal-Gritter, Wendy. *Generous Spaciousness: Responding to Gay Christians in the Church*. Grand Rapids: Brazos Press, 2014.

Verhey, Allen. "'Playing God' and Invoking a Perspective." In *On Moral Medicine: Theological Perspectives in Medical Ethics*, 2nd ed., edited by Stephen E. Lammers and Allen Verhey. Grand Rapids: Eerdmans, 1998.

Wadell, Paul J. *Friendship and the Moral Life.* Notre Dame: University of Notre Dame Press, 1989.

————. *Becoming Friends: Worship, Justice, and the Practice of Christian Friendship.* Grand Rapids: Brazos Press, 2002.

Winthrop, John. "A Modell of Christian Charity." In *American Sermons.* New York: Library Classics of the United States, 1999.

Index of Names and Subjects

Index of Scripture References